The Old Testament in
Modern Research

The Old Testament in Modern Research

HERBERT F. HAHN

With a Survey of Recent Literature
by
HORACE D. HUMMEL

Fortress Press

Philadelphia

First issued in 1954 by Muhlenberg Press

Expanded edition issued in 1966 by Fortress Press

© 1966 BY FORTRESS PRESS

Library of Congress Catalog Card Number 66-18995

3058B66   Printed in U.S.A.   UB749P

Preface

The purpose of the present study is to examine the various approaches to the interpretation of the Old Testament that have predominated in biblical studies since the "higher critics" revolutionized the basic principles of research with reference to the Scriptures. It is the hope of the writer that such a survey may provide the necessary background for appraisal of the alternatives confronting Bible scholars today.

No attempt has been made here to be exhaustive regarding the hypotheses and conclusions brought forth by the various approaches to the Old Testament. The survey attempts simply to suggest the main trends of research in each field and to illustrate them with the typical and most significant treatments. In particular, the intention has been to show the effect of each approach upon the interpretation of the religious history contained in the Old Testament. For the religious history most directly involves the basic problems of interpretation.

The nature of the undertaking required the examination of more books and monographs than could be discussed within the limits which the writer set himself. For guidance in selecting pertinent areas for investigation and aid in finding significant material, he owes a great debt to Professor S. W. Baron of Columbia University. But the scope and the nature of the treatment are the writer's own.

Quotations from works in German or French have been translated by the present writer, except where an existing English translation is specifically referred to as the source.

For permission to quote from copyright material, grateful acknowledgment is hereby made to the following publishers:

American Schools of Oriental Research, New Haven
Columbia University Press, New York
E. P. Dutton and Co., New York
Harper & Bros., New York
The Johns Hopkins Press, Baltimore
Alfred A. Knopf, New York
The Macmillan Company, New York
Oxford University Press, New York
Fleming H. Revell Company, Westwood, N. J.
University of Chicago Press, Chicago

Permission to quote from periodicals was also kindly granted by the Dropsie College for Hebrew and Cognate Learning, Philadelphia, publisher of the *Jewish Quarterly Review;* the National Association of Biblical Instructors, Boston, publisher of the *Journal of Bible and Religion;* and the University of Chicago Press, Chicago, publisher of the *Journal of Religion.* To each of these publishers the writer expresses his heartfelt thanks.

NOTE ON THE SECOND EDITION

The reprinting of this volume has provided an opportunity to correct a number of typographical errors in the first edition and to make a few verbal improvements in the interests of accuracy and clarity.

H. F. H.

October, 1965

Contents

List of Abbreviations

AASOR	*Annual of the American Schools of Oriental Research*
AJSL	*American Journal of Semitic Languages and Literature*
ARW	*Archiv für Religionswissenschaft*
BA	*Biblical Archaeologist*
BASOR	*Bulletin of the American Schools of Oriental Research*
BJRL	*Bulletin of the John Rylands Library*
BR	*Biblical Research*
BZAW	*Beiheft zur Zeitschrift für die alttestamentliche Wissenschaft*
CBQ	*Catholic Biblical Quarterly*
DLZ	*Deutsche Literaturzeitung*
ET	*Expository Times*
ETL	*Ephemerides Theologicae Lovanienses*
EvT	*Evangelische Theologie*
HTR	*Harvard Theological Review*
HUCA	*Hebrew Union College Annual*
IDB	*The Interpreter's Dictionary of the Bible*, ed. G. A. Buttrick (4 vols.; New York and Nashville, 1962 ff.)
IEJ	*Israel Exploration Journal*
Int.	*Interpretation*
JAOS	*Journal of the American Oriental Society*

JBL	*Journal of Biblical Literature*
JBR	*Journal of Bible and Religion*
JNES	*Journal of Near Eastern Studies*
JPOS	*Journal of the Palestine Oriental Society*
JSOR	*Journal of the Society of Oriental Research*
JSS	*Journal of Semitic Studies*
MGWJ	*Monatsschrift für Geschichte und Wissenschaft des Judentums*
MVAG	*Mitteilungen der vorderasiatischen Gesellschaft*
OLZ	*Orientalistische Literaturzeitung*
PEFQS	*Palestine Exploration Fund Quarterly Statement*
PEQ	*Palestine Exploration Quarterly*
RB	*Revue Biblique*
RHPR	*Revue d'histoire et de philosophie religieuses*
RHR	*Revue de l'histoire des religions*
SVT	*Supplements to Vetus Testamentum*
TZ	*Theologische Zeitschrift*
ThLZ	*Theologische Literaturzeitung*
VT	*Vetus Testamentum*
ZAW	*Zeitschrift für die alttestamentliche Wissenschaft*
ZDMG	*Zeitschrift der deutschen morgenländischen Gesellschaft*
ZTK	*Zeitschrift für Theologie und Kirche*

Introduction

Interpretation of the Bible in the present day has reached a point of crisis. Until recently scholars were moving forward with confidence and widespread approval toward a rational exposition of the meaning of the Old and New Testaments. In place of the traditional view that the sacred Scriptures contained a timeless revelation concerning God's relation to the world, they elaborated the view that the Scriptures were really a literary record of man's slow growth in moral and religious understanding and of his striving toward a deeper apprehension of the spiritual aspects of life. Now, in some quarters, the assumptions upon which this interpretation was based have been called into question, and the validity of the methods used to establish the conclusions has been denied. Doubts have been expressed regarding the adequacy of the man-centered point of view and the philosophy of historical development which lay behind the interpretation. A seeming return to the age-old emphasis on the doctrinal content of Scripture and its essential unity throughout the sacred books—a return to traditionalism which nevertheless denies that it is a step backward—has dominated recent discussion of biblical interpretation to the point where it must be regarded as an important phenomenon.

The crisis grows out of a loss of confidence in the historical approach on the part of many who formerly favored it. They have come to doubt whether a detached and objective method of investigation can interpret the inner meaning of religious literature. The historical method had been content to discover the origin and growth of religious ideas in the Bible and to place them in proper perspective in the religious history of mankind. But, of late, the conviction has been growing that historical understanding divorced from a commitment to belief is unproductive of true insight where religious conceptions are concerned. Basically, the crisis is one of attitude. Historical interpretation was allied with the optimistic belief in mankind's progress toward a better social order and a firm faith in the ability of human reason to discover and apply general principles for successful living. The new orthodoxy, taking its point of departure from the appalling fact of unreason in human behavior which the political and social turmoil of a quarter century has revealed, emphasizes the necessity of going back to the eternal verities for the solution of mankind's problems. The revival of traditional dogmas is part of the reaction to conservative ways of thinking in an age which has found easy optimism and unrealistic idealism wanting in many respects.

In these circumstances, the main question is whether the new orthodoxy represents the path forward out of the difficulties it professes to find in the exegesis of the past century; or whether it is a reaction that, by concentrating entirely upon theological exegesis, may obscure the real gains of the historical approach to the interpretation of the Bible. If the former, it is a summons to scholarship to re-examine the bases of biblical research, to admit the error or the incompleteness of its previous conclusions, and to compensate for any inadequacy in its approach. If the latter, it is a challenge to modern exegesis to justify its techniques of investigation and to maintain the line of its advance toward fuller understanding by building on the foundations already laid.

I

The Critical Approach to the
Old Testament

The Rise of the Critical Spirit in Biblical Exegesis

Until the latter part of the nineteenth century, biblical studies had usually taken the form of theological exegesis. The prevailing view was that the Bible contained a timeless, universal, and final teaching which was fundamentally the same in all the various books. "Biblical Theology" was therefore mostly a matter of presenting the teachings of the Bible in systematic form. But, since the theologian tended to equate the dogmas of orthodoxy with the teachings of the Bible, his interpretation of Scripture was a highly subjective one. He usually found in the sacred writings what he sought there, and what he sought was determined by his theological prepossessions. The results frequently obscured the real meaning of the passages he expounded. Even the doctrine of divine inspiration did not always persuade the theologian to listen to what the "word of God" might actually be saying. He heard in it the echo of other voices to which his ear had long been trained.

It required an entirely different approach to the Bible to expound it according to its original intention and meaning—a different conception of the nature of the Bible which would permit more objective principles of exposition. Such a new conception became possible when the tendency generated by humanistic studies to regard all ancient literature as the product of human culture had removed the old distinction between sacred and profane writings. All were expressions, in varying degrees of profundity, of mankind's most characteristic thoughts and aspirations.

1

The Bible, therefore, among liberal scholars, came to be regarded as a body of religious literature amenable to study and appraisal by the same principles of scholarly research as were applied to any other ancient book. These principles, known as the "higher criticism," which came to dominate biblical studies in the second half of the nineteenth century, did not themselves produce an exposition of the meaning of the biblical literature; they were a necessary preliminary to the successful accomplishment of that end. The prerequisite was an analysis of the Bible by objective literary and historical methods for the purpose of determining the internal structure of the individual books, the actual authorship of the various parts, and the historical circumstances under which they were produced. The goal of such an analysis was to reconstruct the historical development of the biblical literature. Its ultimate objective, however, was to gain an understanding of the spiritual history recorded in the documents. For through the latter, and only through the latter, did the critics believe they could recover the real meaning of the literature.

This objective required the avoidance of any preconceived notion regarding the nature of "sacred history," for the documents must be allowed to tell their own story. Sometimes, it is true, interpretation of the data was still affected by one or another theological viewpoint, such as the doctrine that the Old Testament was but the preparation for the New. But, at its best, the higher criticism refused to be fettered by traditional views. It tried to make a place in biblical studies for that sort of free inquiry which had proved fruitful in other historical disciplines. Freedom of inquiry was, after all, the essence of the Protestant tradition, however much it had been hedged about by theological controversy in the centuries after Luther. Given its opportunity in the nineteenth century by the rise of the scientific spirit, it came to fruition in the liberal Protestant approach to the biblical literature.

The critics soon found that the facts did not permit that conception of the Old Testament which had been usual up to that time. Instead of a unified body of literature which presented a single history unfolding according to the divine plan, they found a rich and manifold literature which expressed a number of different religious viewpoints, each reflecting the conceptions of a particular age. There were varying depths of religious insight and an apparent history of growth in understanding of the basic conceptions of Old Testament religion. The critics, therefore, regarded their task as an investigation into the actual historical development implied in the documents. They did not deny that the Old Testament generally taught a specific doctrine of divine control over human history. But they insisted that, if the true significance of the Old Testatment as an expression of human religious aspiration was to be comprehended, they must go behind the official theology and search out the actual facts of religious development as objectively as possible.

No historian of the nineteenth century, trained in the methods of scientific research, undertook to expound a historical development without first examining the available written sources critically. The initial task of the higher critics, accordingly, was a purely technical one: the careful analysis of the composition of the books of the Old Testament. Even in the eighteenth century, J. G. Eichhorn, "the father of Old Testament criticism," had seen clearly that, before criticism could proceed with its task of investigating the historical circumstances under which the writings had been produced, the problem of defining the textual limits and the special characteristics of the underlying sources must be solved.[1] It had long been suspected, but could not be proved before the rise of scientific methods of literary analysis, that the Pentateuch was really a composite work, in spite of the tradition of its unity, and that it contained various sources of diverse age and origin. A

[1] On Eichhorn, see Thomas Kelly Cheyne, *Founders of Old Testament Criticism* (London, 1893), pp. 21–26.

clue to the identification of such sources had been discovered as early as 1753 by Jean Astruc, who used the fact that two different names for God (Elohim and Yahweh) occurred in the book of Genesis as a means of distinguishing two interwoven narratives running through the book.[2] Then Eichhorn discovered additional criteria for defining and describing these narrative documents in repetitions and duplicate stories, diversities of style, and characteristic words and phrases peculiar to one or the other of the documents. It was the task of his successors in the nineteenth century to follow these parallel lines of narrative beyond the book of Genesis by applying the same criteria of identification to the rest of the Pentateuch.

At first, it seemed to the critics that the "Elohistic narrative" was the most comprehensive document in the Pentateuch, for it included the bulk of the legal material in the middle books of Exodus, Leviticus, and Numbers. Since its narrative portions seemed to provide a chronological framework for the whole, the early critics called it the Foundation Document; and, because of the numerous archaisms in its vocabulary, they considered it the oldest of the sources of the Pentateuch.[3] The "Yahwistic narrative" was, in their view, a later supplementary addition; and the Book of Deuteronomy—or its original legal nucleus (chaps. 12-26), which had already been identified by W. M. L. De Wette[4] with the "Book of the Law" found in the Temple during the reign of Josiah—was a still later addition. But Hermann Hupfeld in 1853 showed that the Foundation Document was really the work of two writers who had used the name Elohim for the deity. He accordingly divided

[2] See Adolphe Lods, "Astruc et la critique de son temps," *RHPR*, IV (1924), 109-39, 201-37.

[3] The theory, first suggested by J. J. Stähelin in his *Kritische Untersuchungen über die Genesis* (Basel, 1830), was fully elaborated in his *Kritische Untersuchungen über den Pentateuch* (Berlin, 1843). The name Foundation Document was proposed by J. C. F. Tuch in his *Kommentar über die Genesis* (Halle, 1838).

[4] In his doctoral dissertation (1805), reprinted in his *Opuscula* (Berlin, 1833).

it into a separate Elohistic narrative and an extensive "Priestly Document." [5] A dozen years later, K. H. Graf demonstrated that the Foundation or Priestly Document was not the most ancient but the latest of the sources of the Pentateuch.[6]

Thus, as the result of a century of critical study, four major documents had been identified in the Pentateuch and their relative sequence had been determined. Each document had an individual character, both in contents and in general point of view; and, although they had been skilfully interwoven, their special characteristics made it possible, for the most part, to trace the extent of each through the books of the Pentateuch. The earliest was the Yahwistic Document (to which the symbol J was assigned, being the first letter of the divine name which was its characteristic feature). It was followed soon after by the Elohistic Document (E). Both were narrative histories with some legal material embedded in them. They had a charming literary style and displayed great skill in the portrayal of human nature. These two documents were thought to have been composed in the early monarchical period, probably in the ninth and eighth centuries respectively. The book of Deuteronomy (D), which gave a narrative framework to the "Book of the Law" promulgated by Josiah in the seventh century, was primarily a law code based on prophetic principles. The Priestly Document (P), a universal history and extensive legal code, was chiefly concerned with matters of cultus and was dominated by the priestly interest in prescribing the correct ritual for each ceremonial occasion. In contrast to the first two documents, it had a precise and formal style, was given to stereotyped expressions, and lacked human interest. K. H. Graf assigned it to the postexilic age and connected it with the promulgation of "the Law" by Ezra in the fifth century.

[5] *Die Quellen der Genesis und die Art ihrer Zusammensetzung* (Berlin, 1853).

[6] *Die geschichtlichen Bücher des Alten Testaments: Zwei historisch-kritische Untersuchungen* (Leipzig, 1865).

The process whereby these four documents were combined to form the Pentateuch was described in terms of successive "redactors" (editors) of the original documents. A "prophetic redactor" first combined the two old narrative histories, even before the appearance of Deuteronomy, and did it so successfully that critical analysis was not always able to distinguish the parts. Many scholars therefore spoke of the combined work as a single source document (JE). It reflected the "prophetic" point of view regarding the nation's history; that is, it taught there was a causal relationship between the prosperity or misfortunes of the people and their righteousness or sinfulness. This greater history underwent revision when the book of Deuteronomy was appended to it, to make it conform to the teachings of the latter. Traces of the "Deuteronomist redactor" could be found throughout the whole, in characteristic turns of phrasing or the addition of "Deuteronomic" ideas. Finally, the Pentateuch itself was created by the combination of this composite work with the great Priestly Document, the latter supplying a framework for the whole. A final revision was made in harmony with its spirit and its leading conceptions by the "priestly redactor."

The attempt to date the various documents of the Pentateuch had taken the critics beyond literary criticism into the field of historical criticism, their second task as scientific historians. In this type of research, which required the comparison of the data of the documents with the facts of history (as revealed by the historical and prophetic books of the Old Testament), the critics achieved equally illuminating results. The relative sequence in which the documents had been composed had already been established by comparing the legal material of each document with that of the others. There were perceptible differences in their cultic regulations which could be arranged in a logical sequence showing the progressive development of cultic practice. Now the further comparison of these implied stages of ritual development with the

facts of actual cultic practice in Israel's history made it possible
to determine the period of religious development to which each
corresponded. W. M. L. De Wette, whose researches frequently
anticipated the final conclusions of the higher critics, had demonstrated, by such a comparison with reference to the ritual regulations of the Levitical legislation,[7] that these laws could neither
have been promulgated in the age of Moses nor have been the
product of the early monarchical period. For the historical books
showed that the most important regulations were either unknown
or ignored in the early days of Israel's history. Wilhelm Vatke next
argued that the elaborate ritual system of the Levitical legislation
must have been the product of a long process of development.[8]
Basing his investigation on Hegelian theories regarding the growth
of religious institutions, he concluded that Israel's religion had
progressed through three stages of development, to which there
had apparently been three corresponding stages of ritual legislation.
There was, first of all, the age of primitive worship portrayed in
the books of Samuel and Kings and reflected in the Yahwistic and
Elohistic documents; then the age of ethical consciousness initiated
by the prophets, to which the Deuteronomic Code corresponded;
and finally the age of the more external, ceremonial religion represented by the Levitical legislation.

The final proof that the Levitical legislation of the Priestly
Code was actually the latest stage of cultic regulation was provided
by K. H. Graf, as already indicated. His conclusion, drawn from
the apparent history of ritual development, was supported a few
years later by Bernhard Duhm's argument for a parallel development of religious ideas.[9] Duhm demonstrated that the teachings

---

[7] *Beiträge zur Einleitung in das Alte Testament* (2 vols., Halle, 1806–07).

[8] *Die biblische Theologie wissenschaftlich dargestellt: Die Religion des Alten Testaments nach den kanonischen Büchern entwickelt* (Berlin, 1835). On Vatke, see Otto Pfleiderer, *The Development of Theology in Germany since Kant* (London, 1890), pp. 252–56.

[9] *Die Theologie der Propheten als Grundlage für die innere Entwicklungs-geschichte der israelitischen Religion* (Bonn, 1875).

of the prophets did not presuppose the ceremonial conceptions of the Priestly Code, but were themselves presupposed by both the Deuteronomic and the priestly legislation. Moreover, while the Deuteronomic law drew most of its fundamental conceptions from the prophets, it drew none from the priestly legislation. The conclusion was evident that the prophets preceded Deuteronomy, while the Priestly Code followed both.

The "Grafian hypothesis" that the Levitical law was the product of the postexilic age became the most significant conclusion of historical criticism. For it affected a great deal more than the date of the Priestly Code; it necessitated a radical revision of the traditional view of Israel's religious history. The transfer of the "Mosaic law" from the beginning to the end of the history did away with all theories based on the supposition that the religious institutions of the Levitical legislation were characteristic of the age of Moses. With these elaborate institutions shifted to the end, the history of Israel's religion no longer appeared as a continual struggle to maintain an ideal system established at the beginning; instead, it took on the character of gradual growth from the simple to the complex, with the Levitical institutions as the climax of the whole development. This new interpretation made the history more rational and comprehensible than the confusing sequence of events resulting from the traditional dating. The latter had separated the promulgation of the "Mosaic law" from the time of its effective influence on the institutions of the people by a long period in which its prescriptions were apparently unknown and the existing religious institutions were primitive by comparison. The evolutionary conception proved of great value in ordering and explaining various phenomena of this sort which had puzzled earlier scholars. Now the characteristic ideas and institutions of each age could be understood as parts of the continuous process of development through which Israel's religion had gone.

The first attempt to describe the successive stages of Israel's religious development in line with the new chronological arrangement of the sources was Abraham Kuenen's history of the religion of Israel.[10] Like Vatke, he distinguished three successive forms of the religion: the primitive religion of popular worship, the spiritual religion of the prophets, and the ritualistic religion of the Law. But, unlike Vatke, who had used Hegelian philosophy and intuitive insight to trace the evolution of the religion, Kuenen made his reconstruction of the historical process strictly on the basis of a careful analysis and criticism of the sources. He blunted the point of some of the opposition to the "Grafian hypothesis" from conservative scholars, by demonstrating that the postexilic origin of the Priestly Code did not imply the same late date for all of its contents. There were among its laws some regulations covering much older practices, built into a ritual system which was itself late.[11] With this clarification, the chronological order of documents established by historical criticism became the framework for a persuasive reconstruction of the religious history of Israel.

The conception of historical development was the chief contribution of the liberal critics to the exegesis of the Old Testament. It is true, of course, that this conception did not grow merely from an objective reading of the sources. In a larger sense, it was a reflection of the intellectual temper of the times. The genetic conception of Old Testament history fitted in with the evolutionary principle of interpretation prevailing in contemporary science and philosophy. In the natural sciences, the influence of Darwin had made the theory of evolution the predominant hypothesis affecting research. In the historical sciences and in the areas of religious and philosophical thought, the evolutionary concept had begun to exercise a powerful influence after Hegel had substituted the notion of "becoming" for the idea of "being." He had arrived at the notion

[10] *De Godsdienst van Israël* (2 vols., Haarlem, 1869–70); English translation: *The Religion of Israel to the Fall of the Jewish State* (3 vols., London, 1874–75).

[11] See, *ibid.* (English trans.), II, 252–58.

by *a priori* reasoning without testing it by scientific application to observable fact, but Hegel was none the less the intellectual progenitor of the modern point of view. In every department of historical investigation the conception of development was being used to explain the history of man's thought, his institutions, and even his religious faiths. It was not strange that the same principle should be applied to the explanation of Old Testament history. In every age exegesis has conformed to the thought forms of the time, and in the latter half of the nineteenth century thought was dominated by the scientific method and an evolutionary view of history.

This is not to say that the work of a liberal critic was no more objective than that of a conservative theologian. There is a great difference between a dogma assumed to be true from the start and a hypothesis to be tested in the light of the facts. The liberal critics would have been the first to agree that the evolutionary view of Old Testament history could be maintained only as the result, not the presupposition, of a critical examination of the relevant evidence. But the conception of historical development seemed to them an inevitable deduction from the evidence of successive changes in the religious institutions of Israel. The only historical reconstruction possible on the basis of the sources was one which showed an evolutionary growth.

As a result, then, of the liberal Protestant approach, the task of Old Testament scholarship was to apply the current rules of scientific criticism to the Old Testament records and to uncover the line of evolution in the religious history of Israel. By the beginning of the twentieth century, theological exegesis as the paramount concern of biblical scholarship had been supplanted by the scientific-historical conception of the scholar's task.

BIBLIOGRAPHICAL NOTE

For general surveys of the history of criticism in the nineteenth century, see Thomas Kelly Cheyne, *Founders of Old Testament Criticism* (London,

1893); Heinrich Holzinger, *Einleitung in den Hexateuch* (Freiburg, 1893), pp. 40-70: "Geschichte der Kritik"; William Edward Addis, *The Documents of the Hexateuch* (2 vols., London, 1893), I, xiii-xciv; J. Estlin Carpenter, *The Bible in the Nineteenth Century* (London, 1903), chaps. III-IV; Otto Eissfeldt, *Einleitung in das Alte Testament* (Tübingen, 1934), pp. 173–201; Joseph Coppens, "L'histoire critique de l'Ancien Testament, I: Ses origines," *Nouvelle revue théologique*, LXV (1938), 513–50; English translation by E. A. Ryan and E. W. Tribbe, *The Old Testament and the Critics* (Paterson, N. J., 1942), chap. I.

More limited in scope but also useful are: Stanley A. Cook, "Notes on Old Testament History, VII: Literary and Historical Criticism," *Jewish Quarterly Review*, O.S. XIX (1906–07), 342–62; idem, "The Present Stage in Old Testament Research," in H. B. Swete (ed.), *Essays on Some Biblical Questions of the Day* (London, 1909), pp. 53–89; Leroy Waterman, "A Half-Century of Biblical and Semitic Investigation," *AJSL*, XXXII (1915–16), 219–29; D. C. Simpson, *Pentateuchal Criticism* (London, 1914; rev. ed., 1924).

A systematic and detailed justification of the conclusions arrived at by literary and historical criticism was presented by Abraham Kuenen in the second edition of his *Historisch-kritisch Onderzoek . . . van den Boeken des ouden Verbonds* (3 vols., Leiden, 1885–93); German translation: *Historisch-kritische Einleitung in die Bücher des Alten Testaments* (3 vols., Leipzig, 1887–94); English translation (of Part I only) by Philip H. Wicksteed: *An Historico-critical Inquiry into the Origin and Composition of the Hexateuch* (London, 1886). See also Alexandre Westphal, *Les sources du Pentateuque* (2 vols., Paris, 1888–92); Charles A. Briggs, *The Higher Criticism of the Hexateuch* (rev. ed., New York, 1897); J. Estlin Carpenter and G. Harford-Battersby, *The Hexateuch* (2 vols., London, 1900).

The Position of Julius Wellhausen in the History of Criticism

The most cogent presentation of the critical theory of the origin and composition of the Pentateuchal documents and the best exposition of those conclusions which seemed to grow logically out of the critical approach to Old Testament religious history were to be found in the work of Julius Wellhausen. His position in Old Testament criticism is somewhat analogous to that of Darwin in the intellectual history of modern times. The central idea which he made common property had already been broached by others before him, but he gave the theory its classic formulation and applied it with assurance to a wide range of data, assembled in a comprehensive synthesis and unified by a dominant theme. What was new and original in Wellhausen's presentation was the way in which he combined the various lines of argument developed by his predecessors and drew the conclusions toward which the literary and historical criticism of a century had been tending.

In a volume which came to be recognized as the most important contribution to Old Testament criticism of the nineteenth century,[12] Wellhausen gave a convincing demonstration that the Mosaic legislation of the Pentateuch was not the starting point of Israel's religious institutions but the fundamental law of the Jewish community after the Exile. By combining Graf's method of arranging the ritual laws in logical sequence with Vatke's program for studying the religious institutions of successive historical periods, he was able to show not only that there was an intimate connection between the succession of the law codes and the evolution of religious practices, but also that these parallel developments were intelligible only in the sequence which placed the Priestly Code and the priestly institutions at the end. Thus Wellhausen both confirmed the "Grafian hypothesis" and erected thereon a detailed history of the cultus, which worked the multifarious data into a coherent and rational scheme. It disclosed the progressive development which had taken place from simple observances of a spontaneous and natural character, through the reforms in practice initiated by the prophets, to the predominance of ceremonial and priestly elements.

In a subsequent account of the history of Israel,[13] Wellhausen described more fully how the results of criticism affected the interpretation of Old Testament religious history. His exposition was a prime example of the liberal approach to the exegesis of the Old

---

[12] *Prolegomena zur Geschichte Israels* (Berlin, 1883); English translation: *Prolegomena to the History of Israel* (Edinburgh, 1885).

[13] *Israelitische und jüdische Geschichte* (Berlin, 1894; 3d ed., 1897).

Testament. Wellhausen omitted the theological interpretation entirely and emphasized the factor of historical causation instead. He consciously based his exposition on the evolutionary view of history. The fact that he also displayed an extensive knowledge of the sources and critical acumen in their interpretation lent persuasiveness to his conclusions. Among his followers, Wellhausen's reconstruction of the religious history of Israel became the standard interpretation. It inspired and served as the model for a number of critical histories of Old Testament religion during the next generation.[14]

As Wellhausen reconstructed it, the history of Israel's religion began with the Exodus, not with the patriarchs. From the evolutionary point of view, which assumed that development invariably took place from lower to higher forms, it was inconceivable that the nomadic ancestors of the Israelites could have held the lofty, monotheistic conceptions ascribed to Abraham in the patriarchal narratives; and, from the critical view, these narratives were untrustworthy sources for religious history before the Exodus, since they reflected the conceptions of the later age in which they were written. "We can begin the history of the religion," said Wellhausen, "only with the history of the people, that is, with Moses at the earliest."[15] It was Moses who had created the people from a group of loosely related tribes by giving them a community of interests for the first time and a common religion centered around the figure of a national deity. The religion which they took with them into the promised land was not monotheism, for the existence of the gods of other nations was not denied. Nor had it yet outgrown some of the primitive religious conceptions which the Hebrews had inherited from their nomadic background. But it was a genuine type of religion, toward which Wellhausen felt

---

[14] See the Bibliographical Note at the end of this section.
[15] "Israelitisch-jüdische Religion," in Paul Hinneberg (ed.), *Die Kultur der Gegenwart*, Div. I, Vol. IV, Part I (Berlin, 1906), p. 7. Cf. Wellhausen's *Prolegomena* (Berlin, 1883), pp. 363–65.

quite sympathetic. He portrayed its ritual acts as a natural expression of religious feeling and tried to show how worship grew out of life, being conducted at the local shrines in intimate connection with the activities of the people.[16] This interpretation reflected the humanistic appreciation of religion first expressed by Herder in the eighteenth century.

Following the evolutionary mode of interpretation, Wellhausen proceeded to show how the religion developed into a more complex form, as the Israelites adopted various cultic practices from the Canaanites among whom they had settled. But the significant development of the second period of their religious history was the transformation of the simple, monolatrous religion of the early Israelites into strict monotheism. This was the work of the prophets. In the course of their polemic against the way in which ritual worship developed, they "created" the transcendent, divine figure of God and transformed his relationship to man from a national into an ethical one. The truly formative power in the religion of Israel was not the Mosaic law, as traditionally assumed, but the teaching of the prophets. In Wellhausen's view, it represented the real climax of the whole development.[17]

Paradoxically, it was the prophets, according to Wellhausen, who introduced into Israel's religion the concept of law which later transformed their spiritual point of view into a legalistic preoccupation with the ritual forms of worship. So emphatically were they impressed by the universal significance of God's justice as the supreme law of the whole world that they brought the principle of conformity to it into the very center of their thinking and made it the fundamental basis of religion. They made righteousness (justice) the basic requirement of religious ethics, hoping thereby to transform the social order of the day. But, while the principle was embodied in the Decalogue and Deuteronomy and inspired the

---

[16] See *Israelitische und jüdische Geschichte* (3d ed., 1897), chap. II.

[17] See, *ibid.*, chaps. VII and IX.

reformation under Josiah, the permanent influence of the prophets was not so much in social reform as in the region of the cultus. The prophetic conception of monotheism led to the centralization of the cultus at a single shrine, the temple in Jerusalem; and this was the beginning of a process of ritual development that reached its climax in the elaborate cultus of the Priestly Code.[18]

Wellhausen felt that this ritual development resulted in a type of worship which contrasted greatly with the spontaneous and natural worship of the early period. "With the appearance of the Law the old freedom came to an end, not only in the region of the cultus . . . but also in the realm of the religious spirit." [19] For, when the cultus became the subject of detailed legislation, worship was deprived of its spontaneity, by being reduced to a set of prescribed religious exercises. Moreover, since the centralization of the cultus gave a strong impetus to the creation of a hierocracy, the reform of the social order contemplated by the prophets ended instead in the transformation of the nation into an ecclesiastical state. "There arose that artificial product, the holy constitution of Judaism." [20] However, the formalized institutions of Judaism formed a protective shell for the kernel of ethical monotheism that preserved it in a world not yet ready to accept it.[21]

Thus, in contrast to old-fashioned summaries of Old Testament history, Wellhausen offered a reconstruction. Its characteristic feature was that less attention was paid to the pre-Mosaic period and a greater emphasis was placed on the importance of the prophets. This shift in emphasis was accompanied by a reinterpretation of the restoration of Judaism after the exile. The most striking feature of Wellhausen's interpretation was the sharp contrast that he drew between the formalized wor-

[18] See, ibid., pp. 111–12, 131–32.
[19] Prolegomena (Berlin, 1883), p. 427.
[20] Ibid., p. 447.
[21] In general, see Israelitische und jüdische Geschichte (3d ed., 1897), chap. XIII.

ship of postexilic Judaism and the vital, natural religion of the early Israelites. He portrayed two different spiritual climates in the respective periods and set them in opposition to each other. "In Hebrew antiquity worship was natural; it was the expression of life." [22] In the later period, the cultus "became an end in itself, set apart in its own sphere," with the result that "the old practices were denatured and rendered lifeless." [23] The force with which Wellhausen felt the contrast was the result of his lively appreciation of the wide difference between the "natural" world which he found in the historical and prophetic books and the "holy" community described in the Priestly Document. The superiority of the former was the dominant theme of his exposition.[24] He preferred the "primitive" society of the Israelites because he found it to be a genuinely integrated world in which religion was the very essence of life. The world of postexilic Judaism, on the other hand, was divorced from reality because it separated the ceremonial expression of religion from secular life. Its dominant tendency was "legalism." Wellhausen regarded the increasing complexity of the ritual law as exemplifying a certain decay in the original vitality of Israel's religion. In place of religious individualism, which once had flourished free of institutional restrictions, the principle of conformity had become the basis of the socioreligious system.

In Wellhausen the higher criticism had arrived at the point of expounding the meaning of Old Testament history. All the preceding work of criticism, with the exception of Vatke's, had been no more than the preparation of the technical groundwork. Wellhausen built upon it an imposing structure of interpretation. How much his interpretation differed from the theological exegesis of the past is obvious. It combined a careful scrutiny of the religious

---

[22] *Prolegomena* (Berlin, 1883), p. 80.

[23] *Israelitische und jüdische Geschichte* (3d ed., 1897), p. 182; *Prolegomena* (Berlin, 1883), p. 185.

[24] See, especially, *Israelitische und jüdische Geschichte* (3d ed., 1897), pp. 16–30; *Prolegomena* (Berlin, 1883), pp. 436–37.

data with a genuine feeling for their significance in human history. Taken as a whole, his critical and historical work answered the needs of the times so completely that his conclusions were widely accepted. He had evolved a view of Old Testament history, covering literature, religion, and law, which accounted for most of the facts and answered most of the problems brought forth by the higher criticism. His relatively simple scheme of three major periods in Old Testament history provided the framework into which all else fitted easily. No other system of interpretation has been suggested since his time as comprehensive in its scope or as satisfactory in its solutions, even though his judgment of postexilic Judaism has rendered his historical reconstruction somewhat less than satisfactory to those of a later generation who do not share his ruling conceptions.

If a distinction is made between the results of Wellhausen's critical study of the Old Testament and his characteristic interpretation of the religious history, much of value remains from his work. His dominant theme had no necessary connection with the analysis of the Pentateuch into its major sources or the consequent division of Old Testament history into its major periods. These have been the common property of scholarship ever since, for they were achieved by scientific methods of literary and historical criticism. The real importance of Wellhausen in the history of criticism lies not in his exegetical conclusions but in the critical methods by which he worked. He stands as "the symbol of nineteenth century criticism" chiefly because, in elaborating the theory of the documents and the succession of periods in Old Testament history, he assembled the relevant facts in that objective way which is characteristic of the critical spirit at its best. Wellhausen did not speak the last word on Old Testament exegesis, but he had perfected the method of research initiated by Eichhorn.

BIBLIOGRAPHICAL NOTE
On Wellhausen's work and influence, see Johannes Meinhold, "Well-

hausen," *Die christliche Welt*, XI (1897), 461–65, 487–92, 539–43, 555–57, 578–83; Eduard Schwartz, "Julius Wellhausen," *Nachrichten von der K. Gesellschaft der Wissenschaften zu Göttingen: Geschäftliche Mitteilungen* (Berlin, 1918), pp. 43-70; Otto Eissfeldt, "Julius Wellhausen," *Internationale Monatsschrift für Wissenschaft, Kunst und Technik*, XIV (1920), 193–208, 325–38; Ernst Sellin, "Julius Wellhausen," *Deutsches biographisches Jahrbuch: Ueberleitungsband II, 1917–1920* (Berlin, 1928), 341–44; Walther Baumgartner, "Wellhausen und der heutige Stand der alttestamentlichen Wissenschaft," *Theologische Rundschau*, II (1930), 287–307; William A. Irwin, "The Significance of Julius Wellhausen," *JBR*, XII (1944), 160–73.

The most important critical introductions to the Old Testament, based on Wellhausen's literary and historical criticism, were: C. H. Cornill, *Einleitung in das Alte Testament* (Freiburg, 1891; 5th rev. ed., 1905); English translation by G. H. Box: *Introduction to the Canonical Books of the Old Testament* (London, 1907); Samuel Rolles Driver, *An Introduction to the Literature of the Old Testament* (Edinburgh, 1891; 9th rev. ed., 1913); Lucien Gautier, *Introduction à l'Ancien Testament* (Lausanne, 1906; 2d rev. ed., 2 vols., Paris, 1914); Carl Steuernagel, *Lehrbuch der Einleitung in das Alte Testament* (Tübingen, 1912); George Buchanan Gray, *A Critical Introduction to the Old Testament* (London, 1913); W. O. E. Oesterley and Theodore H. Robinson, *An Introduction to the Books of the Old Testament* (London, 1934).

The chief critical histories of Old Testament religion, based on Wellhausen's reconstruction, were: Bernhard Stade, *Geschichte des Volkes Israel* (2 vols., Berlin, 1887-88)—see also his *Biblische Theologie des Alten Testaments, I: Die Religion Israels und die Entstehung des Judentums* (Tübingen, 1905); Rudolf Smend, *Lehrbuch der alttestamentlichen Religionsgeschichte* (Freiburg, 1893; 2d rev. ed., 1899); Karl Marti, *Geschichte der israelitischen Religion* (Strassburg, 1897); Karl Budde, *Die Religion des Volkes Israel bis zur Verbannung* (Giessen, 1900); English version: *The Religion of Israel to the Exile* (New York, 1899); Johannes Meinhold, *Studien zur israelitischen Religionsgeschichte* (Bonn, 1903).

The Successors of Wellhausen in Old Testament Criticism

Wellhausen believed that he had succeeded so well in establishing the value of the critical method in Old Testament studies that he devoted no more attention to the history of Israel's religion but turned to the books of the New Testament instead, in order to apply the same critical method to the problem of the Synoptic

Gospels—a problem as complex and challenging as that of the Pentateuch had been.

But the critical spirit did not rest content with past achievements. Wellhausen's followers continued to dig for facts in the Old Testament field, using his methods and working within the framework of his critical conclusions. His influence on younger scholars was profound and far-reaching. For a full generation he dominated Old Testament scholarship not only in his own country but in France, England, and America.[25] All the more important histories of Israel, of Hebrew literature, and of Old Testament religion, as well as a host of commentaries and introductions, were based more or less directly on the Wellhausen system of Old Testament criticism. The commentaries, especially, in the series edited by Wilhelm Nowack and Karl Marti,[26] and in the *International Critical Commentary on the Holy Scriptures*, represented the liberal Protestant type of exegesis at its best; neither theological nor homiletical in their emphasis, they were strictly critical and historical.

Although Wellhausen's influence was international, Germany remained the chief center of biblical studies, especially with reference to the Old Testament; and the problem of the Pentateuch which had dominated all research in that field continued to be the chief subject of investigation. The methods of critical research had been firmly established, but the results of the documentary analysis were not universally agreed upon. Even the most convinced advocates of the theory of documents sought to pursue the literary analysis still further, feeling that it had not been carried out in sufficient detail, particularly with reference to the assignment of

[25] See Antonin Causse, "Notes sur le développement des études d'Ancien Testament en France . . . depuis un demi-siècle," *RHPR*, XX (1940), 47–76; H. Wheeler Robinson, "The Contribution of Great Britain to Old Testament Study," *Expository Times*, XLI (1929–30), 246–50; J. M. Powis Smith, "The Contribution of the United States to Old Testament Scholarship," *ibid.*, pp. 169–71.

[26] *Handkommentar zum Alten Testament*, edited by Wilhelm Nowack (15 vols., Göttingen, 1892–1903); *Kurzer Handkommentar zum Alten Testament*, edited by Karl Marti (20 vols., Freiburg, 1897–1904).

verses to the J and E documents. Confining themselves more strictly to the technical problems than Wellhausen had done, the younger members of the Wellhausen school made new analyses of the scope and structure of the major documents, reconsidered the number of source documents, and advanced new hypotheses concerning the literary history of the Pentateuch.

The most important change made in the critical theory after Wellhausen had left the field resulted from the reconsideration of the scope and structure of the chief sources. It had usually been assumed that each of the major documents was a unified literary work, produced in answer to the needs of a particular time. Now, after recalling certain hints and suggestions of earlier critics, Wellhausen's successors re-examined the possibility that each of the documents had acquired its final form by a process of accretion. On the basis of internal evidence, it had been clear even to Wellhausen that neither J nor E could be regarded as the work of a single author. Each contained a number of obviously older elements, originally independent, which had been taken up into the body of the document; each had apparently been supplemented from time to time with later historical material; and each had undergone a certain amount of editorial revision in an effort to co-ordinate and harmonize the various elements in the style of the original. The additional materials were so extensive that it was better to regard the documents as products of literary or religious schools than as the work of individual authors. Much attention was now given to the sources behind the documents and the editorial processes by which they had been combined to make the present texts.[27]

The consequent tendency of criticism was to cut the materials of the Pentateuch ever finer. Deuteronomy, when subjected to new analysis, was found to contain some fragments of older legis-

[27] The chief works of the Wellhausen school along this line included Heinrich Holzinger's *Einleitung in den Hexateuch* (Freiburg, 1893), Rudolf Smend's *Die Erzählung des Hexateuch auf ihre Quellen untersucht* (Berlin, 1912), and Wilhelm Eichrodt's *Die Quellen der Genesis von neuem untersucht* (Giessen, 1916).

lation and to show traces of several stages of redaction.[28] The Priestly Code, which had impressed even the early critics as consisting of a huge mass of disparate legal materials, was also found to contain within its bulk some originally separate groups of laws, some of which were probably pre-exilic.[29] The late date given to the document by Graf applied only to the final redaction; it did not cover the separate groups of laws or, as Kuenen had pointed out, all the practices regulated by them. Intensive critical investigation of the documents along these lines greatly enriched the stock of knowledge concerning their internal structure, although the results made the analysis of the Pentateuch seem extremely intricate. However, the broad outlines of the document theory—the identification of four major sources and the establishment of their relative historical sequence—were not basically affected by the conclusion that the documents had been expanded through the insertion of additional materials.

Early in the history of criticism it had become evident that the J and E documents not only could be traced through the Pentateuch but extended into the book of Joshua as well. Scholars therefore spoke of the documents of the "Hexateuch" and even attempted to trace them farther into the historical books.[30] So basic were their conclusions for the reconstruction of religious as well as literary history that the prophetic and poetical books also received a searching examination, for the purpose of determining what effect the new conclusions had upon the interpretation of

[28] See, e.g., Willy Staerk, *Das Deuteronomium: sein Inhalt und seine literarische Form* (Leipzig, 1894); A. F. Puukko, *Das Deuteronomium: eine literarkritische Untersuchung* (Leipzig, 1909); Johannes Hempel, *Die Schichten des Deuteronomiums* (Leipzig, 1914).

[29] Cf. Carl Steuernagel, *Lehrbuch der Einleitung in das Alte Testament*, pp. 227, 252.

[30] See, e.g., Rudolf Smend, "JE in den geschichtlichen Büchern des Alten Testaments," *ZAW*, XXXIX (1921), 181–217; I. Benzinger, *Jahvist und Elohist in den Königsbüchern* (Berlin, 1921); Otto Eissfeldt, *Die Quellen des Richterbuches* (Leipzig, 1925), and *Die Komposition der Samuelisbücher* (Leipzig, 1931).

these other classes of literature in the Old Testament.[31]

However, with the passage of time critical research tended to concentrate almost exclusively upon the analysis of "documents," as though that were an end in itself. The critics, of course, never lost sight entirely of the historical goal which was the only justification for literary criticism. But more and more time was spent in isolating subdocuments and assigning disputed passages, or in the still more minute work of dividing paragraphs and even single sentences into two or more original elements. The result was a somewhat artificial criticism that defeated its ultimate purpose by grinding away forever at the same mill. The literary criticism which at first had seemed significant and productive now became increasingly sterile. Small wonder, then, that a kind of reaction, akin to a feeling of surfeit, set in against the methods of critical analysis, combined with an attempt to return to older views regarding the composition and history of the Pentateuch.

Conservatives, in particular, seized upon the exclusive splitting up of the Pentateuchal documents as a *reductio ad absurdum*. They rejected the critical approach to the Old Testament as not only illegitimate in principle but without constructive value in its results. Anxious to preserve as much of the traditional viewpoint regarding the Pentateuch as possible, they attacked the very foundations of the documentary analysis, including the criterion of the divine names.[32] But the conservative opponents of criticism could not

---

[31] Wellhausen had made the first critical study of the Minor Prophets in *Die kleinen Propheten* ("Skizzen und Vorarbeiten," No. 5; Berlin, 1892). The important work on the major prophets was done by Bernhard Duhm, *Das Buch Jesaja* (Göttingen, 1892; 4th ed., 1923), *Das Buch Jeremia* (Tübingen, 1901), and *Israels Propheten* (Tübingen, 1916). Duhm also did the pioneer work on the Psalms, in *Die Psalmen* (Tübingen, 1899; 2d ed., 1922).

[32] See, e.g., Johannes Dahse, "Textkritische Bedenken gegen den Ausgangspunkt der Pentateuchkritik," *ARW*, VI (1903), 305–19; or his fuller treatment in *Textkritische Materialen zur Hexateuchfrage* (Giessen, 1912). This attack on the "divine names" criterion was successfully refuted by John Skinner, *The Divine Names in Genesis* (London, 1914). See the convenient summary of his arguments in S. R. Driver, *Introduction to the Literature of the Old Testament* (9th ed., 1913), pp. xxvi-xxxiii.

discredit analysis as such. Pointing out the excesses of literary criticism as practiced by the less cautious members of Wellhausen's school was not equivalent to invalidating the method itself when sanely and soberly applied. Refuting minor points in the details of critical theory regarding the scope of the documents did not negate the necessity for criticism where the phenomena of the Pentateuch were concerned. The conservatives did not succeed either in explaining away the internal difficulties of the Old Testament or in elaborating an acceptable alternative to the Graf-Wellhausen theory. In its major outlines, the latter still offered the best explanation for the critical problem of the Pentateuch. Such modifications as were required in the light of various points raised by the conservatives affected peripheral elements, not the main conclusions of critical analysis.

More vulnerable, however, than the critical school's methods of literary analysis were some of the conclusions growing out of its historical criticism. Opposition to the critical reconstruction of Old Testament history from those who were motivated by an essentially theological interest[33] can be disregarded at this point. Theirs was the normal reaction to every advance achieved by a scientific method which aims to be objective. Their sincerity cannot be questioned, but their failure to understand the purposes of historical research made their criticisms irrelevant. A more significant type of opposition came from one who tried to meet the critical school's arguments on its own ground. B. D. Eerdmans submitted its reconstruction of Old Testament history to a searching examination and attempted some corrections of critical theory without sacrificing scientific objectivity.

Eerdmans argued, first of all, that the critical school had erred in refusing to credit the traditional picture of the Hebrew patriarchs simply because the patriarchal narratives were contained in

---

[33] As, for example, James Orr, *The Problem of the Old Testament* (London, 1906).

supposedly late documents.[34] He rejected the critical view that the early Hebrews must have been simple nomads and called for greater confidence in the historicity of the narratives which showed them pursuing a settled way of life, not only raising flocks but also tilling the soil whenever circumstances were favorable.[35] In Eduard Meyer's phrase, their mode of life was "semi-nomadic." [36] The point of Eerdmans' argument was that the distinction between a nomadic and an agricultural stage in Old Testament history, which neatly fitted the evolutionary interpretation, had never actually existed. The Hebrews had been agriculturists from the beginning and their way of life much farther advanced than Wellhausen had supposed. This view of the matter gave a new importance to the patriarchal period as a time of cultural origins. "We are not justified," Eerdmans declared, "in considering the moral feeling and the ethical content of early Semitic religion so primitive as it was formerly considered." [37]

Eerdmans tried in similar fashion to restore the importance of the Mosaic period, showing more confidence in the reliability of Israel's traditions about the origins of its ritual institutions than was accorded to them by the critics. He argued that the rituals embodied in the Levitical legislation were older than the laws themselves, because they seemed to reflect ideas belonging to a very early age.[38] From the literary point of view, he agreed, the law codes were all late; but, from the point of view of substance, he maintained, they contained much ancient material. The priests who compiled the Priestly Code had brought long forgotten prescriptions into the foreground. Eerdmans described these prescriptions as authentic reproductions of the ancient practices of Mosaic times,

[34] *Alttestamentliche Studien, II: Die Vorgeschichte Israels* (Giessen, 1908), pp. 28-34.

[35] See, *ibid.*, chap. II (esp. pp. 38-43).

[36] *Die Israeliten und ihre Nachbarstämme* (Halle, 1906), p. 303.

[37] *Alttestamentliche Studien, III: Das Buch Exodus* (Giessen, 1910), p. 126.

[38] *Alttestamentliche Studien, IV: Das Buch Leviticus* (Giessen, 1912); see esp. pp. 143-44.

thus carrying the origin of the ritual institutions much farther back than Kuenen had suggested. He did not go so far as to revive the precritical, traditional view that all of Israel's religious institutions had existed from the beginning; but he felt that the critical theory had gone to the other extreme by placing the chief ceremonial institutions last in the history of ritual development. The critics had been led to declare many things that must have been ancient the inventions of a later age because of their evolutionary preconceptions, which prevented them from accepting the existence of highly developed rituals in an early period of history. Wellhausen, it is true, had not made the mistake of assuming that the ritual system of the Levitical legislation had been wholly manufactured by the priests during and after the Exile; he agreed with Kuenen that the compilers of the Priestly Code had "systematized and reduced to writing what they had formerly observed in practice." [39] But he had strongly emphasized that the basic rituals had gone through a progressive evolution, as indicated by the three successive strata of legislation concerned with ritual. Accordingly, he had described the ritual practices of Mosaic times as primitive and the elaborate ceremonials of the priestly legislation as the climax of the whole development. But Eerdmans, who rejected the evolutionary dogma that every historical process must have simple beginnings, saw no reason to deny that the Mosaic era was the time when the Levitical ritual system took substantial form.

Eerdmans' conclusions, however, did not convince those who regarded the history of Old Testament religion in the tradition of Wellhausen. He had bolstered his views regarding the high stage of cultural and ritual development among the early Hebrews by appealing to the evidence which archaeological discoveries had begun to supply concerning the existence of a well-developed state of culture throughout the ancient East. But his deductions from the oriental data with regard to the early Hebrews struck his

[39] *Prolegomena* (Berlin, 1883), p. 429.

contemporaries as no more than assumptions based on analogies. Because of the large measure of uncertainty involved, his arguments failed to win acceptance, at that time, either for his thesis regarding the cultural maturity of the patriarchs or for his view of the advanced state of ritual in the Mosaic era. Nevertheless, he had helped to reveal how complex were the historical questions involved. Although some theory of development was obviously demanded by the facts of Old Testament history, the unilinear development of Israel's religion expounded by the Wellhausen school apparently needed modification. Just where modification was to be made, however, and how far it was to be carried were still open questions.[40]

The basic difficulty was that, up to this point, criticism had been working entirely with the Old Testament materials themselves and interpreting them exclusively from within. The critics lacked a comprehensive knowledge of that ancient oriental world which constituted the larger milieu of Old Testament history. Consequently, they had been unable to set the Old Testament records against a wider historical background or to interpret them through comparisons with developments in contemporary cultures. Being unfamiliar with the wealth of data supplied by the archaeological exploration of the Near East, it did not occur to them to investigate the possible influence of external factors upon the origin and development of Old Testament religion. But new methods of investigation, based on the comparative principle, were beginning to make their appearance and promised fresh insight into the historical problems of the Old Testament. Historical anthropology, the general history of religions, comparative literature, and sociology, each approaching the historical picture from a different

[40] Almost twenty years later Eerdmans himself attempted such a modified interpretation of Old Testament religious history in his *Godsdienst van Israël* (2 vols., Huis ter Heide, 1930). For a summary and critical evaluation, see Otto Eissfeldt, "Zwei Leidener Darstellungen der israelitischen Religionsgeschichte (Kuenen und Eerdmans)," *ZDMG*, LXXXV (1931), 172–95. A revised edition of Eerdmans' history later appeared in English: *The Religion of Israel* (Leiden, 1947).

direction, altered the perspectives from which it could be viewed. Whatever might help toward an understanding of the soil out of which religious phenomena grew and whatever might contribute to an appreciation of the conditions that determined the processes of development was being brought under scrutiny. The field of investigation was consequently greatly enlarged and new sciences auxiliary to literary and historical criticism demanded the attention of Old Testament scholars.

BIBLIOGRAPHICAL NOTE

General summaries of the work accomplished in literary criticism by the Wellhausen school may be found in John Edgar McFadyen, "The Present Position of Old Testament Criticism," in Arthur S. Peake (ed.), *The People and the Book* (Oxford, 1925), pp. 183–220; Arthur S. Peake, "Recent Developments in Old Testament Criticism," *BJRL*, XII (1928), 47–74; Walther Baumgartner, "Alttestamentliche Einleitung und Literaturgeschichte," *Theologische Rundschau*, VIII (1936), 179–222; Otto Eissfeldt, "Literarkritische Arbeit am Alten Testament in den letzten zwölf Jahren," *ibid.*, X (1938), 255–91; English translation of same: "Modern Criticism," in H. Wheeler Robinson (ed.), *Record and Revelation* (Oxford, 1938), pp. 74–109.

Old Testament Criticism during the Last Generation

Among the generation of critics who came to maturity after World War I the insights provided by the new approaches to the Old Testament made the higher criticism of the preceding generation seem less than adequate. The feeling was general that this type of Old Testament research had done its work: it had accomplished much in separating the existing sources into historical strata and arranging them in chronological order so that a history might be deduced from them. But it was now clear that literary analysis and historical criticism had their limitations and that further progress toward elaborating the history was to be made along other lines.[41] In a programmatic survey of the problems of research in the new era that had begun, Hugo Gressmann declared that "in

---

[41] Cf. Rudolf Kittel, "Die Zukunft der alttestamentlichen Wissenschaft," *ZAW*, XXXIX (1921), 84–99.

our field we need not more but less literary-critical research. The higher criticism has generally exhausted the problems which it could and had to solve." [42]

Nevertheless, the critical approach was never wholly abandoned and has survived to the present day. Other problems might pre-empt the foreground of Old Testament study, but the analysis of the Hexateuch continued to receive some attention. For fresh points of view reopened some of the old problems or put them in a new light. Otto Eissfeldt divided the Yahwistic document into two parallel strands of narrative, the older of which he character-ized as an early collection of popular tales embodying the traditions and reflecting the viewpoints of the people in nomadic times.[43] Julian Morgenstern identified a few surviving fragments of a still older document which had contained a narrative of Moses and his relations with the Kenites.[44] Robert H. Pfeiffer thought he detected the existence of another old document which had originated some-where to the south of Palestine, probably in Edom.[45] These identi-fications of hitherto unobserved documents independent of the major sources increased the complexity of literary criticism. But, in broad outline, the theory of four basic documents in the Hexa-teuch was still maintained.

However, in the critical work of the generation after World War I, it was not the continued analysis of the textual scope of the documents that drew the most attention, but their age and prove-nance. This historical criticism was more radical in its conclusions and, for a time, threatened to force a major change in the accepted theory regarding the history of the documents. After the critical studies of the previous generation had uncovered old materials in supposedly late documents, it was inevitable that the tendency of

---

[42] "Die Aufgaben der alttestamentlichen Forschung," *ZAW*, XLII (1924), 8.
[43] *Hexateuch-Synopse* (Leipzig, 1922).
[44] "The Oldest Document in the Hexateuch," *HUCA*, IV (1927), 1–138.
[45] "A Non-Israelitic Source of the Book of Genesis," *ZAW*, XLVIII (1930), 66–73; *An Introduction to the Old Testament* (New York, 1941), Part II, chap. III.

the Wellhausen school to date the sources of the Hexateuch as late as possible should be challenged. Ernst Sellin, for example, questioned the theory that the J and E documents were no earlier than the ninth and eighth centuries B.C. respectively. The J document, he thought, had been composed in the time of King Solomon to provide a proof of the divine authorization of Israel's claims to Palestine. The E document, likewise, contained narrative materials which had been completed by the end of Solomon's reign, although the final composition of the document must be dated somewhat later.[46]

Similarly, Adam C. Welch argued from the presence of archaic material in Deuteronomy that the original law book was considerably older than the classic date in the reign of Josiah.[47] He broke the historical connection with the king's reform by denying that the chief purpose of the Deuteronomic Code was the centralization of the cultus in the temple at Jerusalem. As Theodor Oestreicher had already suggested,[48] the purpose of the original law book was not the centralization of the cultus at one shrine but its purification at all shrines. Welch's theory was that Deuteronomy contained old laws from the northern kingdom of Israel, inspired by prophetic teaching against the contamination of the cultus by Canaanite influences. That the genesis of these legal principles lay even farther back in history Welch considered a strong possibility, for he regarded the Deuteronomic Code as the outcome of that religious and national movement which had its beginnings in the work of Samuel. An attempt to fix the origin of the Deuteronomic legal principles definitely in the time of Samuel was subsequently made by Edward Robertson,[49] who credited Samuel himself with

---

[46] *Einleitung in das Alte Testament* (5th ed., Leipzig, 1929), pp. 34, 41.

[47] *The Code of Deuteronomy: A New Theory of Its Origin* (London, 1924).

[48] *Das deuteronomische Grundgesetz* (Gütersloh, 1923).

[49] In a series of articles originally published in the Bulletin of the John Rylands Library, 1936–1949, and gathered together in his *The Old Testament Problem* (Manchester, 1950).

the compilation of the Deuteronomic Code from the various traditions and laws of the local sanctuaries of the premonarchical period.[50]

With regard to the Priestly Document, neither Sellin nor Welch denied the postexilic date of its final redaction. But they gave further support to the thesis that late sources could and did contain old elements. Sellin maintained that the narrative portions of the Priestly Document were as old as the narratives of J and E,[51] while Welch argued in favor of a pre-exilic date for the bulk of the legislation.[52] Pointing out the presence of rituals of a really primitive character, such as the rituals of the scapegoat and the red heifer, he strengthened Eerdmans' thesis that the Priestly Code was no new creation of a late epoch but, in large measure, a compilation and codification of old laws and customs. The code, as a code, had a long history behind it, and a history of some complexity.

This tendency to regard much of the narrative and law in the Pentateuch as of more or less antiquity brought into question what had once been accepted as "the assured results of criticism." It was not, however, the effect of a conservative reaction against scientific criticism; it was a sincere attempt on the part of the critics to discover the actual outlines of a true historical picture. How much of this represented a permanent advance in critical theory and how much was mere groping in blind alleys is open to question. Sellin's shifting backward of the dates of J and E merely illustrates the fact that historical criticism had never been able to date these documents except within very broad limits. Without the use of other criteria than the internal literary phenomena of the documents, his theory was neither more nor less convincing than previous theories had been. A clearer understanding of the actual provenance of

---

[50] Robertson's theory is questionable, however, because it does not accord with what is known of the activity of "prophets" in the premonarchical period.

[51] *Einleitung in das Alte Testament* (5th ed., Leipzig, 1929), p. 55.

[52] "On the Present Position of Old Testament Criticism," *Expositor*, XXV (1923), 364–65.

these early narratives was possible, however, on the basis of the "form criticism" initiated by Hermann Gunkel, to which consideration must be given later.[53]

The attempt of Welch and Oestreicher to shift the date of Deuteronomy, thus dislodging the keystone of Wellhausen's scheme of history, was a more serious attack on the classic theory of the documents. If sustained, it would have involved a radical readjustment in the whole critical position, for the validity of the critical view of Old Testament literary and religious history depended on the essential correctness of the identification of the Deuteronomic Code with the Book of the Law found in the temple in 621 B.C. This dating of Deuteronomy had been the central point from which the critics had worked forward and backward to determine the age and the relative sequence of the other law codes and documents; and the description of Deuteronomy as the immediate inspiration for the reform and centralization of the cultus had been the starting point for Wellhausen's reconstruction of the religious history of Israel. With the date of Deuteronomy the whole critical edifice stood or fell. However, Welch's earlier dating did not win many critics away from the classic theory. His argument not only involved a denial of the identity between Deuteronomy and Josiah's Book of the Law but a rejection of the account in II Kings 22–23 of how the Book of the Law had been found in the temple—radical positions which most critics were not willing to accept.[54] The arguments first adduced by De Wette for connecting Deuteronomy with the reform of Josiah had an inherent persuasiveness which

---

[53] See below, chap. IV.

[54] See Hugo Gressmann, "Josia und das Deuteronomium," *ZAW*, XLII (1924), 313–37; Karl Budde, "Das Deuteronomium und die Reform König Josias," *ZAW*, XLIV (1926), 177–224. The problem was discussed in its more general aspects by William C. Graham, "The Modern Controversy about Deuteronomy," *Journal of Religion*, VII (1927), 396–418; Julius A. Bewer, "The Case for [*sc.* against] the Early Date of Deuteronomy," *JBL*, XLVII (1928), 305–21. Cf. the review article by Walther Baumgartner, "Der Kampf um das Deuteronomium," *Theologische Rundschau*, I (1929), 7–25.

made the standard view of the book's date and purpose still generally acceptable.[55] After all, it was not impossible to combine the
view that many of the individual laws had an early origin with the
accepted theory that the body of the book was the product of the
seventh century B.C.[56]

Something of the sort had been the end result of Welch's discussion of the Priestly Code. His view was strengthened a decade
later by certain conclusions of Otto Eissfeldt regarding the nature
and history of the Pentateuchal law.[57] Having identified within
the code various small *corpora* of laws, each of which was a distinct
unit dealing with a single subject and formulated in a single style,
Eissfeldt argued that they must be the literary deposit of earlier
stages of legislation. For although the cultic regulations in their
present form reflected the practice of the temple in the late
monarchical period, the rituals they had reference to were almost
all old, drawn from the cultus of earlier generations at the local
shrines. Since the latter must also have been controlled by rule
and regulation, Eissfeldt assumed that the small groups of laws
went back "not only in content but in formulation" to earlier types
of cultic regulations, perhaps even to a stage when they were transmitted in the form of oral tradition.[58]

This theory, of course, represented a great change from the old
view of how the Priestly Code had come into existence. Wellhausen had recognized the antiquity of many of the practices embodied in its ritual laws, but he had denied the antiquity of the laws

[55] See George Dahl, "The Case for the Currently Accepted Date of Deuteronomy," *JBL*, XLVII (1928), 358–79.

[56] Such a position was taken by A. R. Siebens in *L'origine du code deuterono-
mique* (Paris, 1929).

[57] *Einleitung in das Alte Testament* (Tübingen, 1934), pp. 26-32.

[58] Compare this view with the thesis of Edward Roberston, mentioned above.
See also R. Brinker, *The Influence of Sanctuaries in Early Israel* (Manchester,
1946). The theory that separate groups of cultic regulations originated at the
local shrines raises the possibility that the duplications and inconsistencies in the
Pentateuchal law may have been due to independent, parallel developments rather
than successive stages in the history of the law (cf. the theory of Ezekiel Kaufmann, below).

themselves. Now it was clear that much of the legal content of the code was pre-exilic, in form as well as substance. This insight, derived from the theories of Eerdmans and Welch and expressed most clearly by Eissfeldt, was a permanent gain in critical theory. It counteracted the critical school's preoccupation with the latest stage of legal development—a preoccupation which had been the result of Wellhausen's overemphasis upon the dominant interest of the postexilic priesthood in codifying the ritual system. By showing that an interest in ritual legislation was not a new phenomenon in the postexilic period but characteristic of every period in Israel's history, the new theory shifted some of the weight of interpretation forward to the earlier stages of legal development and restored the feeling for gradual growth in the history of the law. The "formalism" of the cultic regulations in the Priestly Code, which Wellhausen had contrasted unfavorably with the "natural" treatment of the cultus by the Yahwist and the Elohist, could no longer be regarded as the result of a "legalistic" orientation in the postexilic period alone.

As a matter of fact, it could now be argued that the priestly tradition in cultic legislation was entirely pre-exilic. Ezekiel Kaufmann regarded it as the oldest and most characteristic tradition in Israel's religious history and even argued that the priestly literature in the Old Testament was the oldest stratum of the writings preserved there.[59] His theories did not spring from a traditionalist bias but grew out of the same sort of literary and historical criticism as the Wellhausen school had practiced. Kaufmann believed that, once the data of the respective law codes were compared with each other apart from any evolutionary preconceptions, it could be shown that the legislation of P, rather than enlarging and elaborating upon the legislation of D, antedated it in every important

---

[59] See his series of articles under the general title of "Probleme der israelitisch-jüdischen Religionsgeschichte," *ZAW*, XLVIII (1930), 23-32, 32-43; LI (1933), 35-47.

particular, being much closer to the formulations of JE.[60] More important, however, in establishing the priority of P, was the fact that the ideological content of the priestly literature was quite independent of prophetic teaching and reflected an age in which conditions were more nearly like those of the premonarchical and monarchical periods than those of the prophetic or the postexilic age.[61] The "congregation" of Israel, far from being an ecclesiastical community chiefly interested in religious exercises, was conceived as a camp of the hosts of Israel; the "high priest" of this congregation stood beside, not in place of, the leader of the people and aided him with advice obtained through oracles; the "tent of meeting," being first and foremost the place of revelation of such oracles, corresponded more closely to the character of an early shrine, as implied in JE, than to the function of the second temple. The priestly literature, therefore, Kaufmann believed, was not the successor of previous religious writings but a parallel and independent tradition developing from beginnings which actually antedated the other traditions.[62]

Thus Old Testament criticism in the decades between World War I and II had considerably altered the Wellhausen system of hypotheses and conclusions. The problems to be investigated were stated differently and the solutions proposed led to modifications and adjustments in the imposing scheme of literary history which Wellhausen had constructed. As a matter of fact, the attack upon its fixed points was made from two sides at once. While the origin

[60] See, especially, *ibid.*, XLVIII (1930), 32-36.

[61] See, *ibid.*, pp. 27-32.

[62] These theories Kaufmann has since been developing, with many an original observation that merits serious consideration, in his multi-volumed history of Israel's religion in Hebrew: *Toledoth ha-emunah ha-yisraelith* (Tel-Aviv, 1937–?), Vol. I, 3 parts; Vol. II, 2 parts; Vol. III, 2 parts—to date. Cf. the summary of Vol. I by Efraim Urbach, *"Neue Wege der Bibelwissenschaft,"* MGWJ, LXXXII (1938), 2-14.

See Moshe Greenberg, "A New Approach to the History of the Israelite Priesthood," *JAOS*, LXX (1950), 41-47; H. L. Ginsberg, "New Trends in Biblical Criticism," *Commentary*, X (1950), 282-84.

of much of the law was being moved back in time, the alternative possibility that the final dates of the law codes should be moved down was also considered. Gustav Hölscher abandoned the pre-exilic date of Deuteronomy altogether and questioned the identification of the Priestly Document with Ezra's law book.[63] Dating each of them considerably later than the Wellhausen school had done, he cut these sources loose from their anchors in history (the reforms of Josiah and Ezra), thus weakening the close connection which Wellhausen had established between the literary and the religious history of Israel. Hölscher ignored the proof of Wellhausen and his school that Deuteronomy was essentially prophetic in point of view and, making it essentially priestly in character, classed it with the other legal literature of the postexilic period. But his theory crowded the entire legal development from Deuteronomy to the Priestly Code into a brief period of about fifty years—a period which seems too short for the development of so many differences as separated the two codes.

Modifications that were proposed on the margins of the Wellhausen system did not yet represent a sufficiently consistent point of view to form the basis of a new theory of Old Testament literary history. On the other hand, the younger generation of critics had been attacking the Wellhausen system at one point or another for so long that the consensus of acceptance which had once prevailed no longer existed. But, with all the fluctuations of critical theory, it is significant that there was no return to precritical arguments to find a basis for qualifying the theories propounded by Wellhausen. Although such scholars as Welch and Hölscher thought of themselves as outside the main stream of the Wellhausen tradition, their work was in no sense anticritical. In their attempt to improve upon critical theory, they appealed to evidence and induc-

[63] "Komposition und Ursprung des Deuteronomiums," *ZAW*, XL (1922), 161–255; "Die Bücher Esra und Nehemia," in Emil Kautzsch (ed.), *Die Heilige Schrift des Alten Testaments* (4th ed., Tübingen, 1923), II, 491–502; *Geschichte der israelitischen und jüdischen Religion* (Giessen, 1922), pp. 132, 142.

tion like other critics, differing from them only in the adequacy and soundness with which they used critical methods.

The same phenomenon appeared even in the ranks of the conservatives who were interested on *a priori* grounds in annihilating the exegetical position represented by the name of Wellhausen. The decade of the thirties witnessed a decided reaction in the direction of reviving the traditional theory that the Pentateuch was the work of a single great author. A small group of conservatives labored hard to restore a semblance of the ancient view. But, in contrast to the conservatives of an earlier generation, they did not attempt to refute the results of criticism by discrediting the methods of literary analysis. They made use of the methods of criticism to establish new positions which challenged the previous results of criticism. Thus a situation arose in which those who rejected Wellhausen's rationalistic approach and his evolutionary philosophy of history nevertheless paid him the tribute of adopting his technique of analysis. Their work was based upon an apparatus of criticism ostensibly as scientific as that of the objective critics, though they arrived at totally different conclusions.

Umberto Cassuto, for example, maintained that the linguistic and stylistic criteria for identifying the documents did not represent distinct and separate sources but purposeful variations in the style of a single author.[64] Benno Jacob had already argued that many of the stylistic peculiarities on which the dissection of sources had been based were simply the effects of oriental modes of thought and expression.[65] He now defended the unity of the book of Genesis with the thesis that the compiler was the real author, since he had created an integrated work by imposing a single viewpoint upon the various types of sources.[66] Similarly, F. Dornseiff, on the

---

[64] *La Questione della Genesi* (Florence, 1934). For a similar use of the argument from style against the documentary theory, see A. Bea, "Der heutige Stand der Pentateuchfrage," *Biblica*, XVI (1935), 192–98.

[65] *Quellenscheidung und Exegese im Pentateuch* (Leipzig, 1916).

[66] *Das erste Buch der Tora* (Berlin, 1934).

basis of detailed comparisons of the literary phenomena of the Pentateuch with the works of classical writers,[67] argued that the Pentateuch was a consciously composed literary unit, the work of a Levite (c. 900 B.C.) whose aim had been to present the cultic, ethical, and civil laws of the Israelites in a colorful historical framework.[68] But none of these theories can be said to have offered a satisfactory alternative to the critical theory. Cassuto's technique of taking each of the literary criteria separately and showing how it failed to support the accepted theory of documents ignored the chief contention of criticism that the strongest argument for the theory was the consistent occurrence of several types of criteria in conjunction with each other. The arguments of Benno Jacob regarding oriental modes of expression were drawn from the narrative art of a much later age than that which produced the Pentateuch. Dornseiff's argument from analogy with the literary criticism of classical literature failed to give sufficient weight to the results of biblical criticism, for it made the priestly legal codifications and the old popular tales the products of the same hand. Only Jacob's thesis that the compiler of the ancient traditions had tried to unify them under a single religious viewpoint was a valuable contribution to the understanding of biblical literature. It reappeared in the work of others, who did not, however, avoid the task of also seeking to understand the significance of the original traditions so unified.[69]

Symptomatic of the conservative reaction which accompanied the halting progress of critical scholarship was the further fact that some of those who were themselves heirs of the critical tradition joined in the attempt to reassert the basic unity of the Pentateuch. Max Löhr rejected the Priestly Document as a literary entity and

[67] "Antikes zum Alten Testament," ZAW, LII (1934), 57–75; LIII (1935), 153–71; LV (1937), 127–36.
[68] "Die Abfassungszeit des Pentateuchs und die Deuteronomiumsfrage," ZAW, LVI (1938), 64–85.
[69] See below, chap. IV, pp. 150–56.

put forward the view that Ezra and his school had created the Pentateuch, not from continuous documentary sources, but from smaller groups of laws and narratives upon which they stamped a relative unity in the interests of the priestly point of view.[70] Paul Volz and Wilhelm Rudolph attempted to explain away the Elohistic document by an analogous theory.[71] They recognized the presence in Genesis of only one narrator, the Yahwist, whom they exalted to a primary position such as he had not enjoyed under the four-document theory. They described him as an author of great skill and deep religious purpose, who in the time of Solomon had gathered the ancient traditions of Israel and grouped them into a consecutive narrative. The portions of Genesis usually assigned to the Elohist or the priestly narrators they said were either original parts of the great Yahwistic narrative or merely the work of later editors interested in emphasizing certain theological or cultic principles.

But these attempts to cancel the long established results of literary and historical criticism by means of criticism itself failed to convince the majority of critics. The tendency apparent in the work of some to build theories affecting the whole Pentateuch from a consideration of the phenomena in Genesis alone[72] was a glaring weakness of method; and the wide variation in dating, as well as the failure to work out a circumstantial history of the composition of the Pentateuch, left these theories as inconclusive as those of Welch and Hölscher had been.

Finally, there has been the rather striking phenomenon of criticism being applied to books in the Old Testament which had

---

[70] *Untersuchungen zum Hexateuchproblem, I: Der Priesterkodex in der Genesis* (Giessen, 1924); see the convenient summary of his argument in "Zum Hexateuch-problem," *OLZ*, XXIX (1926), 3-13.

[71] *Der Elohist als Erzähler ein Irrweg der Pentateuchkritik?* (Giessen, 1933).

[72] Wilhelm Rudolph later extended the theory he and Volz had worked out for Genesis to the rest of the Hexateuch in *Der "Elohist" von Exodus bis Josua* (Giessen, 1938). His analysis, however, was confined to the narrative portions of the Hexateuch, leaving out of consideration the large body of legal material.

hitherto escaped the scalpel of the literary dissectors. When William A. Irwin was invited to issue a revised edition of J. M. P. Smith's handbook on the prophets,[73] he found it necessary to rewrite completely the chapter on Ezekiel, because of the great change that had taken place in the critical view of the book of Ezekiel since Smith wrote. Ezekiel had been the one book in the Old Testament regarding which the critics had thought it possible to accept the traditional view of authorship and date with complete confidence. But even that tradition has now been corroded by the acids of criticism. An entirely new view of both the prophet and his book was presented by Gustav Hölscher in 1924,[74] and the clue he offered to the understanding of the book was quickly followed up by others until the accepted view of Ezekiel was no longer recognizable. Hölscher had made a distinction between the man Ezekiel and the book which bore his name. The man, he tried to show, had been a true prophet with the stylistic gifts of a poet, not the legalist obsessed by ritual which tradition made of him. The book, he argued, in its present form was a complete transformation of the prophet's original oracles, made by priestly writers who had added all the legalistic and ritual matter. In other words, a simple prophet of the people had been turned into a teacher of the law. The traditional Ezekiel had never existed; he was a fiction created by the priestly editors of his writings.

The startling aspect of this change in the long accepted view of Ezekiel was that it threatened to destroy the theory of the Wellhausen school regarding the history of Judaism. Wellhausen and his followers had made Ezekiel a key figure in the development of exilic and postexilic religion, a priest-prophet who drew up a program for the restoration of Judaism after the Exile. His book, according to their view, played a major role in preparing the final

---

[73] J. M. P. Smith, *The Prophets and Their Times* (Chicago, 1925). Second edition, revised by William A. Irwin (Chicago, 1941).

[74] *Hezekiel: der Dichter und das Buch* (Giessen, 1924).

triumph of the priestly over the prophetic point of view. Hence he could be called "the father of Judaism" and the critics always regarded him as such. Now Hölscher's new view of the prophet made that impossible. But the priestly book of Ezekiel could still play the role once assigned to the man, for Hölscher did not date the priestly compilation much later than the critics had done. Other scholars, however, moved the period in which the priests had worked on the book so far down that the book now followed the Priestly Code instead of preparing the way for it.[75] Torrey, for example, considered Ezekiel a pseudepigraphic writing composed entirely in Palestine in the third century B.C.[76] Such a radical revision of the book's dating would have destroyed the historical sequence established by the Wellhausen school. But since Torrey's view was related to his thesis that the Babylonian Exile itself was a myth created by the Palestinian priests,[77] it did not find general acceptance.[78] Nevertheless, subsequent scholarship recognized that at least some part of the book originated in Palestine, but it attempted to preserve the tradition of the book's origin in Babylonia by supposing that the original prophecies of the pre-exilic prophet had been edited and given a Babylonian framework by a second "author" during the Exile.[79] William A. Irwin, however, in his own work on Ezekiel,[80] supported the conclusion that the book must be regarded as the offspring, not the progenitor of Judaism. The prophet Ezekiel, as he appeared after his genuine prophecies had

[75] Millar Burrows, *The Literary Relations of Ezekiel* (Philadelphia, 1925); C. C. Torrey, *Pseudo-Ezekiel and the Original Prophecy* (New Haven, 1930).
[76] James Smith, in *The Book of the Prophet Ezekiel: A New Interpretation* (London, 1931), also considered the book wholly Palestinian in origin but ascribed it to a pre-exilic prophet Ezekiel.
[77] First presented in his *Ezra Studies* (Chicago, 1910) and restated in subsequent works.
[78] Cf. the refutation by Shalom Spiegel, "Ezekiel or Pseudo-Ezekiel," *HTR*, XXIV (1931), 245–321.
[79] See Volkmar Herntrich, *Ezechielprobleme* (Giessen, 1932); J. B. Harford, *Studies in the Book of Ezekiel* (Cambridge, 1935); I. G. Matthews, *Ezekiel* (Philadelphia, 1939).
[80] *The Problem of Ezekiel* (Chicago, 1943).

been disentangled from the rest, stood out from Irwin's analysis as a truly prophetic personality. But the book appeared as largely a commentary on the original words of the prophet, made by many editors over a long period of time. There the problem of Ezekiel rested, for the time being, three different periods of history having been suggested for the origin of the book.[81]

This review of activity in the field of Old Testament criticism during the last quarter century[82] has revealed a chaos of conflicting trends, ending in contradictory results, which create an impression of ineffectiveness in this type of research. The conclusion seems to be unavoidable that the higher criticism has long since passed the age of constructive achievement. This does not mean that it has failed to vindicate the purposes which generated it in the beginning or that it has lost the fruits of its early victories. The principle of objective research according to scientific methods is still the basic preliminary to Old Testament interpretation, and there is a large body of common knowledge concerning the history of Old Testament literature and religion which is the permanent legacy of scientific criticism. But the fact remains that criticism seems to have lost its way in a dense tangle of minor problems of analysis.[83] Having reached the point of steadily diminishing returns, it no longer occupies its former position as the paramount method of research.

[81] For a review of the problem of Ezekiel, which arrived at a conclusion similar to Irwin's, see George Dahl, "Crisis in Ezekiel Research," in Robert P. Casey (ed.), *Quantulacumque: Studies Presented to Kirsopp Lake* (London, 1937), pp. 265–84.

[82] For a more detailed survey of the same, see C. R. North, "Pentateuchal Criticism," in H. H. Rowley (ed.), *The Old Testament and Modern Study* (Oxford, 1951), pp. 48–82; and N. H. Snaith, "The Historical Books," *ibid.*, pp. 84–114. See also Otto Eissfeldt, "Die neueste Phase in der Entwicklung der Pentateuchkritik," *Theologische Rundschau*, XVIII (1949), 91–122, 179–215, 267–87.

[83] See the most recent attempt to carry literary analysis to the utmost limits of detailed verse-division: Cuthbert A. Simpson, *The Early Traditions of Israel: A Critical Analysis of the Pre-Deuteronomic Narrative of the Hexateuch* (Oxford, 1948), esp. pp. 280–322. Cf. Otto Eissfeldt's severe criticism of this book in *Die ältesten Traditionen Israels* (Giessen, 1950).

Perhaps the basic reason for the decline in popularity of criticism is the fact that, even with all the work it had done, it had failed to fulfill the promise of the liberal, humanistic approach to religious literature. It had failed to explain the Old Testament as a significant expression of religious aspiration, the most important product in all human history of the mind and heart of man. To be sure, criticism had accomplished its purpose of describing the spiritual history recorded in the documents. But, in doing so, it had avoided the Old Testament's own view of the meaning of that history and so had missed the real key to the significance of the Old Testament as the supreme example of man's striving toward an understanding of his place in the world and in history. Criticism had also accomplished much toward showing that Old Testament literature was the product of the religious culture of its times. But it might better have attempted to explain how the Old Testament's view of history grew out of the spiritual experience of its authors. That would have fulfilled the objectives of the humanistic approach to Old Testament literature more adequately.

However, the idea that a religious culture, rather than divine inspiration, was the source of the literature had been so new when criticism began that the necessity of making plain the nature and history of that culture appeared to be the primary task of scholarship. In the attempt to accomplish the task as objectively as possible, criticism did not see the problem of explaining that culture's attitude toward history as the real problem. It set aside the Old Testament's "philosophy of history" as a tendentious interpretation of historical events by the redactors of the various documents. Instead, it sought to extract the kernels of historical fact from the interpretations overlaid upon them. To portray the history of Israel's literature and religion in the same objective manner as would be used in portraying the history of any other cultural development was a useful and necessary work. But the more the critic adhered to the spirit of scientific objectivity, the less he attempted to interpret the inner significance of the religious literature with which he dealt. Criticism contributed greatly to the increase of knowledge; it did not deepen understanding.

But, even in terms of its own objectives, criticism did not fully accomplish the task it set itself. Its reconstructions of Old Testament literary and religious history suffered the limitations of a specialized method of research which did not look beyond the particular materials of its own field. To broaden the significance of its results, Old Testament research needed a deeper insight into the nature of religious belief and practice and a wider perspective on the historical manifestations of religion in the ages when Old Testament religion was developing. It needed to approach the history of the Old Testament writings from a broader literary point of view than was afforded by the strict analysis of internal structure. And it needed a better understanding of how religious development was affected by social and economic trends in the life of a people. These broader approaches to the study of the Old Testament had been made available by the auxiliary sciences of anthropology, comparative religion and literature, and sociology. Too often, however, literary and historical criticism was carried on in isolation from these other disciplines, although they had much to offer by way of supplementing the results of criticism. It is time to turn to a consideration of their contributions to the interpretation of the Old Testament.

II

The Anthropological Approach to the Old Testament

The Nature and Purpose of Anthropological Research in the Field of Religion

The first broadening of the horizon of Old Testament studies came from the field of anthropology. Here was a science—completely independent of biblical studies, but developing at the same time as the higher criticism—which eventually supplied a much wider perspective for the study of Old Testament religion. It approached religion as a general feature of the cultural history of mankind, and what it discovered regarding the basic characteristics of all religions made it possible to view the Old Testament in the broad light of the universal experience of humanity.

Much of the work of the early anthropologists was quite hypothetical in nature; yet they achieved certain worthwhile results in the sphere of methodology. They demonstrated the value of comparing the beliefs and practices of different areas and different epochs in order to determine the common, fundamental features of religion; and they widened the horizons of research by extending their investigations beyond the literary sources pertaining to the historical religions and bringing the rites of primitive peoples and oral traditions within their purview.

The anthropologists' concern with the religion of primitive races was based on the assumption that the best index to the nature of an institution was its original, elementary form. In the religious beliefs and practices of primitives, it was believed, would be found the fundamental features of religion. Similarly, in the subject matter of folklore, it was assumed, there lay hidden a wealth of information regarding the basic characteristics of religion. The superstitious practices, the popular beliefs, and the legends and tales of the common people in modern civilized nations embodied ideas that were remnants of the religious culture of much earlier times. As isolated fragments of a former "climate of belief," such ideas no longer had a living meaning; but, when studied in relation to similar conceptions in primitive cultures where they were still vital factors, they acquired significance as "survivals" of the earliest beliefs of mankind.[1]

Comparative study of the copious data gathered from such sources in all quarters of the globe revealed that amid the great variety of belief and practice there were certain similarities in the ways religion was expressed and a certain uniformity in the underlying conceptions. Primitive customs and ideas, at the same level of development and in a similar environment, seemed to take the same forms, even when the social groups in which they originated were widely separated in time and place. Adolf Bastian, the first of the nineteenth century anthropologists, propounded the theory that the ultimate explanation of religious behavior would be found in a uniform, if rudimentary, mode of thinking common to all primitive races of mankind.[2] Thereafter an interest in the psychology of primitive religion was one of the major features of anthropology.

But while all anthropologists subscribed to the doctrine that primitive man was everywhere psychologically the same, not all were agreed on the exact nature of primitive mentality. Bastian described it as consisting of potentialities latent in the individual mind, which were brought into play only under the stimulus of a social frame of thought, comprising the attitudes and conceptions

[1] See Leon Marillier, "Le folk-lore et la science des religions," *RHR*, XLIII (1901), 166–83.
[2] See Richard Schwarz, *Adolf Bastians Lehre vom Elementar- und Völkergedanken* (Leipzig, 1909), pp. 36–39.

of the group mind.[3] But his sociopsychological explanation was generally passed over, at the time, in favor of theories which concentrated on the psychology of the individual. The dominant theory in the nineteenth century regarding the nature of primitive religious thinking was Edward B. Tylor's theory of "animism," according to which primitive man conceived of everything in terms of himself and hence ascribed a living essence, a "soul," to all things in his environment: animals, plants, and even inanimate objects. Since primitive man felt himself subject to the influence of all the "souls" that constantly surrounded him, yet able to influence them in turn through various simple propitiatory acts, the "animistic" type of thinking, according to Tylor, was the basis from which all subsequent religious beliefs and practices were developed.[4]

How the fundamental features of religion had developed from the primitive base was a secondary concern of the anthropologists. Because of their emphasis on the original as basic, they tended to devote most of their attention to the primitive. But they attempted also to establish the line of development which religion had traversed by collecting from all the available sources examples of the basic conceptions and institutions in varying stages of complexity, which, when arranged in logical order according to the degree of complexity, would provide an ideal scheme showing the process of growth. Behind this methodology was not only the hypothesis that religion, like other aspects of human culture, had evolved from elementary forms of belief and practice to higher and more complex forms, but also the assumption that cultural evolution was a uniform process that went through the same stages everywhere. This assumption, of course, was not peculiar to the anthropologists. But, for more than a generation after Herbert Spencer had popularized the notion that biological evolution had an analogue in the

---

[3] See, *ibid.*, pp. 39–40.

[4] *Primitive Culture* (2 vols., London, 1871), Vol. I, chap. XI (esp. pp. 384–88).

cultural history of mankind, the ideas of unilinear evolution and parallel development dominated anthropological research.

The Initial Application of Anthropological Principles to Old Testament Research

The anthropological approach to the study of religion was first applied to the Old Testament by William Robertson Smith.[5] Whereas Wellhausen had studied the religious institutions of the Hebrew people almost exclusively from the data given in the Old Testament itself, Robertson Smith endeavored to go back to the primitive Semitic origin of the Hebrew beliefs and practices. In line with the usual anthropological view, he believed that the primitive form of an institution provided the basis for understanding its real nature in a more developed stage. Hence, he proposed to investigate the primitive nomadic religion with which the critical school assumed the Hebrews had entered Palestine, by analyzing the religious beliefs and practices of the nomadic tribes of Arabia in the pre-Islamic era—a collateral branch of Semitic religion which he believed could throw some light on the nature of early Hebrew religion.[6]

The general trend of Robertson Smith's interpretation was determined by the view, common to anthropologists, that religion was an integral part of life. It could not be treated as an entity separate from the social and political culture of a people. Like Wellhausen, but for a different reason, Robertson Smith believed that this union of the religious and the other elements in human life was more complete in primitive societies than in advanced cultures. Both scholars maintained that the modern distinction between religious and secular matters would have had no meaning for the primitive

[5] See J. Sutherland Black and George Chrystal, *The Life of William Robertson Smith* (London, 1912), chap. XIII.

[6] His major work on this subject was *Lectures on the Religion of the Semites* (Edinburgh, 1889; 2d ed., 1894; 3d ed. edited by Stanley A. Cook with Introduction and copious notes, London and New York, 1927).

mind. But Wellhausen had laid great stress on the "spontaneity" with which the individual conformed to the social pattern; Robertson Smith, more realistically, recognized the restrictive force of social compulsion. He understood that in a primitive society the individual was autonomous only up to a point; since the individual had no significance except as a member of a group, he had to conform to the pattern of the social will or perish. In the sphere of religion, belief was not a matter of personal conviction but of inherited custom; religious practice was embodied in fixed forms, the proper observance of which was a social obligation rather than a matter of free choice. Robertson Smith, obviously, was closer to Bastian's view of primitive society; Wellhausen favored the individualistic interpretation of primitive psychology. The latter was the more popular interpretation at the time, but Robertson Smith showed the depth of his insight into primitive culture by maintaining the social interpretation long before the bulk of scholarly opinion swung around in that direction.

Robertson Smith's own contribution to the interpretation of primitive religion was the method he proposed for recovering the basic conceptions without which no religion could be understood. He maintained that the nature of primitive belief could best be ascertained through a study of *ritual* institutions. Since these tended to remain unchanged from the earliest times to the historical period, they reflected the fundamental beliefs which stood at the beginning of religious development. The task of the anthropologist was to analyze the original meanings of those practices which survived from generation to generation in the crystalized form of ritual custom.

The most universal and characteristic ritual in ancient times was sacrifice. To the background of ideas behind sacrifice, therefore, Robertson Smith devoted primary attention. From his point of view, the conceptions expressed in sacrificial ritual were the most important clue to the essential nature of primitive religion.

In particular, they offered the best illustration of the ideas implicit in the religion of the kinship group, the characteristic type of social organization in the early nomadic period of history. At this stage of cultural development, when "all religion was the affair of the community rather than of the individual," [7] sacrifice was a public ceremony of the whole clan. Its significance, according to Robertson Smith, lay in the fact that it was essentially a communion meal. To the participants, who partook of a sacred animal slaughtered "in the presence of" their god, it was a sacred act by which they "cement and seal their mystic unity with one another and with their god." [8] An important corollary to this conception was the idea of atonement (at-one-ment). Whenever "the physical oneness of the deity and his community is impaired or attenuated," it could be restored by the "solemn ceremony in which the sacred life is again distributed to every member of the community." Atonement, in this sense, was "simply an act of communion designed to wipe out all memory of previous estrangement" by bringing the community "again into harmony with its alienated god." [9]

The two notions of communion and atonement, Robertson Smith believed, were the basic conceptions in primitive Semitic religion. His interpretation brought out clearly the integrated nature of the religion of the early Semites by showing how a ritual which symbolized their social organization gave expression to their most fundamental beliefs. Robertson Smith believed it was "the original type of religion, out of which all other types grew." [10] Some of the most important and constant features of the later forms of Semitic religion could be traced back to the fundamental factor of group kinship in the primitive stage of social organization.

All other forms of sacrifice, for example, were lineal derivatives from the sacrificial customs of the early kinship group. The gift

---

[7] *Religion of the Semites*, p. 253.
[8] *Ibid.*, pp. 312–13.
[9] *Ibid.*, pp. 319–20.
[10] *Ibid.*, p. 51.

type of sacrifice, which E. B. Tylor had postulated as the fundamental type,[11] and its analogue, the tribute type of sacrifice, according to Robertson Smith were later evolutionary developments from sacrifice as an act of communion. They reflected the same basic beliefs, although they had naturally been adapted to the changes in social organization that had taken place in the meantime. The rise of the institution of private property made possible the conception of sacrifice as a gift to the deity, and the change from nomadic life to an agricultural economy resulted in the conception of sacrifice as tribute paid to the "lord" of the land. But the basic conception of a natural bond between the deity and his worshipers had merely reappeared in altered forms.[12]

Another basic conception of primitive Semitic religion was to be found behind certain practices associated with places of worship. The fact that sanctuaries were always hedged about with restrictions which regulated the conduct of men within the sacred precincts was, to Robertson Smith, a survival of the primitive notion of "holiness." This did not involve the later and more familiar conception of sanctity, for it had nothing to do with an inherent quality. The notion originally expressed the relationship of certain things, places, or persons to the god: they were "set apart" for his service and belonged to him. That which was "holy" must be preserved from all contact with the common, except when the latter was itself "sanctified" by proper preparation or the observance of certain necessary precautions. For the gods would not tolerate the use of their holy places and holy things except in prescribed ways.[13]

This emphasis on the careful observance of detailed rules of ritual, even in early times, was the most arresting feature of Robertson Smith's discussion of the concept of holiness. Wellhausen had

[11] *Primitive Culture*, Vol. II, chap. XVIII.
[12] See *Religion of the Semites*, pp. 244–45, 249–51.
[13] See, *ibid.*, pp. 140–58.

maintained that an anxious care to fulfill ritual requirements was characteristic only of postexilic Judaism. Robertson Smith showed that it had existed among all the Semites from the earliest stage of their religious development, and that it was based on an ideological background of which Wellhausen had no inkling when he emphasized the spontaneity and freedom from restrictive regulations of the "original" religion of the Israelites. Robertson Smith recognized, of course, that the forms of ritual and the ideas attached to them were different among the Israelites of the monarchical period from the system and the theory of ritual in the postexilic period. But he emphasized that "ritual was never deemed unimportant in a religion so little spiritual as that of the mass of Israel" and that "an interest in correct ritual never died out." [14] The intensification of ritualistic religion in the postexilic period did not have for him quite the paramount significance it had for Wellhausen. Robertson Smith echoed Wellhausen in contrasting early times, when every locality had its altar and "a visit to the local sanctuary was the easy and obvious way of consecrating every important act of life," with the later period, when "no such interweaving of sacrificial service with everyday religion was possible under the new law." [15] But he did not divide the history of Old Testament religion into antithetical epochs. He had a stronger feeling for the quality of continuous development through successive periods—a progressive development which, at the same time, preserved elements fundamental to the religion from the beginning. Instead of emphasizing the differences between the important stages in religious history, Robertson Smith was primarily concerned with those permanent features of religion—the basic beliefs and the rituals through which they were expressed—which recurred "with striking uniformity" in the successive periods.

The dissimilar manners in which Wellhausen and Robertson

---

[14] *The Old Testament in the Jewish Church* (2d rev. ed., London, 1892), p. 242.
[15] *Religion of the Semites*, pp. 215-16; cf. *Old Testament in the Jewish Church* (2d ed., 1892), pp. 245-48, 378-80.

Smith made their interpretations of Israel's religious history grew out of the different perspectives from which each conducted his investigations. Wellhausen concentrated on the climactic point of his critical analysis: the conclusion that the priestly institutions and the priestly point of view were a late development in Old Testament history. Robertson Smith faced toward the period of beginnings, looking for the original meanings of the religious institutions of the historical periods. From this perspective, which brought a longer range of religious development into view, he saw that certain ideas labeled "priestly" by the critical school, such as holiness and atonement, had early origins. The value of studying the primitive stage of Semitic religion lay in the very fact that it revealed the rudimentary forms of religious beliefs dominant in the later periods. With this insight Robertson Smith was able to show the persistence of a basic core of religious belief through various changes in the interpretation of ritual practice. Successive periods represented advances in religious perception, but they made new formulations of the basic conceptions without abandoning the essence of the original ideas.

The unique element in Robertson Smith's interpretation was his belief that the process did not end with the last stage of Old Testament religion. For him, Christian doctrine and ritual were the climax of the whole development. The basic ideas of communion, atonement, and holiness, which he had traced from the social religion of the kinship group through the "natural" religion of the agricultural stage to the prescriptive religion of the Law, had passed over as fundamental conceptions into Christianity. In the long process of development from their primitive forms, ideas which originally had been conceived in merely physical terms were gradually freed from their material connotations, until they became the "spiritual truths" expressed in the theological doctrines of Christianity.[16]

[16] *Religion of the Semites,* pp. 439-40.

Thus, Robertson Smith found in the Judeo-Christian heritage "a consistent unity of scheme" which ran through its whole historical development. It was not the unity of a traditional body of doctrine, such as theologians sought in the Old Testament, but the unity of a continuous development from a crude and imperfect understanding of religious truth to a clear and full perception of its spiritual significance. This interpretation was, of course, a speculative reconstruction which itself bordered on the theological. But Robertson Smith, like so many of the nineteenth century anthropologists, was essentially a theoretical thinker, not a mere gatherer of facts. He did assemble a wide range of data, but his purpose was to illustrate a theory regarding the nature of religious belief and practice. His treatment of the data, perhaps even his selection of the data, was determined by his assumption of what was fundamental in religious belief. However, his sacramental interpretation of sacrifice and his emphasis on the ideas of communion and atonement as the most vital elements in religious belief resulted in "too simple a theory of the history of religion." [17] No more than Wellhausen's interpretation did it provide a final and complete interpretation of Old Testament religious history. Yet Robertson Smith's method of going back to the origins had the merit of giving a broader panorama of the development of Old Testament religion than had been possible from the critical standpoint.

Sir James G. Frazer's Anthropological Researches and Their Bearing on the Old Testament

Among those who considered themselves as belonging to the school of Robertson Smith, Sir James G. Frazer did most to broaden still further the scope of investigation into the nature of Old Testament religion. Robertson Smith had studied the primitive Semitic religion entirely through such literary sources as survived in the

[17] Stanley A. Cook, in the Introduction to the third edition of *Religion of the Semites*, p. xlii.

Hebrew, Arabic, and classical literatures. Important and indispensable as these were for establishing the nature of Semitic custom and belief, they were yet too meager to reconstruct fully the life and culture of the early Semites. Frazer extended the reach of the comparative method by bringing within the scope of his research the anthropological data on the uncivilized races of mankind. He proposed to study the historical religions, including the biblical, by means of comparisons with the customs and rites of primitive peoples. As the best means of penetrating to the essence of religious belief, he used Robertson Smith's technique of studying rituals rather than theologies; but Frazer applied it to a much wider range of data gathered from all parts of the world.

Accepting the theory of the essential uniformity of primitive thinking among all races, Frazer set himself the task of tracing the growth of primitive human thought through all the variations of particular belief in as many areas of primitive culture as possible. With indefatigable labor and a keen eye for analogies, he spent a lifetime collecting data on the basic thought forms of savage races. He sought particularly for parallel phenomena from which to deduce a single, typical line of development. In this respect, his work corresponded to the attempt of the nineteenth century anthropologists to construct an ideal scheme of the process of evolution through which all religion was assumed to have gone. Frazer did not succeed in actually elaborating a universal theory of religious growth, but his work was pervaded by a general sense of the uniformity of development among all peoples.

The results of Frazer's labors were presented with great erudition in his famous work, *The Golden Bough*,[18] which grew, as he continued to assemble data, from two volumes in the first edition of 1890 to twelve in the third edition twenty years later. This widely ramified study of the traditional rites and the superstitious

[18] *The Golden Bough: A Study in Magic and Religion* (2 vols., London, 1890; 2d ed., 3 vols., 1900; 3d ed., 12 vols., 1910–15; one-volume abridgement, New York, 1922).

practices of primitive peoples and peasant populations in various times and places presented a great number of suggestions regarding the evolution of primitive religion. But the vast accumulations of illustrative data were frequently more impressive than the conclusions based upon them. Frazer showed greater facility in amassing the data than in correlating them into fresh interpretations. His conclusions were the usual ones of nineteenth century anthropology. Through the successive editions of his major work, there was no development in his views on the nature of primitive thought to match the advances his contemporaries were making.

Frazer, for example, consistently described primitive religion in animistic terms. The theory of animism, in Tylor's sense that the primitive mind peopled the world with personal "souls," was never entirely superseded; but by the early years of the twentieth century most anthropologists no longer accepted animism as the starting point of religion. An alternative theory had been developed which described a type of thinking psychologically more primitive, hence prior to animism in the evolutionary scale.[19] This "pre-animistic" type of thinking involved a completely impersonalized conception of "divinity" in nature. The primitive mind, according to this theory, regarded everything, living or inanimate, as imbued with a generalized life-force which had no separate identity or will of its own.[20] Thus, modern anthropologists made a distinction between animism, the doctrine of individual "souls," and dynamism, the more primitive doctrine of impersonal force. Frazer confused the two as aspects of one and the same crude thought process.

Nevertheless, *The Golden Bough* was a quarry of useful information on primitive religious belief and practice. The materials Frazer gathered with such prodigality provided the basis for a mass of interesting comparisons that were often quite illuminating with

[19] See R. R. Marett, "Pre-animistic Religion," *Folk-lore*, XI (1900), 162–82.
[20] See Fritz Schultze, *Psychologie der Naturvölker* (Leipzig, 1900), pp. 217–18, 251–52.

regard to the nature of specific rites and customs among primitive peoples in widely separated areas.

Armed with the insights of his comparative studies in general anthropology, Frazer turned to the specific field of the Old Testament. As he had traced the elements of primitive belief through the ritual customs of "savage" races, he now attempted to do the same with the religion of the Hebrew people.[21] Frazer explored the Old Testament for relics and survivals of the earlier stages of religious belief through which the ancestors of Israel had presumably passed in prehistoric times. Such relics, he believed, were embedded in great numbers in the literature of the Old Testament and awaited the eye of the comparative anthropologist to be recognized as indices to the primitive religion of the early Hebrews. The method for determining the original significance of the relics and survivals was to relate them to those earlier and cruder stages of thought and practice exemplified by the beliefs and customs of existing primitive peoples.

This attempt to seek parallels to the ideas and institutions of the Old Testament in a wider area than the Semitic world was the new feature which distinguished Frazer's work from that of Robertson Smith. Frazer supplied the element that had been lacking in the work of his master: copious data, collected without thought as to how they fitted into a theory of interpretation. He was the gatherer of facts *par excellence* and complemented Robertson Smith's theoretical interpretations with illustrative materials drawn from all parts of the world. But Frazer's studies in biblical anthropology by no means superseded those of Robertson Smith. Frazer made no attempt to co-ordinate his studies into a set of general conclusions regarding Hebrew religion. His discussions were more often descriptive and anecdotal than systematic or theoretical. Frazer was not a systematic thinker. Each passage in the Old

[21] *Folk-lore in the Old Testament: Studies in Comparative Religion* (3 vols. London, 1918).

Testament which he discussed was treated separately, so that his work had the character of an intermittent commentary rather than a well-ordered study of Hebrew belief and practice. He went through the Old Testament more or less at random, stopping only where something of interest to him occurred, and proceeded to illustrate some particular feature of the passage with examples of similar beliefs or practices in the religious behavior of primitive peoples. As in *The Golden Bough*, the analogies he assembled for comparative purposes were marshaled in great abundance and described with infinite detail, but they frequently seemed included for their intrinsic interest instead of their bearing upon the subject in hand. However, if Frazer did not always succeed in presenting his data in a logical relationship, he often set a number of apparently unrelated facts in illuminating juxtaposition. The comparative method, as he practiced it, served to throw light on many an obscure text which had been left untouched or was hurriedly passed over by the critical school as of little importance.

In Frazer's hands, the Old Testament was treated not so much as the record of a nation's religious growth as a sourcebook from which to study the primitive aspects of belief or the origins of ritual custom. His task, as he saw it, was to illustrate the survival of very primitive features under the surface of later religious conceptions, as a means of recovering the original beliefs of the Hebrews. He contented himself, therefore, with the role of supplying supplementary explanations of individual obscure points. In discussing the mark of Cain, for example, he explained the enigmatic sign as a mark set upon the murderer to camouflage him from his brother's ghost, who otherwise would have haunted him and eventually wreaked vengeance upon him.[22] Frazer was not concerned with the meaning which the story had for the writer of the text but with a long forgotten meaning behind the practice which it described. Similarly, in the numerous stories of Abraham,

[22] See *Folk-lore in the Old Testament*, I, 78–100.

the only feature that interested him was a certain detail in the account of how the patriarch made a covenant with God (Gen. 15). The hitherto inexplicable rite of passing between the severed halves of a sacrificial animal in ratifying the covenant Frazer explained, by comparison with a number of similar rites among primitive peoples, as a bit of sacramental magic which had the character of a purification ritual.[23]

Yet there was a danger in thus emphasizing only primitive survivals. Frazer's method of interpretation unintentionally made the religion of the Hebrews seem compounded entirely of primitive elements. That animistic notions, magic, and taboo were factors in the religion of the early Hebrews was highly probable. But Frazer equated their religion too much with the religion of modern primitives, to the neglect of other elements which were probably more characteristic. Similarly, he made the religion of the historical period seem much more primitive than the Old Testament records justified, by his habit of concentrating upon certain curious details which reflected primitive ideas surviving into late times. The details which he chose for study were seldom distinctive features of Israel's religion. It was all very well, for example, to suggest that the survival of demonology accounted for such phenomena as placing a fringe of golden bells on the raiment of the high priest in order to scare away evil spirits;[24] but the question inevitably arises whether the Israelites of the historical period actually had any memory of such primitive superstitions—granted that the superstition had existed in the beginning. Frazer's concentration upon such survivals too easily led to exaggeration of their significance. His method seemed to make them important clues to characteristic elements of Hebrew belief, instead of keeping them in proper perspective as incidental elements in the total picture.

But the faults of Frazer's methodology were the faults of nine-

[23] See, *ibid.*, I, 392–99, 408–12.
[24] *Ibid.*, III, 446, 480.

teenth century anthropology in general. A persistent preoccupation with the most primitive forms of religious behavior had given even the general interpretations of religion at that time a certain incompleteness.

Sociopsychological and Magical Theories of Religion

Nineteenth century interpretations of religion had been curiously one-sided, not only because they concentrated on the primitive features, but because they attempted to explain these features exclusively in terms of the psychology of the individual. The first major change in anthropological theory came when attention was directed to the social forces that played an equally important part in shaping the basic forms of belief and practice. It was the work of Wilhelm Wundt in the realm of psychological theory that first drew the attention of anthropologists to the importance of social determinants in the development of human thought processes. Wundt felt that the psychology of the individual did not suffice to explain the phenomena of primitive thinking. As Bastian had maintained, the effects of group life upon the subjective experiences of the individual would have to be considered before primitive psychology could really be understood. For the thinking of the individual was dominated by the traditional conceptions and motivations of the group.[25]

The application of Wundt's theories to the interpretation of primitive religion was made by the French ethnological school headed by Emile Durkheim. Starting with Wundt's theoretical reconstruction of the thought processes of early man, Durkheim attempted to arrive at an understanding of the sociopsychological background of religion by making use of actual data on particular primitive races. From the studies of Spencer and Gillen on the natives of Australia, who were nearest to the savage state of early

---

[25] See Wilhelm Wundt, *Völkerpsychologie* (2 vols. in 5 parts, Leipzig, 1900–09), esp. Vol. I, pp. 1–6.

mankind, Durkheim concluded that the earliest form of religion was a system of group belief in an impersonal power inherent in the group, which held the group together and was worshiped by it.[26] Religion, in other words, was an emotional participation in group experience; it had no meaning for the individual apart from the social unit to which he belonged. This linking of religious feeling with social organization was the significant element in Durkheim's exposition.[27]

But the most important aspect of Durkheim's theory was the fact that his conception of the "power" inherent in the social group was akin to dynamistic theories of impersonal force. Durkheim himself identified the power reverenced by the natives of Australia with the mysterious force called *mana* by the Melanesians. This conception of an impersonal force which manifested itself in natural objects, living things, and even men had originally been discovered among the South Sea islanders by R. H. Codrington,[28] and had since become a staple of the dynamistic interpretation of primitive thinking about the nature of the world.[29] Two younger members of Durkheim's school, Henri Hubert and Marcel Mauss, saw in the notion of *mana* a primitive mental category which was the original basis for all magic and religion.[30] Instead of opposing the phenomena of magic to those of religion, as was usually done, they maintained that both stemmed from the same thought process.

[26] *Les formes élémentaires de la vie religieuse* (Paris, 1912), pp. 211–12, 268–72, 314–18. There is an English translation by J. W. Swain (London, 1915).

[27] Cf. Alexander Goldenweiser, "Religion and Society: A Critique of Emile Durkheim's Theory of the Origin and Nature of Religion," *Journal of Philosophy,* XIV (1917), 113–24.

[28] *The Melanesians: Studies in Their Anthropology and Folklore* (Oxford, 1891).

[29] See Edward Clodd, "Pre-animistic Stages in Religion," *Transactions of the Third International Congress for the History of Religion* (2 vols., Oxford, 1908), I, 33–35; K. T. Preuss, *Die geistige Kultur der Naturvölker* (Leipzig, 1914); Edvard Lehmann, "Die Anfänge der Religion und die Religion der primitiven Völker," in Paul Hinneberg (ed.), *Die Kultur der Gegenwart,* Div. I, Vol. III, Part I (Berlin, 1906), 1–27 (see esp. pp. 10–17).

[30] "Esquisse d'une théorie générale de la magie," *L'année sociologique,* VII (1904), 1–146.

Religion was a social phenomenon; its rites were designed to propitiate the invisible powers in the interests of the social group. Magic was practiced by the individual to accomplish purely personal ends by bending the invisible powers to his will. But the "*force mystique*" which the individual exploited in magic was the same which the social group depended upon in its religious rites.[31]

The theoretical basis for such dynamistic interpretations of primitive thought was provided by Lucien Lévy-Bruhl.[32] He described the primitive mentality of savage peoples as "prelogical," by which he did not mean a type of thinking that antedated the development of logical thought nor a type of thinking that was unlogical, in any way, but an early mode of thought that was "mystical" rather than rational. It was a species of imagination whereby things, animals, and men were conceived as participating in various cycles of relationships which existed in the immediate and the supernatural worlds at the same time. The primitive mind did not make the distinction between the material and the spiritual worlds to which the modern mind is accustomed. Hence, primitive man habitually explained everything not by natural causes but by the action of invisible forces. A necessary consequence of the failure to distinguish between the material and the spiritual was the belief that it was possible to use physical means of constraint to render the invisible powers favorable; that is, magic was effective in the sphere of religious practice.[33]

This emphasis on the magical aspect of primitive religion, at first incidental to the sociopsychological explanation of religious

---

[31] See also Karl Beth, *Religion und Magie bei den Naturvölkern* (Leipzig, 1914); Alfred Vierkandt, "Die Anfänge der Religion und Zauberei," *Globus*, XCII (1907), 21-25, 40-45, 61-65.

[32] *Les fonctions mentales dans les sociétés inférieures* (Paris, 1910), *La mentalité primitive* (Paris, 1922), and *L'âme primitive* (Paris, 1927). English translations: *How Natives Think* (London, 1926), *Primitive Mentality* (New York, 1923), and *The "Soul" of the Primitive* (London, 1928). A convenient summary of his theories is provided by G. van der Leeuw, "La structure de la mentalité primitive," *RHPR*, VIII (1928), 1-31.

[33] See *Les fonctions mentales*, pp. 344-45.

belief and practice, became a dominant theme in anthropological theory. While ethnologists had finally caught up with Robertson Smith's insight into the importance of collective factors in the formation of primitive ideas, they went off on a tangent for a time, seeking to establish the magical nature of ritual actions used in the service of religion.

Hubert and Mauss, for example, attempted to demonstrate the intimate connection between the magical mode of thinking (constraint of the invisible powers) and the practice of offering sacrifice.[34] They could not accept either Tylor's theory that sacrifice was originally conceived as a gift of propitiation to the supernatural powers or Robertson Smith's explanation of sacrifice as a means of establishing communion with the gods. Both theories assumed the existence of a personal conception of the supernatural powers, such as the most primitive peoples had not attained. Hubert and Mauss sought to identify the "pre-animistic" element in the original conception of sacrifice. This they thought they found in the basic procedure of all types of sacrifice, which consisted in establishing some sort of communication between the sacred and profane worlds through the intermediary of a victim. Sacrifice, originally, was a means of tapping the resources of power usually designated by the term *mana*. By various preliminary ceremonies the mysterious power was concentrated in the sacrificial victim and then discharged to the benefit of gods (in the gift types of sacrifice) or of men (in atonement sacrifices) through the destruction of the victim, either by burning or by slaughter.[35] Thus Hubert and Mauss related the various forms of sacrifice to a single primitive mode of thought, instead of tracing them back, as Tylor and Robertson Smith had done, to a single *type* conceived as the original from

---

[34] "Essai sur la nature et la fonction sociale du sacrifice," *L'année sociologique*, II (1899), 29–138. Reprinted in their *Mélanges d'histoire des religions* (Paris, 1909). pp. 1–130.

[35] *Mélanges*, pp. 64–65, 124–25.

which all other types were derived in the course of an evolutionary development.

As applied to the Old Testament (one of the sources from which Hubert and Mauss drew their data), this method of interpretation betrayed a fault that was all too common whenever ethnologists who were not themselves Old Testament scholars attempted to interpret it in terms of some theory derived from the observation of external data. Hubert and Mauss imported into the Old Testament a primitive mode of thought without considering the point of view the Old Testament itself may have reflected. In the process, in order to fit the data into their scheme of interpretation, they treated the Old Testament as all of a piece, ignoring the possibility of variation in viewpoint or of historical growth in the ideas expressed. Declaring that their purpose was to make a general analysis of sacrifice, not a historical study of its forms, they took the whole Pentateuch as their base, disregarding the critical analysis of its parts and paying little or no attention to the data which criticism had amassed regarding the historical development of sacrificial customs among the Israelites.[36] More confidence in the validity of their conclusions would have been possible if they had taken into account the results of other approaches to the Old Testament.[37]

The same uncritical procedure appeared in the study of Israel's religion made by Richard Kreglinger,[38] another French ethnologist who was not a specialist in the Old Testament but a historian of religions in general. Attempting to interpret the biblical evidence in the light of the new theories regarding the nature of primitive religion, he devoted the body of his work to a lively description of

[36] See, ibid., pp. 9–10, note.

[37] Later students of the subject, critical scholars who made use of ethnological data to throw light upon Old Testament belief and practice, took care to consider the possible diversity of conceptual motifs behind the institution of sacrifice. Cf. Alfred Loisy, Essai historique sur le sacrifice (Paris, 1920); G. Buchanan Gray, Sacrifice in the Old Testament: Its Theory and Practice (Oxford, 1925); Adolf Wendel, Das Opfer in der altisraelitischen Religion (Leipzig, 1927); W. O. E. Oesterley, Sacrifices in Ancient Israel (London, 1938).

[38] La religion d'Israël (Brussels, 1922).

the popular religion of the Israelites, in which survivals of primitive elements were to be found in the greatest number. But Kreglinger did not always make clear whether he was describing the primitive religion of the Hebrews before the adoption of the cult of Yahweh, the religion of the Israelites after their settlement in Canaan, or the Canaanite religion itself. He tended to reduce them all to one great mass of religious phenomena, instead of separating them into successive stages or contemporary states of religion. Like Hubert and Mauss, he lacked the sense of historical development. Moreover, Kreglinger's interpretation of the data was guided by his predominant interest in the dynamistic conceptions of primitive religion.[39] He went so far as to equate the Semitic generic term for the deity, *el* or *elohim*, with the notion of *mana*.[40] There was no doubt that primitive conceptions, including the dynamistic point of view, survived in portions of the Old Testament;[41] but Kreglinger's preoccupation with such notions led him to devote more space to survivals than to the more distinctive features of Israel's religion.

The work of the French ethnologists manifestly suffered the same limitation as Sir James G. Frazer's. Anthropological research in the twentieth century eventually broadened its scope to include the totality of a religious culture. But for the time being the effort persisted to explain the belief and practice of ancient Israel in terms of magical notions, in spite of the resulting danger of making Israel's religion seem more primitive than it was. Examples of the supposed influence of magical notions on Israelite thinking were pointed out by the Norwegian scholar, Sigmund Mowinckel, in a series of studies on the Old Testament psalms. He made the ingenious observation that the "evil" complained of in the supplication psalms was really the magic art, as practiced by the "enemies"

[39] See especially, *ibid.*, chap. VI.
[40] *Ibid.*, pp. 66-72.
[41] Cf. Alfred Bertholet's exposition of the dynamistic basis of Old Testament sacrifice, "Zum Verständnis des alttestamentlichen Opfergedankens," *JBL*, XLIX (1930), 218-33.

of the suppliants in order to work harm upon them.[42] Similarly, the formulas of blessing and of cursing scattered through the psalms, Mowinckel believed, had been used in conjunction with rituals of benediction and malediction which were magical in their fundamental assumptions.[43] Since so many of the psalms seemed to reflect the primitive belief in the effectiveness of magical actions, Mowinckel rejected the postexilic date which the critical school had adopted for their composition and placed their origin in the early historical period. If his general thesis was sound, it indicated that, spiritually, Israel was still a primitive folk in whose thinking magic and sorcery played a large part, as it did among primitive peoples generally.[44]

But Mowinckel probably read the original magical significance of the term "evil" too frequently into expressions that may have had no more than a metaphorical connotation by the time the psalms were composed. If the psalmists made use of primitive magical terms to describe the sources of evil, the faith they expressed in the source of deliverance rose above the mechanical level of exorcism and rested quite upon a spiritual plane. Mowinckel's error was to assume the survival of the magical notions behind the cultic expressions down into a period much later than the history of Israel's religion warranted.[45] Similarly, with regard to the formulas of blessing and cursing, the conceptions behind them no doubt had their roots in magical notions, but by the time of the early monarchical period the primitive ideas had been sublimated into more genuinely religious conceptions.[46] As Alfred Bertholet

[42] *Psalmenstudien, I: Awän und die individuellen Klagepsalmen* (Kristiania, 1922).

[43] *Psalmenstudien, V: Segen und Fluch in Israels Kult und Psalmendichtung* (1924).

[44] See also Nicolai Nicolsky, *Spuren magischer Formeln in den Psalmen* (Giessen, 1927).

[45] Cf. Hermann Gunkel's criticism in *Einleitung in die Psalmen* (Göttingen, 1928), pp. 196–203.

[46] This was the argument of Johannes Hempel, "Die israelitischen Anschauungen von Segen und Fluch im Lichte altorientalischer Parallelen," ZDMG, LXXIX (1925), 20–110.

pointed out, the religion of Israel in historical times had outgrown the primitive dynamistic type of thinking and had achieved a strongly personal conception of deity which was distinctive in the ancient world.[47]

Mowinckel, however, found the magical mode of thinking a convenient explanation for another group of ideas implicit in the psalms. There was a strong admixture in some of these hymns of mythological allusions to the creation, the combat with a dragon, and the judgment of the "enemies," which Mowinckel took to be the surviving traces of a cult-myth describing the accession to his throne of the Divine King, the Creator, who was victor over primeval chaos. The psalms which contained these allusions Mowinckel assumed had once formed the liturgy for an annual celebration of the enthronement of Yahweh,[48] the rituals of which were based on magical notions usually associated with agricultural rites. An important feature of the New Year celebration, during which Mowinckel assumed the enthronement of Yahweh took place, was a solemn procession which marched round the Temple with the fruits of the harvest and poured out water from the pool of Siloam. Both actions corresponded to ancient vegetation rites, originally believed to have magical potency in ensuring the fertility of the soil and inducing an abundant rainfall during the coming year.[49] Sir James G. Frazer had found similar rites among various primitive peoples who depended upon agriculture for their sustenance and had interpreted them as "magical in intention," since the purpose always was to induce the desired outcome by imita-

---

[47] *Der Beitrag des Alten Testaments zur allgemeinen Religionsgeschichte* (Tübingen, 1923).

[48] *Psalmenstudien, II: Das Thronbesteigungsfest Jahwäs und der Ursprung der Eschatologie* (1922). Cf. Hans Schmidt's summary of Mowinckel's theory for nontechnical readers: *Die Thronfahrt Jahwes am Fest der Jahreswende im alten Israel* (Tübingen, 1927). The theory had been anticipated, without Mowinckel's knowledge, by Paul Volz, *Das Neujahrsfest Jahwes* (Tübingen, 1912).

[49] On the magical character of the ritual of pouring water over the altar, cf. Robertson Smith, *Religion of the Semites* (2d ed., 1894), p. 231.

tion.[50] Mowinckel interpreted not only these rituals but the whole ceremony of the enthronement of Yahweh as magical in intention. It was not a mere commemorative ceremony but a ritual designed to bring into being the things it typified. It was "creative drama" that not only represented but actualized Yahweh's annual reassumption of his royal power and his re-creation of heaven and earth (in the form of rainfall and fertility).[51] Moreover, it assured the realization of the hopes of those who took part in the ceremonies. The Israelite who followed the Ark into the Temple, singing one of the "accession" psalms which proclaimed Yahweh's kingship, was confident that, with Yahweh's assumption of power for another year, the enemies of his people would be reduced to impotence.[52]

As described by Mowinckel, such an enthronement ceremony must have been the most important feature of the New Year's rituals performed at Jerusalem. Yet it was nowhere mentioned in those parts of the Law or the Prophets which described or referred to the festivals of the religious year. Mowinckel simply assumed its existence from the analogy of the Babylonian New Year's ritual and from the fragmentary traces of the supposed cult-myth surviving in the psalms. The evidence was extremely tenuous; yet he made it the basis for an elaborate theory regarding the existence in Israel of a faith in the magical efficacy of ritual actions.

Perhaps this continued emphasis on the survival of the magical mode of thinking in connection with the performance of religious rituals was due to the confusion of religion with magic for which Hubert and Mauss were responsible. They had emphasized the similarity of the technique of constraint in magical rites and in ritual actions but had confused the object toward which the respec-

---

[50] *The Golden Bough*, Vol. VII (3d ed., 1912), pp. 92–104.
[51] See *Psalmenstudien*, II, 19–22. Cf. his article, "Drama, religionsgeschichtlich," in Hermann Gunkel *et al.* (eds.), *Die Religion in Geschichte und Gegenwart* (2d rev. ed., 5 vols., Tübingen, 1927–32), I, 2000–03.
[52] See *Psalmenstudien*, II, 126–27.

tive practices were directed. Where the act of constraint was thought of as bending an impersonal force, conceived in dynamistic terms, to the will of the practitioner, it was an act of magic. But where the ritual was addressed to a power conceived as individualized and as acting with a will of its own, the act was an essentially religious one. This distinction was clarified with reference to Old Testament practice by Alfred Bertholet in a short monograph[53] which not only summarized the evidence for dynamistic conceptions in the thinking of the Israelites but also showed how successfully their conception of deity had advanced to a personal definition of divine power. The dynamistic notion of exploiting an impersonal power through magical actions had been sloughed off in their religious rituals. Only in the area of private usage did magic remain as the dynamistic point of view warped to selfish ends.[54]

By and large, the bypath of a magical interpretation of Old Testament religious practice proved to be a blind alley. A more profound and substantial interpretation of the religious ideology behind Old Testament religion was Johannes Pedersen's comprehensive survey of the concepts and thought forms implicit in the belief and practice of ancient Israel.[55] Pedersen sought to explain Israel's religious culture by analyzing the characteristic conceptions of the Hebrew mentality and describing them in systematic form. Insofar as the original ideas of the early Israelites could be recovered from the ancient sources, they revealed—at least, as Pedersen described them—that dynamistic notions of the nature of existence were still living conceptions in the thinking of the Israelites. Pedersen never used the term *mana* in this connection, but his discussion of the two fundamental notions of "soul" (in Volume

[53] *Das Dynamistische im Alten Testament* (Tübingen, 1926).

[54] Cf. his "Das Wesen der Magie," *Nachrichten von der Gesellschaft der Wissenschaften zu Göttingen: Geschäftliche Mitteilungen* (1926–27), pp. 63–85.

[55] *Israel, I-II* (Copenhagen, 1920), *Israel, III-IV* (1934); English translation: *Israel: Its Life and Culture*, Vol. I (London, 1926), Vol. II (1940). All references are to the English translation. Oxford University Press.

I) and "holiness" (in Volume II) showed that these conceptions corresponded in essence to the primitive notion.

The "soul," for example, to an Israelite was not something separate and separable from the body, as in modern thinking; it was "man in his total essence." This unity of the personality expressed itself as *will*, which was the total personality acting as a conscious entity.[56] Associated with this conception of the soul were certain basic concepts of Israelite thought, such as blessing, honor, and shame, which corresponded in essential meaning to dynamistic notions. "Blessing" was the vital power of the soul, through which it was able to act and bring happiness to itself and others. As "souls" differed from each other, so did the nature of their "blessing." Great souls like David had great blessing, which constantly increased, and which multiplied the happiness of those around them. With souls like Saul, on the other hand, blessing decreased; and the peculiar "power" of his soul only contributed to the unhappiness of others. Thus, the success or failure of a person depended upon the "strength" of his soul, the amount of blessing (i.e., effective energy) that was within him.[57] Blessing gave a man "honor," a certain "weightiness," as the etymology of the Hebrew word suggested. "Honor is not that which the man himself or others, with more or less justice, think of him. Honor is that which actually fills the soul and keeps it upright." [58] Shame, on the other hand, was the effect of a lack of "blessing" in the soul. Weakness and failure were *dis*-honor. "Not to possess sufficient courage [i.e., spiritual power] to maintain one's honor is shame." [59] The similarity of these definitions to the primitive conception of a person's *mana* is implicit in Pedersen's phraseology.

"Holiness," too, as Pedersen described it, was a spiritual power,

[56] See, in general, *ibid.*, I, 99–104.
[57] See, *ibid.*, I, 183, 184–89. Cf. the similar discussion by Aubrey R. Johnson, *The Vitality of the Individual in the Thought of Ancient Israel* (Cardiff, 1949).
[58] Pedersen, *op. cit.*, I, 213; cf. pp. 234, 237.
[59] *Ibid.*, I, 239; cf. pp. 239–41.

closely related in conception to the "blessing" of the soul. "Holiness
. . . is the extraordinary, the greatly increased strength of the
soul." [60] It was a quality which the leader in battle, the prophet in
his ecstatic experience, and the priest in daily contact with holy
things could have in great measure.[61] Actually, "holiness is a force
which is felt in all spheres of life; it is, indeed, at the root of all
other kinds of energy." [62] Pedersen thus made the conception mean
much more than it had signified in Robertson Smith's definition,
where it was restricted to the area of "separated" things associated
with the cultus. Pedersen acknowledged that holiness attached
especially to sacred places and cultic objects, which were "marked
by an immense concentration of sacred strength." [63] But he equated
the conception with the primitive notion of *mana* rather than
tabu.[64] Consequently, he gave a somewhat different interpretation
of the cultus from that of Robertson Smith. He defined the purpose of sacrifice as "the renewal of holiness" in the soul. "Atonement especially expresses the change that takes place in the soul
when it is freed from all that inhibits it." The rite "brings about
a close communion between the worshiper and the source of holiness and power." [65] Robertson Smith had emphasized the establishment of this bond as the purpose of atonement; Pedersen made
the resulting access of spiritual power the significant element in
the ritual.

Still other conceptions, that were ethical in nature, Pedersen
explained not merely in terms of primitive thought but in terms
of their social implications. For he believed, with the twentieth
century anthropologists, that there was an intimate connection between the psychology of a people and its social system. He pointed

[60] *Ibid.*, II, 267.
[61] See, *ibid.*, II, 34–35, 111–12, 266–67, respectively.
[62] *Ibid.*, II, 264.
[63] *Ibid.*, II, 198.
[64] See, *ibid.*, II, 267–70.
[65] *Ibid.*, II, 359, 361.

out that in early Israelite thinking, in apparent correlation with the tribal organization of nomadic society, the individual and the social group were never conceived as independent entities.[66] The typical Israelite thought in terms of group entities (the tribe) of which the individual units (the members of the tribe) were but particular representatives. Israelite psychology was not individualistic; it operated with the mental category of corporate personality.[67] "The soul only exists in organic connection with other souls, and it can only act through being united with others."[68] To live rightly, therefore, meant to live in community. To an Israelite, solitude was unnatural and isolation inhuman; such spiritual states signified that a person lacked "blessing" or stood under a curse. But to live in community with others meant to share blessing with them and to partake of the spiritual "harmony" of the group. The word used to designate this harmony was "peace." Etymologically, it meant "wholeness"; but it referred not so much to the wholeness of an individual soul as the harmonious unity of the social group.[69]

Similarly, the idea of "righteousness" signified not merely the spiritual health of the individual but the social health of the community. As applied to the individual, righteousness meant that condition of the soul in which it was in complete conformity with its own being.[70] But, since the soul had no real existence apart from its membership in the community, the ideal of righteousness also signified the social condition in which individuals co-operated in maintaining the harmony proper to the social group.[71]

These examples suffice to show that Pedersen's attempt system-

[66] See, ibid., I, 110, 485.

[67] Cf. H. Wheeler Robinson, "The Hebrew Conception of Corporate Personality," in Paul Volz (ed.), Werden und Wesen des Alten Testaments (Berlin, 1936), pp. 49–62.

[68] Pedersen, op. cit., I, 340. Cf. J. Philip Hyatt, "The Old Testament View of Man," Religion in Life, XIV (1945), 526–34.

[69] See, in general, ibid., I, 263–64, 311–13.

[70] See, ibid., I, 336–38.

[71] See, ibid., I, 345.

atically to define the fundamental notions of Hebrew belief resulted in a distinctive and self-consistent picture of the thought
forms of ancient Israel. Yet, the question has been raised by a
number of his critics whether Pedersen drew a true picture of the
actual psychology of the Israelites, or whether he did not read into
the biblical texts a few basic notions derived from too theoretical
a conception of primitive psychology. Gustav Hölscher, for example, asked whether such a primitive mode of thought as the
dynamistic conception of the soul was still effective in the thinking
of even the earliest Israelites.[72] Acknowledging that "dynamistic
conceptions . . . are echoed in the Hebrew legends, just as similar
notions live on in the tales and folklore of modern times," Hölscher
nevertheless maintained that "the Israelites must have left off thinking in dynamistic thought forms much earlier than Pedersen
assumed." [73]

If Pedersen failed to estimate correctly the maturity of religious
thought among the Israelites, the probable reason was that he gave
inadequate consideration to the historical evolution of the basic
conceptions he dealt with. He was rightly aware of the influence
upon Israelite thinking of historical changes such as the gradual
dissolution of the tribal organization and the transition from the
nomadic to the agricultural mode of life. But only infrequently
did he show how the development of particular conceptions was
given a new turn by these external factors, as when he pointed out
how the ancient conception of "honor" was transformed after the
settlement in Palestine into the conception of personal power.[74]
Apart from an occasional sidelight of this sort, Pedersen made no
attempt to study the basic beliefs of the Israelites historically.
Instead of tracing an idea chronologically through the process of
its development, he gathered the evidence for an analysis of its

---

[72] In a review of Pedersen's volumes, in *Theologische Studien und Kritiken*,
CVIII (1937–38), 238.
[73] *Ibid.*, p. 248.
[74] See Pedersen, *op. cit.*, I, 225.

psychological content without reference to the stages of Israel's history to which the data belonged. Like Hubert and Mauss, he approached the Old Testament as a sourcebook, all parts of which were equally valuable for his purpose of constructing a systematic description of the fundamental thought forms. The method made for consistency of theory, but it eliminated almost completely any sense of historical development from the presentation of the data. Pedersen's work, in other words, suffered the limitations of most anthropological research into the "phenomenology" of religion. It was descriptive rather than historical, hence "ideal" rather than actual.

Pedersen, however, has had great influence on Old Testament scholars. They have approved his attempt to explain the religious conceptions of the Israelites by detailed analysis of their thought processes. Some have gone even further in probing the psychology of religious experience in Israel. Where Pedersen had contented himself with defining the intellectual categories which shaped religious thinking, others have attempted to fathom the emotional responses of the typical Israelite. Johannes Hempel, for example, in his study of the way the Israelites expressed their experience of the relation between God and man,[75] drew attention to an aspect of Israel's religious life that had not previously been taken into account. Hempel argued that Israelite psychology could be most clearly understood in terms of a continual alternation between two poles of religious feeling: the feeling of remoteness from God and the consciousness of union with him. By applying this concept of polarity to the interpretation of particular portions of Israel's spiritual history, Hempel showed how the interacting influence of the two emotions determined the specific character of religious feeling in each successive period. Hempel's exposition of the deeper meaning that Israel's religion had for its adherents preserved the historical method of presentation which Pedersen's analysis

[75] *Gott und Mensch im Alten Testament* (Stuttgart, 1926; rev. ed., 1936).

lacked; yet it seems no more complete, for it applied only one principle of interpretation to the religious psychology of the Old Testament, missing the distinctive emotions expressed in particular portions of the literature.[76]

In the light of results achieved up to this point, the value of the sociopsychological approach to Old Testament religion is difficult to assess. The use of the theories of prelogical, magical, or dynamistic thinking as principles of interpretation illuminated this or that aspect of Israel's religious psychology but resulted in limited interpretations of the nature of Israel's religion. Each scholar applied a single theory to the phenomena; and, since each theory usually embodied a point of view derived from the study of primitive religions, the belief and practice of the later periods tended to appear as primitive as that of the earlier periods. The failure to make clear how the transition from a primitive mentality to the highly developed conceptions of a later age had been accomplished was chiefly due to a general neglect of the more distinctive features of Old Testament religion. Adequate consideration of the characteristic elements would have prevented the assumption that prelogical thinking, the magical point of view, or the dynamistic mode of thought was the fundamental feature of Israel's religion at its height.

The Historical Approach in Anthropology: Its Effect on Old Testament Research

Since the days of E. B. Tylor, anthropologists had been trying to explain the whole of primitive religion in terms of one or another basic phenomenon. Even after the important shift in perspective brought about by Wilhelm Wundt, the social anthropologists had been seeking a single clue to the fundamental basis of religion. Their objective was a worthy one: to discover the nature and function of

[76] A similar survey of the historical development of one specific idea was made by Hans Schmidt in his systematic presentation of the successive attempts in the Old Testament to solve the problem of suffering: *Gott und das Leid im Alten Testament* (Giessen, 1926).

religion in its general or universal aspect. But continued research in the field of primitive culture had begun to raise doubts whether the religion of the primitives contained the key to the basic character of religion. For with the progress of research the primitive phenomena became less and less amenable to a single principle of interpretation. What the early anthropologists had taken for simplicity turned out to be characterized by a confusing complexity. They had erred, therefore, in assuming that one or another of the aspects of primitive religion was the primary feature that determined all the rest.

The error was due to the assumption that primitive peoples everywhere had gone through the same stages of development. The theory of uniform development, however, was called into question by the bewildering variety of forms revealed by the accumulation of new evidence. Primitive phenomena were not always the simplest in a series, and the stages of development did not always follow the same order. Sometimes conceptions and institutions believed to have been universal were entirely absent from a particular milieu. The assumed uniformity was contrary to the facts.[77] Anthropology, therefore, could not hope to give a schematic outline of the cultural development of all mankind. It could only describe the behavior of particular groups under particular circumstances.

The more intensively the data regarding primitive belief and practice were examined, the more obvious it became that to appreciate their true significance a more scientific method must be applied to their study. To begin with, the data must be considered in their own context and explained in relation to the thought forms and institutions characteristic of their own milieu. For, if primitive religion was not one thing that could be described in general terms but many distinct kinds of belief and practice, a truly objective

---

[77] See Franz Boas, *The Mind of Primitive Man* (New York, 1911), chap. VII; Robert H. Lowie, *Primitive Society* (New York, 1920), pp. 289-323, 414-28; Alexander Goldenweiser, *Early Civilization* (New York, 1922), pp. 115-28.

method would require the study of each kind as a separate body of ideas and customs. Not theoretical reconstruction of the psychology of primitive man, but scientific analysis of actual data was needed, with a view to reconstructing the actual history of definite phenomena. Moreover, the possibility of external influence upon the phenomena of belief and practice must be taken into account and the assimilation of borrowed elements described as fully as the development of the native elements. It had been a fault of the older anthropology to neglect the evidence for borrowing of culture traits by one social group from another. As a consequence, an adequate understanding of the role played by foreign contacts in the development of ideas and institutions was generally lacking.

The value of the historical method in anthropology had not been unappreciated even in the nineteenth century. There were always a few students who were conscious of the inadequacies of theoretical anthropology.[78] But the historical approach did not become paramount until it was evoked by the massive authority of Franz Boas. He constantly insisted that native cultures were to be studied in their historicogeographical environments and in relation to their contacts with surrounding cultures.[79] Hence, instead of "primitive culture" as a generalized phenomenon, assumed to represent the original condition of all mankind, the Boas school of ethnologists studied distinct "cultures" in specific local areas. They devoted primary attention to the "pattern" of culture in each area and the adaptation of borrowed elements to the local pattern.[80] These concepts of the "culture area" and the "cultural pattern" were the chief contributions of the American school to modern ethnology.

[78] E.g., H. J. Sumner Maine, in his *Lectures on the Early History of Institutions* (London, 1875), and *Dissertations on Early Law and Customs* (London, 1883).

[79] "Limitations of the Comparative Method of Anthropology," *Science*, N.S. IV (1896), 901–8; "The Methods of Ethnology," *American Anthropologist*, XXII (1920), 311–21.

[80] See Alexander Goldenweiser, "Diffusionism and the American School of Historical Ethnology," *American Journal of Sociology*, XXXI (1925–26), 19–38.

One of the most forceful advocates of the new "historical" approach was the British Old Testament scholar, Stanley A. Cook. In the extensive "Notes" which he appended to the third edition (1927) of Robertson Smith's *Lectures on the Religion of the Semites*, the effect of the new approach was made clearly evident. What Cook attempted in these comments on his master's classic work was primarily a re-examination of correct methodology in the study of religion. Since "correct methodology" was largely a matter of establishing definitions devoid of preconceptions, Cook's notes were a series of dissertations of varying length but of great intrinsic value upon such subjects as the nature of magic and religion, the conception of holiness, the doctrine of atonement, and the relation between the individual and the group in the development and practice of religion.[81] But, more particularly, Cook was concerned with historical method in the treatment of the data. In place of the theory of progressive evolution from the simple to the complex, Cook advocated recognizing that even primitive cultures were characterized by complexity. Instead of attempting to illustrate a generalized scheme of religious evolution, he emphasized the significance of individual cultural systems. A cultural system he defined as "a system of interrelated sentiments, ideas, and aims," thus approximating the idea of a cultural pattern. Pointing out how successfully Robertson Smith had grasped the close integration of all secular and religious aspects of primitive life,[82] Cook declared that "the really vital problem for modern research is . . . the varying relations between the 'religious' and the 'non-religious' phases of life and their mutual interaction"—in other words, the pattern of religious and social life in an integrated cultural area.[83] Moreover, as a student of primitive Semitic religion, he gave due

[81] See *Lectures on the Religion of the Semites*, edited by Stanley A. Cook (3d ed., London, 1927), pp. 679, 548–54, 645–54, 590–94, respectively.

[82] See above, pp. 47–48.

[83] *Op. cit.*, p. xlvi. Cf. the way in which Cook described the integration of religious with social and political life in "The Semites," *Cambridge Ancient History*, Vol. I (Cambridge, 1923), chap. V (pp. 181–237).

consideration to the possibility of cultural diffusion between the various culture areas of the ancient Orient.[84]

The theory that a "culture pattern," at least in the sphere of religious belief and practice, had been diffused through all the culture areas of the ancient Orient was fully developed by a group of British anthropologists under the leadership of Samuel H. Hooke. Finding the idea of a pattern of thought useful for explaining such phenomena as Sigmund Mowinckel had discussed, they undertook to prove that a specific set of myths and rituals, intimately associated with each other, had been wide-spread in the ancient East.[85] Religious texts from Babylonia and Egypt indicated that certain religious festivals, notably that of the New Year, were celebrated by the recitation of cult-myths in conjunction with rituals that included acting out the stories of the myths.[86] The New Year's festival in Babylon, for example, for which the evidence was most complete,[87] took the form of a great drama, centering in the figure of the "divine" king, who played the chief role in the ceremonies and at the same time represented the god in the myths symbolized by the rituals.[88] Hooke was impressed by the interrelated structure of the rituals. This "pattern," he believed, provided a better key to the nature of religious thinking in Babylonia than some arbitrary

[84] See his chapter, "The Religious Environment of Israel," in Arthur S. Peake (ed.), *The People and the Book* (Oxford, 1925), pp. 41–72.

[85] See the two omnibus volumes edited by Samuel H. Hooke, *Myth and Ritual* (Oxford, 1933) and *The Labyrinth* (London, 1935), especially the initial essay by the editor, "The Myth and Ritual Pattern of the Ancient East," in *Myth and Ritual*, pp. 1–14.

[86] See Heinrich Zimmern, *Das babylonische Neujahrsfest* (Leipzig, 1926); Kurt Sethe, *Dramatische Texte zu altägyptischen Mysterienspielen* (Leipzig, 1928).

[87] See Samuel H. Hooke, "The Babylonian New Year Festival," *Journal of the Manchester Egyptian and Oriental Society*, XIII (1927), 29–38; Cyril J. Gadd, "Babylonian Myth and Ritual," in *Myth and Ritual*, pp. 40–67.

[88] For a complete description and discussion of the festival, see Svend A. Pallis, *The Babylonian Akitu Festival* (Copenhagen, 1926), chap. IV (pp. 249–306). A survey of the ideas and customs associated with the conception of the "divine king," together with a discussion of supposed parallels in the Old Testament, is to be found in Ivan Engnell's *Studies in Divine Kingship in the Ancient Near East* (Uppsala, 1943).

mosaic of conceptions constructed from isolated elements of primitive belief. As Mowinckel had assumed regarding the ritual of "the enthronement of Yahweh" at Jerusalem, the annual presentation of these mythological rituals was not simply dramatic but magical in intention. They were intended to induce a favorable outcome of the natural processes symbolized in the myths. Even the recitation of the creation epic at the New Year's festival was regarded as a magical incantation of great potency, representing the renewal of the whole creation year by year.[89]

The conception of a pattern of myth and ritual, centered in the person of the king, proved to be a most suggestive contribution to the elucidation of the Old Testament. Used as a working hypothesis, it illuminated several things that were otherwise enigmatic. Sigmund Mowinckel had already applied the conception to the explanation of the New Year's rituals celebrated at Jerusalem.[90] He had attached no special significance, however, to the part played by the king in the ceremonies. That the king did play a part, in his capacity as chief priest of the nation, was proved by Julian Morgenstern[91] but with no implication that the role was magical. Now, one of Hooke's collaborators claimed that even in Israel the king was regarded as the ultimate source of well-being for the people, and that the role he played in the New Year ritual symbolized the renewal of vitality and prosperity in the community for the coming year.[92] There was some question, however, whether this position

[89] See Samuel H. Hooke, *The Origins of Early Semitic Ritual* (London, 1938), pp. 16-19. That the Babylonian myths had a distinct ritual significance was first pointed out by Leonard W. King, *The Legends of Babylon and Egypt in Relation to Hebrew Tradition* (London, 1918), pp. 50-51.

[90] See above, p. 66. Cf. W. O. E. Oesterley, "Early Hebrew Festival Rituals," in *Myth and Ritual*, pp. 122-38.

[91] "A Chapter in the History of the High Priesthood," *AJSL*, LV (1938), 1-24, 183-97, 360-77 (see esp. pp. 5-11).

[92] Aubrey R. Johnson, "The Role of the King in the Jerusalem Cults," in *The Labyrinth*, pp. 73-111; "Divine Kingship and the Old Testament," *Expository Times*, LXII (1950-51), 36-42.

could be fully maintained, in view of the fragmentary nature of the evidence for the ritual myth pattern in the Old Testament.[93]

Hooke and his school did not argue that the whole Near Eastern pattern of ritual and myth had been transmitted to the Israelites intact. Hooke recognized that the diffusion of culture patterns was frequently accompanied by "adaptation, disintegration, and degradation"; and that in the case of Canaanite and Hebrew culture the process had taken the form of disintegration, or the survival of separate fragments of the pattern.[94] Nevertheless, Hooke not only identified remnants of the pattern in the pre-exilic New Year rituals[95] but traced certain of its elements down into the thinking of very late times. He maintained that the magical attributes originally ascribed to the king were carried over into the conception of the Messiah. When the pre-exilic rituals had fallen into desuetude, the mythic elements of the ancient pattern were perpetuated in the new form given them by the apocalyptists.[96]

This approach to apocalyptic thought, whereby Hooke dealt only with an oriental feature surviving in the larger complex of ideas, illustrates how he and his associates allowed their particular theory too often to fill their whole horizon. They were so preoccupied with the similarities between Hebrew and oriental thought forms that they ignored the more distinctive features of Old Testament religion. It had not been Hooke's intention, of course, to do more than describe a particular pattern of thought which had influenced the religious belief and practice of the Israelites in certain respects. But he and his group tended to assume that the ritual

[93] Cf. the more cautious conclusion of C. R. North, "The Religious Aspects of Hebrew Kingship," *ZAW*, 50 (1932), 8–38; and the criticism of this circle of ideas, when applied to the Israelite New Year festival, by Norman H. Snaith, *The Jewish New Year Festival* (London, 1947).

[94] See *Myth and Ritual*, p. 5.

[95] See *The Origins of Early Semitic Ritual*, pp. 51–56.

[96] "The Myth and Ritual Pattern in Jewish and Christian Apocalyptic," in *The Labyrinth*, pp. 213–33.

myth pattern of the ancient East supplied characteristic and even basic motifs to Israelite religious thinking.

Stanley A. Cook, on the other hand, made a better balanced application of the new historical method, by studying the whole complex of ideas peculiar to the specific "cultural system" of Israel in Palestine. While he recognized that many ideas in the Old Testament could be paralleled in the religious conceptions of other peoples, he gave adequate consideration to the reinterpretation—not simply the survival in disintegrated form—of borrowed conceptions. He avoided the common failing of so many anthropologists who, in looking back toward the origins of religious beliefs, were so preoccupied with their original significance that they failed to consider the more important question of what such beliefs had become as a result of the intervening process of reinterpretation. After all, what an Israelite of the historical period actually believed when he took part in a ritual was more to the point than the largely forgotten myth his predecessors may have associated with it. Cook tried to show how completely certain conceptions common to the peoples of the ancient Orient had been remolded in Israelite thinking, with the result that they had become essentially unique.[97] This respect for the individuality of the religious beliefs under scrutiny was characteristic of historical anthropology at its best.

At any rate, recent studies in the field of anthropology have no longer been concerned with the nineteenth century problem of the origin and nature of the general phenomena of religion. Under the stimulus first imparted by Franz Boas, they have been investigating the historical development of specific beliefs and practices in particular areas. When anthropology now uses the comparative method, its purpose is not to abstract the universal meaning of analogous conceptions and usages but to clarify the significance of each in its own context.

[97] See *The Old Testament: A Reinterpretation* (London, 1936), chap. V.

In this respect, anthropological research has approximated the methodology long practiced by the "religio-historical" school. The latter deals with the great historical religions rather than the primitive religions of mankind. But, from the beginning, it has been studying the history of particular religions without preconceived theories of the general significance of religious phenomena. An important part of its research has been the investigation of external influences and of borrowing between religious cultures, but with proper attention to the adaptation of the borrowed elements to their new environment. Because of its emphasis on the historical rather than the primitive, the approach of the religio-historical school to the Old Testament has been even more fruitful than anthropological research in providing explanations of the phenomena of Old Testament religion. Its conclusions constitute another important supplementation of the results of criticism. We therefore turn next to the field of the "history of religions."

III

The Religio-Historical School and the Old Testament

The Rise of the Religio-Historical School of Interpretation

The field of research known in German as *Religionsgeschichte* and in French as *L'histoire des religions* has no convenient name in English. The term "comparative religion" sometimes applied to it rather connotes the early anthropological approach to religion and fails to indicate the important historical aspect which it had. Broadly speaking, it was the application of the historical method to the study of religion under the influence of Positivist principles of investigation, combined with the use of the comparative method as a valuable tool of research. The new approach originated during the revulsion of scholarship against speculative reconstructions of the nature of religion in the early nineteenth century. About the time that Auguste Comte was emphasizing the necessity of taking the concrete and the actual into consideration in philosophy, the "positive" approach in religious studies also came to the fore. Scholars turned away from broad generalizations about religion as such to study the facts regarding actual religions in their historical manifestations. With the recovery of the religious literatures of the Far East, the publication of a large number of inscriptions from the Graeco-Roman world, and the critical re-examination of the surviving documents of classical literature, the new approach acquired rich materials with which to work.[1]

The technique of investigation proceeded on the assumption

---

[1] See E. Hardy, "Zur Geschichte der vergleichenden Religionsforschung," *ARW*, IV (1901), 45–66, 97–135, 193–228.

that the best means of understanding an institution was to study its history: when and where it had originated, how it developed through subsequent changes, and what influences in its environment were responsible for its growth. The historian of religion saw his task as one of tracing the specific phenomena of religious belief and practice through the successive phases of their development from rudimentary to highly developed forms. At first, the "history of religions" was limited to the study of each great religion separately. But it soon became apparent that to investigate the data of one religion exclusively and to establish the major trends of its development alone was not enough to explain its history. Further light could be obtained by comparing the common phenomena and parallel trends of several religions. Those factors in the history of a particular religion that had not been fully understood could perhaps be explained by analogy with the corresponding phenomena in other religions. The historians of religion, however, never went so far as to assume, as the anthropologists were doing, that all religions followed a uniform sequence of stages of development. Their studies of analogies led to a different, more important conclusion.

The comparison of parallel phenomena revealed the fact that the beliefs or the practices of one religion had sometimes been influenced by those of another. This discovery widened the area in which the origins of particular phenomena were to be sought. It was already understood that cultural factors within a religion's native environment gave form to the religion and provided the stimuli to its further growth. Now it became clear that the formative milieu of a religion extended beyond its own cultural environment. Hence the science of religious history came to embrace the study of a religion not only in terms of its own background but in relation to the external influences affecting its development.

In the field of biblical studies, the religio-historical approach first appeared among a group of scholars who had sat at the feet of Albrecht Ritschl, but who broke away from his nonhistorical, speculative approach to the exegesis of Scripture. They desired an objective method of biblical study that would do justice to the new historical point of view which, in their generation, had come to dominate all research into the past. Their inspiration came from the historiography of Mommsen and von Ranke, who, like the Positivists, insisted that the primary requirement of scientific method was a thorough search for the facts contained in the written sources, without any attempt at a philosophical or theological interpretation. The members of the new school were as anxious as others had ever been to understand biblical religion in its breadth and depth, but they were convinced that this objective could best be attained if it were approached from a historical point of view.[2]

Since the Positivist effort to recover all the facts and to interpret them by a scientific historical method required the avoidance of any particular thesis that would betray a dogmatic interest or an apologetic purpose, the religio-historical school put biblical religion on the same plane with other religions as an object of investigation. Its history was interpreted in terms of the same theories of development that were found significant for the history of other religions. Believing that the course of history was an entirely natural process, the Positivist scholars, like the rationalists of the critical school, rejected all supernatural factors as effective causes in religious history. To rationalists like Wellhausen, the natural forces in history were a kind of immanent dynamic; to the Positivists, the determining factors were external to the events. But, for both, religion was the product of human culture, and theological systems were merely data in the history of religious ideas.

Moreover, the members of the new school considered it necessary to place biblical religion in its universal context and to seek its relationships with other religions in the ancient world. They

---

[2] Cf. Hermann Gunkel's remarks along this line, "Die Richtungen der alttestamentlichen Forschung," *Die christliche Welt*, XXXVI (1922), 66.

looked for parallel conceptions that might reveal the full significance of biblical ideas otherwise imperfectly understood, and they
searched out the influences from other religious traditions that
seemed to have penetrated the environment of biblical religion to
a significant degree. For example, the first major study by a member of this group, Hermann Gunkel's investigation into the popular
mythology underlying biblical ideas concerning the beginning and
the end of the world,[3] revealed that much of the Old Testament
and some of the New contained conceptual motifs derived from
external sources—in this case, ancient Babylonian myths in disintegrated form. The previous generation of critics had been unable to
discern and give a proper evaluation to the influence of such factors
upon the development of biblical ideas, since they relied almost
exclusively upon data within the Old Testament itself. But Gunkel
made clear that the history of Old Testament ideas could be truly
understood only after a comparative study of ideas current in
the external environment.

Wellhausen and Robertson Smith had made some comparisons,
it is true, with the religious beliefs of pre-Mohammedan Arabia,
which seemed to offer the closest parallels to early Hebrew religion. But the Arabian phenomena served only for purposes of
illustration; there was no question of influence from cults that were
so much later in time. Even so, the comparisons had reference
only to the early form of Hebrew religion, being confined to
conceptions and usages of a primitive nature. The later stages were
described by Wellhausen and Robertson Smith with almost no
reference to external analogies. For they regarded the growth of
Old Testament religion as a self-contained phenomenon.

This was only natural in view of the conception of history
which Wellhausen and his contemporaries had held. Little was
known, at the time, of cultural exchange between the oriental
nations. The intellectual and spiritual life of each ancient people

[3] *Schöpfung und Chaos in Urzeit und Endzeit* (Göttingen, 1895).

was regarded as having moved in its own sphere without any communication of ideas from one to another. The members of Wellhausen's school thought of Israel as an isolated nation, living in a small corner of the world apart from developments taking place in the great states of the Nile and Euphrates valleys. They saw no evidence of external influence upon it before the time of the Babylonian captivity. It is not surpising, therefore, that they wrote the history of Israel and its religion without any significant reference to the outside world, or that they considered it a much less complex history than it had actually been.[4]

But, even while the work of historical criticism had been going forward, the background against which Old Testament history had taken place was gradually being revealed through archaeological discoveries at the cultural sites of antiquity.[5] Cuneiform tablets were unearthed in large numbers, and their decipherment greatly enriched the former meager stock of knowledge concerning the history and culture of the ancient Orient. The most important discovery of this sort was the finding of the Tell-el-Amarna tablets in 1887. This rich collection of diplomatic correspondence between Egypt, on the one hand, and Babylonia, Assyria, and the petty states of Syria and Palestine, on the other, revealed a new world, the character of which had been hardly suspected. It showed that as early as the fourteenth century B.C. the whole ancient East had been one great area, which embraced a great number of peoples and states, each with its own individual characteristics, yet all united by political and cultural ties that made it impossible to understand them apart from each other.[6] Palestine lay in the

[4] Rudolf Smend's *Lehrbuch der alttestamentlichen Religionsgeschichte* (Freiburg, 1893), the most comprehensive history of Old Testament religion written from the critical point of view, neglected the factor of external influence almost entirely.

[5] The most detailed account of the excavations is given by H. V. Hilprecht and others in *Explorations in Bible Lands during the Nineteenth Century* (Philadelphia, 1903).

[6] See Carl Niebuhr, *Die Amarna-Zeit* ("Der alte Orient," I, 2; Leipzig, 1899; 3d ed., 1913); James Baikie, *The Amarna Age* (London, 1926).

middle of this world and was subject to its influence from early times. The lifting of the curtain gave the first clear view of the land as it had been before the entrance of the Hebrews and revealed a well-developed, though greatly mixed culture, the product of centuries of contact with Egypt and Mesopotamia.[7]

Most Old Testament scholars were still too much occupied, at the time, with the literary problem of the Hexateuch to appreciate the significance of these discoveries for the interpretation of the Old Testament. With reference to questions of philology or secular history, they learned to make use of the literary remains of the ancient civilizations. But with reference to the cultural and religious history of Israel, they continued to depend almost exclusively upon the Old Testament. Wellhausen himself never revised his conclusions in the light of the new knowledge. Showing little interest in the progress of scholarship in the oriental field, he made no use of the Amarna letters to reinterpret the history of the early Hebrews, although Hugo Winckler had made the texts readily available.[8] Even the younger members of his school, who should have been receptive to new information, held to a restricted view of their task. They wrote their histories of Israel's religion along the lines laid down by Wellhausen as though nothing had come to change the picture. When a "Positivist" scholar like Rudolf Kittel insisted on supplementing the results of internal criticism with the extrabiblical evidence,[9] his efforts were not hailed with any great enthusiasm. But Kittel was convinced that the archaeological evi-

---

[7] See Samuel Rolles Driver, *Modern Research as Illustrating the Bible* (London, 1909), pp. 32–37.

[8] Critical edition of the texts: *Der Tontafelfund von El-Amarna* (2 vols., Berlin, 1889–90); German translation: *Die Tontafeln von Tell-el-Amarna* (Berlin, 1896). A better translation was later made by J. A. Knudtzon, *Die El-Amarna Tafeln* (2 vols., Leipzig, 1907–14), and an English translation by S. A. B. Mercer, *The Tell-el-Amarna Tablets* (2 vols., Toronto, 1939). Selected letters have been translated by W. F. Albright in J. B. Pritchard (ed.), *Ancient Near Eastern Texts Relating to the Old Testament* (Princeton, 1950), pp. 483–90.

[9] In his *Geschichte der Hebräer* (2 vols., Gotha, 1888–93); English translation: *A History of the Hebrews* (2 vols., London, 1895).

dence showed that Israel was much more intimately involved in the history and culture of the ancient Orient than its own records suggested.

The first effect of the new perspective, as Kittel showed, was to push the horizon of Old Testament history not only outward to include the oriental world but backward beyond the time of Moses into the Amarna age. Where once the vague and legendary history of the patriarchs was all that filled the empty centuries before Moses, there now appeared a great historical era, rich in events and cultural achievements. Instead of ushering in the history of Palestine, the tribes confederated under Moses seemed like late-comers on the scene. Hence, it was no longer possible to begin the history of Israel with Moses; the preceding ages had an importance of their own and required more attention than had been devoted to them heretofore.

In the second place, the altered perspective on Hebrew history called into question the prevailing opinion that the religion of the Hebrews had started from small beginnings of a primitive kind. The fact that highly developed religious systems had preceded the origin of Old Testament religion suggested that the early Hebrews were familiar with an initial stock of religious conceptions much more complex than the critical school had thought possible. However, the unexpected extent and importance of the evidence led to an initial exaggeration of the theory of cultural influences—as is apt to happen with a new theory that provides illuminating insights. Hugo Winckler, who properly emphasized the necessity of relating the history of Israel to that of the neighboring states and gave the first comprehensive description of the ancient oriental background in terms of the Amarna letters,[10] exaggerated the universality and misrepresented the nature of the culture which overspread the ancient East. He maintained that a unified system of thought, embodying the conceptions of the ancient Babylonians

---

[10] *Geschichte Israels*, Vol. I (Berlin, 1895); *Das alte Westasien* (Leipzig, 1899).

about the nature of the universe and man's place in it, had been the common property of all peoples in the ancient Orient from early times.[11] Many conceptions in the Old Testament, he claimed, were derived from this system of ideas.[12] It was not a question merely of borrowing from an older civilization but of participation in a highly developed intellectual culture common to the whole ancient world.[13]

Winckler's "pan-Babylonian" theory led to the unfortunate controversy over "Bible vs. Babel" in the first decade of the twentieth century. The controversy was started by Friedrich Delitzsch's attempt to show that there was nothing in the Old Testament that was not but a pale reflection of Babylonian ideas.[14] In the facts he dealt with, there was little that was new; but the particular emphasis he gave them aroused a storm of opposition from defenders of the originality of the Old Testament, who objected to his theories on the superiority of Babylonian religion over Israel's religion. The only valuable result of the controversy was that it ended the tendency to consider Old Testament history in isolation from the oriental environment. The explosion had cleared the ground for the building of a new structure on much wider foundations.

Except in the person of Alfred Jeremias,[15] Winckler's most faithful disciple, the pan-Babylonian school did not survive long. Its attempt to systematize a great variety of conceptual motifs into a single thought pattern for the whole ancient world was too arti-

---

[11] "Himmels- und Weltbild der Babylonier als Grundlage der Weltanschauung und Mythologie aller Völker," *Der alte Orient*, III (1901), Nos. 2–3.

[12] *Geschichte Israels*, Vol. II (Berlin, 1900).

[13] On Winckler, see Otto Weber, "Hugo Winckler als Forscher," *MVAG*, XX (1915), 13–24; S. A. Fries, *Moderne Darstellungen der Geschichte Israels* (Freiburg, 1898), pp. 11–13.

[14] *Babel und Bibel* (Leipzig, 1902).

[15] His chief works were *Das Alte Testament im Lichte des alten Orients* (Leipzig, 1904; 3d rev. ed., 1916) and *Handbuch der altorientalischen Geisteskultur* (Leipzig, 1913).

ficial.[16] Its over-emphasis on the extent of Babylonian influence upon the thought pattern of the ancient East could not win the approval of Egyptologists.[17] Most unsatisfactory of all, to Old Testament scholars, was the failure to do justice to the developmental character of religious belief. The theory that Hebrew religious conceptions were derived in fully developed form from a highly mature intellectual background at the very beginning of Old Testament history ran counter to the evolutionary interpretation of religious history popularized by both the critical and the anthropological schools of Old Testament study. However, the point of view from which pan-Babylonism had started—that there were affinities and interrelationships between the culture areas of the ancient Orient and that Israel was somehow intimately involved in them—remained. The problem was to find out what, specifically, Israel could have derived from the neighboring cultures under the circumstances of its early history and to show how each derivation had actually affected the character and development of Israel's religion.

A sober approach to the problem was not made until Gunkel and his colleagues of the religio-historical school had entered the field. With a more judicious use of the comparative method, they examined the materials already available and each new discovery as it was made, in an effort to show the bearing of the oriental data on the problems of Old Testament interpretation. Gunkel guarded against the danger of reading into the biblical literature more than was justified, by working from the Old Testament outward to the influences which had acted upon it, instead of starting with the external data and tracing them into the Old Testament. He be-

[16] See the criticisms of William L. Wardle, *Israel and Babylon* (London, 1925), chap. XII: "The Pan-Babylonian Theory" (pp. 302–30); and Leonard W. King, *History of Babylon* (London, 1915), pp. 291–313.

[17] See, for example, George Foucart, *Histoire des religions et méthode comparative* (Paris, 1912), pp. 305–8 (note).

lieved it was the task of the Old Testament scholar, before searching for external factors that may have influenced the growth of
biblical conceptions, to clarify the meaning of the latter in the
biblical context. After tracing their significance through the Old
Testament texts, he was ready to compare them with parallel conceptions in the oriental literatures. Gunkel's method prevented
such sweeping generalizations as Winckler and his group had made,
because it forced attention upon concrete details.[18]

As a result of the new approach, the nature of Old Testament
research began to change during the early years of the twentieth
century. Literary criticism declined in importance as studies in the
ancient oriental field provided a wealth of new material for investigation. Instead of the problems of the scope and structure of the
Old Testament documents, the "more fundamental" problems of
the provenance and historical development of the basic ideas came
to the fore. The addition of the comparative method to historical
criticism gave the religio-historical school a deeper insight into the
history of ideas in the Old Testament than the critical school of
Wellhausen had attained. For, by giving up the study of Old
Testament religion as though it were an entirely self-contained
phenomenon and investigating its interdependence with other religious traditions, the new school reached a better understanding
of a number of important points, particularly with regard to
origins.[19]

The Religio-Historical Approach to Old Testament Religion

The first important result of the new school's researches was
the conclusion that certain conceptions which were once thought

[18] See Hans Schmidt, "Hermann Gunkel," *Theologische Blätter* XI (1932),
97–103.

[19] See Hermann Gunkel, "Die Religionsgeschichte und die alttestamentliche
Wissenschaft," *Protokoll des fünften Weltkongresses für freies Christentum* (Berlin, 1910), pp. 169 ff. Reprinted separately (Berlin, 1910).

to have been current only in the period after the Exile went back to much older prototypes and had their origin in beliefs extant in the ancient oriental world. Gunkel had shown, in his first major work, that mythological conceptions in the late literature of the postexilic age which Wellhausen had attributed to Babylonian influence during the Exile might very well have been the product of much earlier contact between Israel and Babylonia.[20] Pointing out, for example, that the Babylonian creation myth was known to the Canaanites in the Amarna age, Gunkel maintained that the creation myth of Genesis 1, though existing in a late form, did not necessarily embody only late thinking on the problem of cosmogony. Its highly abstract conception of God the Creator triumphing over the primeval chaos dimly reflected the old Babylonian myth of Marduk's physical combat with Tiamat.[21] In much the same way, Hugo Gressmann tried to demonstrate the antiquity of the mythological ideas embedded in prophetic eschatology.[22] Wellhausen and the critical school had considered the eschatological passages of the prophetic books as late interpolations which frequently contradicted the prophet's original message of doom and expressed the far different hopes of the exilic age. Gressmann pointed out that long before the appearance of prophecy in Israel there had existed in Egypt a literary genre of eschatology similar to that of the late Jewish apocalypses, comprising a description of awful calamities followed by an age of renewal and blessedness.[23] Since the Egyptian examples were of relatively great antiquity, Gressmann thought it possible to assume the early origin of such conceptions in Israel and denied that the eschatological portions of prophetic literature

[20] *Schöpfung und Chaos in Urzeit und Endzeit*, pp. 135–55.

[21] See also Gunkel's articles, "Die jüdische und babylonische Schöpfungsgeschichte," *Deutsche Rundschau*, CXV (1903), 267–86; "Babylonische und biblische Urgeschichte," *Die christliche Welt*, XVII (1903), 121–34.

[22] *Der Ursprung der israelitisch-jüdischen Eschatologie* (Göttingen, 1905).

[23] For examples in English translation, see George A. Barton, *Archaeology and the Bible* (7th rev. ed., Philadelphia, 1937), pp. 522–24, 528–30.

were necessarily postexilic.[24] In a later work,[25] he shifted the basis of discussion from the mythological conceptions associated with the "Last Day" to the central conception of the Messiah, but again he thought it possible to assume Egyptian influence upon the ideology of Hebrew prophecy. In tracing the idea of a Redeemer through the Old Testament, Gressmann found that it had been essentially political at first, being associated with the reigning king, whose figure was clothed in a variety of mythological conceptions, tending to exalt him as divine. Since the idea of the divine king was foreign to native Hebrew thought but widely current in the oriental environment, Gressmann argued that it was a derivative conception, most likely from Egypt, the country where kings were specifically deified.[26]

Thus, without subscribing to the pan-Babylonian theory of a general diffusion of culture throughout the ancient East, Gunkel and Gressmann pointed out certain kinds of influence from the ancient oriental world that could have affected the thinking of the Israelites in the early stages of their history. How this modified older views can be illustrated once more from Gressmann's study of the conception of a heavenly deity.[27] Bernhard Stade, basing his conclusions on the biblical evidence alone and finding references to the God of Israel as a heavenly deity only in late portions of the Old Testament, had argued that Yahweh had "grown into the sky" in the time of Ezekiel as the result of a combination of

[24] *Op. cit.*, pp. 238–43. Cf. C. C. McCown, "Hebrew and Egyptian Apocalyptic Literature," *HTR*, XVIII (1925), 357–411. But also see the more cautious conclusions of Nathaniel Schmidt, "The Origin of Jewish Eschatology," *JBL*, XLI (1922), 102–14; and Theodore H. Robinson, "Die prophetischen Bücher im Lichte neuer Entdeckungen," *ZAW*, XLV (1927), 3–9.

[25] *Der Messias* (Göttingen, 1929).

[26] There was some question, however, whether the oriental conception of the divine king actually carried with it messianic connotations. See Lorenz Dürr, *Ursprung und Ausbau der israelitisch-jüdischen Heilanderwartung* (Berlin, 1925), pp. 15, 36–37.

[27] "Hadad und Baal nach den Amarnabriefen," *Abhandlungen zur semitischen Religionskunde und Sprachwissenschaft* (Baudissin *Festschrift* Giessen, 1918), pp. 191–216.

old Israelitic with new Babylonian conceptions learned during the Exile.[28] Gressmann showed that there was evidence for a Syrian "lord of heaven" in the ninth century B.C., while it was possible that an early Baal referred to in the Amarna letters was also regarded as a heavenly deity. Since it was known that other characteristics of the Canaanite Baal had been transferred to Yahweh, this evidence indicated that the conception of a heavenly deity may have been familiar to the Israelites much earlier than was formerly supposed.[29]

Special studies such as these helped to reveal how much in the realm of ideas, in spite of its embodiment in late literary sources, was to be regarded as old in Israel's religion. There was seldom proof of actual derivation from an older culture at an early age, but the existence of analogies to certain Old Testament beliefs in the more mature cultures which had preceded Israel's was a strong argument against the assumption that such beliefs were necessarily late.

The implication that the development of Israel's religion had been influenced by the rich variety of religious traditions in the older cultures did not pass unchallenged by defenders of the "uniqueness" of biblical religion, who felt that the religio-historical school went too far with its theory of derivations and adaptations.[30] They argued that the investigator who searched for external influences tended to lose sight of the distinctive qualities of Old Testament religion in too much preoccupation with the supposed or actual foreign elements within it. But the survival of Old Testament religion, after all other oriental religions had disappeared, was due to its distinctive features, not to those which it had in common

---

[28] *Biblische Theologie des Alten Testaments* (Tübingen, 1905), I, 104, 290–91.

[29] On the ancient oriental deity, Baal-shamen (Lord of Heaven), and the probability that he was quite familiar to the Israelites, see the more recent study by Otto Eissfeldt, "Baalsamem und Jahwe," *ZAW*, LVII (1939), 1–31.

[30] See, e.g., Carl Clemen, *Die religionsgeschichtliche Methode in der Theologie* (Giessen, 1904); Max Reischle, *Theologie und Religionsgeschichte* (Tübingen, 1904).

with the others. The conservatives, therefore, sought to restore the balance of interpretation by emphasizing those elements in Old Testament religion which had not been borrowed from any external source but were due to the genius of the religion itself.[31] But the religio-historical school had tried to show that comparative studies, rather than detracting from the originality of Old Testament religion, helped to emphasize the greatness of its achievement when properly interpreted.[32] Gunkel pointed out that, although partial imitations and even direct borrowings did take place, the new context into which the derivative elements were transplanted quite often infused them with a different conceptual content and transformed them into vehicles for distinctive beliefs; as when the creation and deluge stories were adapted in such a way that the polytheistic elements were eliminated and a monotheistic emphasis was introduced.[33] The religio-historical method, at its best, did not stop with the search for comparative analogies and derivations but, as Gunkel had insisted, based it upon a study of the history of ideas within the Old Testament, thus making it possible to determine the effect of the oriental environment upon Israel's religion without losing sight of the distinctive part Israel itself played in shaping the basic ideas of the Old Testament.

The Conservative Wing of the Religio-Historical School

So strong was the argument which the evidence of cultural maturity in the ancient Orient presented in favor of the greater antiquity of certain Old Testament beliefs that some scholars rejected the evolutionary view of Israel's religious history and described Old Testament religion as having already reached the full

---

[31] For a critical survey of attempts to define the uniqueness of Old Testament religion, see Johannes Lindblom, "Zur Frage der Eigenart der alttestamentlichen Religion," in Paul Volz (ed.), Werden und Wesen des Alten Testaments (Berlin, 1936), pp. 128–37.

[32] Cf. Gunkel's reply to Reischle in DLZ, XXV (1904), 1100–10.

[33] Die Genesis (Göttingen, 1901), pp. xli–xliii.

development of its most important features in the age of Moses. Paul Volz, for example, argued that the high ethical principles of the Decalogue, which were usually attributed to prophetic inspiration, were known to the Hebrews in Moses' time.[34] Ethical teachings analogous to these could be found in the famous "Negative Confession" in chapter 125 of the Egyptian Book of the Dead, which went back at least to the fifteenth century B.C., and on the second tablet of the *shurpu* incantation texts from Babylonia, written some time between 1500 and 1100 B.C.[35] Since there were examples in other ancient sources of ethical precepts formulated as brief commands, it was not beyond the bounds of possibility that Moses drew up similar precepts. On the basis of this evidence, Volz not only defended the Mosaic authorship of the Decalogue but described the religion of Moses' day in terms which made it ethically as advanced as the teaching of the prophets. Eliminating the conception of subsequent growth from serious consideration, he restored the traditional view of the Mosaic era.[36]

As with religious conceptions, so with ritual practices: because the festival liturgies of the Babylonians and Assyrians showed that highly developed rituals existed in the ancient Orient long before the time of Moses, it was possible to argue, as B. D. Eerdmans had done,[37] that the rituals of the early Hebrews were also well developed. Eerdmans maintained that it was unhistorical to assume as Wellhausen did that the elaborate ceremonies of the "Mosaic" legislation were an innovation of the postexilic period. Since elaborate ceremonial was a common feature of the cultus of ancient peoples, it could have been characteristic of the early Hebrew cultus as well. Eerdmans, accordingly, labeled many of the ritual

---

[34] *Mose: ein Beitrag zur Untersuchung über die Ursprünge der israelitischen Religion* (Tübingen, 1907).

[35] See Anton Jirku, *Altorientalischer Kommentar zum Alten Testament* (Leipzig, 1923), pp. 87–88.

[36] See *op. cit.*, pp. 66–85.

[37] See above, chap. I, pp. 24–25.

practices in the Priestly Code Mosaic in origin.[38] The line of reasoning here pursued was also based on the argument from analogy and likewise failed to reckon with the possibility of subsequent development.

The same type of argument was applied to the early history of Hebrew law. When a stele containing almost the whole code of laws promulgated by Hammurabi came to light in 1902 and revealed the existence in the ancient world of a comprehensive jurisprudence antedating the traditional "Mosaic law," the discovery seemed to nullify the initial assumption of Wellhausen's view of Old Testament legal history, according to which early Hebrew law had been simply customary law reflecting a nomadic stage of culture. Since the first superficial comparisons showed a great similarity between the Babylonian code and the earliest stratum of the Pentateuchal legislation (the Book of the Covenant),[39] the conclusion was immediately drawn that the early Hebrews had derived their legal principles directly from the complex Babylonian legislation.[40] Certain scholars argued that a Mosaic code of laws at the beginning of Hebrew history could no longer be considered an anachronism; and so they restored Moses to the position of chief lawgiver in Israel, on the analogy of Hammurabi.[41]

But the most significant attempt to restore the traditional view of the Mosaic era was Bruno Baentsch's description of Mosaic

[38] *Alttestamentliche Studien, IV: Das Buch Leviticus* (Giessen, 1912).

[39] Joseph Halévy, "Le code d'Hammourabi et la législation hébraique," *Revue sémitique*, XI (1903), 142–53, 240–49, 323–24; M. J. Lagrange, "Le code de Hammourabi," *Revue biblique*, XII (1903), 27–51.

English translations of the code may be found in J. M. Powis Smith, *The Origin and History of Hebrew Law* (Chicago, 1931), pp. 181–222; George A. Barton, *Archaeology and the Bible* (7th ed., 1937), pp. 378–406; J. B. Pritchard (ed.), *Ancient Near Eastern Texts* (Princeton, 1950), pp. 163–80 (translated by T. J. Meek).

[40] Alfred Jeremias, *Das Alte Testament im Lichte des alten Orients* (Leipzig, 1904), pp. 222–23; expanded discussion in the third edition of same (1916), chap. XIX.

[41] Johannes Jeremias, *Moses und Hammurabi* (Leipzig, 1903); Samuel Oettli, *Das Gesetz Hammurabis und die Thora Israels* (Leipzig, 1903). Cf. Paul Volz, *Mose*, p. 70.

religion in monotheistic terms on the ground that "traces of monotheism more or less clearly defined are to be encountered outside the religion of Israel in the ancient Orient."[42] Baentsch pointed out the tendency in Babylonian religion to exalt one deity above all others and to give him cosmic significance. Such a tendency to attribute supremacy to a particular deity, in the midst of a polytheistic system of belief, can hardly be called monotheism in the strict sense.[43] Johannes Hehn, who made the most scholarly and comprehensive survey of ideas and expressions which could be taken as monotheistic in the religions of the ancient Orient,[44] pointed out that the undeniable trend toward the conception of "a universal deity standing above all the others" never resulted in the complete absorption of the other gods and their functions into a single deity.[45] However, Baentsch thought that by "reading between the lines" of the Babylonian religious texts he detected a theoretical monotheism in the esoteric speculations of the priests, who sometimes described the gods "not [as] independent powers but only partial manifestations of the single divine power that exists in the universe."[46] Baentsch was forced to add that "these monotheistic speculations had an absolutely private and purely theoretical character."[47] Nevertheless, since they indicated the early existence of a "tendency toward monotheism" in the ancient Orient, Baentsch assumed, under the influence of Winckler's theory of cultural diffusion, that a monotheistic type of belief had existed in Syria, Phoenicia, and Canaan—at least among the priests of the most important shrines. The polytheism of the Amarna age, he

---

[42] *Altorientalischer und israelitischer Monotheismus* (Tübingen, 1906), p. 1.

[43] Max Müller had invented the term "henotheism" to designate the same phenomenon in the Vedic hymns of ancient India—see *Lectures on the Origin and Growth of Religion* ("Hibbert Lectures," 1878; London, 1880), p. 266; cf. *Lectures on the Science of Religion* (London, 1872)), pp. 141–42.

[44] *Die biblische und die babylonische Gottesidee* (Leipzig, 1913), chap. II.

[45] See, *ibid.*, p. 64.

[46] *Op. cit.*, p. 33.

[47] *Ibid.*, p. 34.

found, was organized as in Babylonia into a monarchical pantheon in which one god was supreme above the others. This "signified, at least for the initiated, a concentration of the conception of deity,"[48] which Baentsch maintained must have influenced the religion of Israel's ancestors. Among the Hebrew tribes brought together by Moses, he believed there had existed a similar "tendency toward monotheism," which reached its climax in the "genuine monotheism" of the cult of Yahweh established by Moses.[49]

However, such attempts to enrich the content of belief and practice in the Mosaic era by reference to conditions in the older civilizations suffered from too great an absorption with the oriental evidence and too little attention to the results of historical criticism of the Old Testament records. The information available regarding the older civilizations certainly warranted the assertion that it was *possible* for the Hebrews to have had a mature culture. But more plausible than the view that the early Hebrews had learned much from the older civilizations was the theory of the critical school that they had entered Palestine in a nomadic stage of culture[50] and then had grown into the higher state of civilization which they found there. In fact, this theory provided a better explanation for such derivations of belief and practice as did take place and left room for the operation of that transforming influence which Israel's own genius exerted upon the elements it borrowed.

For example, the most likely explanation for the evident relationship between the Book of the Covenant and the Code of Hammurabi was that the Israelites, after their settlement in Palestine, took over from the Canaanite milieu and adapted to their own purposes certain of the legal principles which the Canaanites had

[48] *Ibid.*, p. 39.

[49] See, *ibid.*, pp. 55–58, 65–66.

[50] More properly, "semi-nomadic," as Eduard Meyer had pointed out. See above, chap. I, p. 24.

derived from Babylonia during the Amarna age.[51] Early Hebrew law, in other words, was a combination of the customary law which still governed the tribes when they invaded the country and the more advanced legislation of the civilized communities among which they settled. This theory had the advantage of explaining the provenance of the Book of the Covenant without disregarding the fact emphasized by Wellhausen that "it was concerned with Palestinian agricultural life, in which the people seem to have taken root—a situation which Moses could not have presupposed in the desert." [52] The theory thus fulfilled the requirement of taking the results of historical criticism into account when conclusions were being drawn from the comparative study of ancient oriental materials.

It was the failure to take these results into consideration which had vitiated Baentsch's argument on the character of "Mosaic" monotheism. He had demonstrated that, in the light of contemporary phenomena, Moses could have been familiar with an esoteric speculation concerning the nature of deity.[53] But that Moses taught a "genuine monotheism" was highly improbable in the light of historical criticism of the Old Testament sources. The records themselves showed clearly enough, in spite of the tradition so consistently emphasized elsewhere in the Old Testament, that the work of Moses did not involve a denial of all other gods but a choice of one God alone for Israel. This was not even "theoretical" monotheism, but monolatry. To be unclear in the use of the pertinent terminology did not serve the purposes of good scholarship. What Baentsch called monotheism was sometimes no more than mon-

---

[51] See C. H. W. Johns, *The Relations between the Laws of Babylonia and the Laws of the Hebrew Peoples* (London, 1914), pp. vi–vii and 28. But cf. the clarification of this point by Albrecht Alt, below, chap. IV, p. 147.

[52] "Israelitisch-jüdische Religion," in Paul Hinneberg (ed.), *Die Kultur der Gegenwart*, Div. I, Vol. IV, Part I (1906), p. 6.

[53] But note Adolphe Lods's negative answer to the question, "Le monothéisme israélite a-t-il eu des précurseurs parmi les 'sages' de l'ancien Orient?," *RHPR*, XIV (1934), 197–205.

archical polytheism and at other times the henotheistic worship of
one deity in preference to others whose existence was not thereby
denied. It was never the belief in a single, unique deity to the
exclusion of all others.[54]

The use of extrabiblical evidence to supplement internal criticism of the Old Testament records could have great value in
correcting Wellhausen's reconstruction of Israel's religious history.
But conservative scholars like Volz and Baentsch seemed to miss
the essential point of his historical criticism when they accepted
the traditional interpretation of Mosaic times at its face value.
Baentsch did not contradict the results of literary criticism in the
strict sense, which he regarded as firmly established.[55] But he and
the other conservatives gave ground on another important point
where Wellhausen had made a permanent gain. When Wellhausen
insisted that the Old Testament's own interpretation of the origins
of Israel's religion was a tendentious one which required objective
analysis, he was essentially right. The Old Testament record of
the Hebrew past was not a history in the formal sense; its basic
pattern was determined by a theological purpose: to set forth the
ancient traditions in such a way as to present the Hebrew people
as the object of divine guidance from the beginning. There were,
of course, many details in the traditional narratives that reflected
actual historical circumstances; and it was due to extrabiblical discoveries that these details could now be understood much more
clearly than had been possible in Wellhausen's day. But nothing
in the new evidence altered the fact that the Old Testament was
not so much a record of events as an interpretation of their spiritual
significance. The critical school, unfortunately, failed to appreciate

[54] It is interesting to note that the latest study of this question, Bruno Balscheit's
Alter und Aufkommen des Monotheismus in der israelitischen Religion (Berlin,
1938), is quite emphatic in defining monotheism in the strict sense. Balscheit
regards the conceptual formulation of monotheism impossible without an express
denial of the existence of other gods. Hence, he finds no genuine expression of
monotheism in Israel before the teachings of the prophets.

[55] See *Monotheismus*, p. 108.

the importance of the interpretation as itself a factor in Israel's religious history. But emphasizing the point that the interpretation could not be taken as objective history was a better preparation of the groundwork for an understanding of its real significance than the attempt of the conservatives to work toward the restoration of the traditional view.

The Mediating Position of Rudolf Kittel and Ernst Sellin

The conservative wing of the religio-historical school had tried to make the ancient oriental data support that interpretation of Old Testament history which served its conservative interests. The Positivist wing, on the other hand, showed that it was possible to confirm some aspects of the traditional history—and thus to correct Wellhausen's strictly evolutionary interpretation—without disregarding the principles of objective method. Rudolf Kittel extracted a kernel of historical truth from the traditions regarding Moses, without accepting them uncritically or making debatable arguments from analogy. He, too, had been persuaded by the rich complexity of ancient oriental culture to assume a greater degree of maturity among the early Hebrews; but he did not exaggerate it or forget the possibility of subsequent growth in religious understanding.[56]

More than his predecessors had done, Kittel concentrated attention upon the cultural situation in Palestine itself. When the oriental background of Old Testament history had first been opened up, it was only natural that attention should have been directed mainly to the great civilizations surrounding Palestine; but, since a complex culture had also been revealed in the land of Canaan, the possibility of influences upon Hebrew religion more direct than those of Babylonia or Egypt had to be taken into account. Kittel investigated everything of a cultural or religious nature that contributed

[56] See Johannes Hempel, "Rudolf Kittel," ZDMG, LXXXIV (1930), 78–93.

to an understanding of the immediate environment into which the Hebrews entered with their first appearance in history.[57]

As a result of his comprehensive study of the Palestinian background, Kittel believed he could support that aspect of the traditions regarding Moses which implied that he had a well-developed conception of deity—not the "genuine monotheism" assumed by Baentsch, but a somewhat more exalted conception than the critical school had thought possible in the supposedly primitive environment of those days. The nature of religious belief and practice in Canaan in the pre-Israelitic period was difficult enough to establish, but Kittel accepted the evidence for a highly developed conception of deity to be found in the monarchical system of gods elaborated by the Canaanites at an early date. He agreed that the more thoughtful element in the population may even have advanced to a speculative generalization of the nature of deity; for the occurrence of the plural form *elohim* ("gods") as a singular noun in the Amarna letters, in Phoenician inscriptions, and in the Old Testament itself seemed to indicate that the conception of deity as a higher unity had already taken form.[58] But, said Kittel, "That is not yet monotheism by far, although it is a viewpoint which has spiritualized polytheism in conception and can easily lead to genuine monotheism, once it has been thought through logically." [59] Since the conception implied the worship of El as a supreme being by the Canaanites, and since there were traces in the biblical traditions of a nearly suppressed memory of El-worship among the early Hebrew patriarchs,[60] Kittel believed that here was the nucleus from which Moses derived his exalted conception of deity.

The terms in which Kittel described the Mosaic conception of deity identified it as a kind of ethical monolatry.

[57] *Geschichte des Volkes Israel, I: Palästina in der Urzeit: Das Werden des Volkes* (2d rev. ed., Gotha, 1912).
[58] See, *ibid.*, pp. 188–97.
[59] *Ibid.*, p. 195.
[60] See, *ibid.*, pp. 396–97, 405–6.

It can hardly be maintained [he said] that Moses . . . [taught] an absolute instead of a relative monotheism—the singleness of God in the strict sense instead of his unique character. . . . The distinctive feature that lifted Moses' religion above the heathen religions . . . was that it conceived of its God not merely as a powerful ruler but at the same time as . . . a lawgiver and judge.[61]

As lawgiver and judge, Moses' God showed a profound concern for ethical behavior on the part of his worshipers. It was this ethical element in the religion of Moses which gave Israel's religion its basic character through all its subsequent development. Kittel recognized that the high type of religion instituted by Moses had been succeeded almost immediately by a much lower plane of spiritual and moral understanding, as a result of assimilation with the Baal-worship of the later Canaanites. But he pointed out that the monolatrous and ethical ideal of Moses maintained itself in certain circles among the Israelites through the centuries of decline in the post-Mosaic era, until it eventually flowered into full expression in the ethical monotheism of the prophets.[62]

Kittel's discussion of the course of Israel's religious development showed how the balance of historical interpretation was being gradually restored to a middle position. Where radical historical criticism had brought the basic ideas of the Old Testament down into relatively late periods, Kittel maintained that the ethical ideals and the conception of deity taught by the prophets were not entirely new manifestations of religious insight but the heightening of original features of Israel's religion. At the same time, Kittel's emphasis on the subsequent development of the original elements counteracted the conservative trend of traditionalist interpretation, which had attempted to restore the basic ideas of the Old Testament in fully developed form to the period of origins under Moses. This mood of cautious reserve toward both extremes was also

[61] *Ibid.*, pp. 557, 561.
[62] See, *ibid.*, pp. 550–51.

displayed in the work of Kittel's contemporary, Ernst Sellin.[63] Sellin traced back to earlier ages than Wellhausen would have allowed conceptions which the latter and his school thought of as late products of an evolutionary development. But, while the conservatives had rejected the conception of development entirely, Sellin maintained the subsequent growth of the richer content of ideas which he placed at the beginning of Israel's religious history. The conception of Yahweh which Moses impressed on his followers and the covenant relationship he established between them and the deity did not constitute ethical monotheism in fully developed form; but, by a natural extension, the religious ideas of Moses provided the content for the prophetic conception. Like Kittel, Sellin maintained that the spirit of loyalty to Israel's God alone and to the ethical ideal for which he stood was the basic aspect of Israel's religion in every age of its history. But, unlike Paul Volz, who had argued that the fundamental principles of Israel's religion were the full-blown achievement of Moses at the very beginning, Sellin attributed to Moses only the germ of religious ideas which later came to flower in the teaching of the prophets.

Kittel and Sellin both argued that the basic conceptions taught by Moses acquired the richer meaning they ultimately had as the result of a constant struggle between two opposing tendencies: the effort of a few to uphold the principles of Moses and the tendency of the many to fall away from them. This tension between a high plane of religious thought among the spiritual leaders and the lower religious beliefs of the people was the "dynamic" element in the development of Israel's religion. Thus Kittel and Sellin changed the currently accepted interpretation of Old Testament religious history in an important respect. Instead of an evolutionary scheme of religious development through three con-

---

[63] *Alttestamentliche Religion im Rahmen der andern altorientalischen* (Leipzig, 1908).

secutive stages of popular, prophetic, and priestly religion (as described by the school of Wellhausen), they portrayed the interacting tension between different levels of religious insight existing contemporaneously among the Israelites.[64] The critical school had identified the cultic religion of the masses, in which the conception of Yahweh was almost submerged beneath Canaanite conceptions of deity, as the real religion of Israel in the preprophetic stage of its development. Kittel and Sellin did not deny that a colorful mixture of Yahweh, Baal, and El worship was the religion of the great majority of the people at that time. But they thought that the critical school had overlooked the existence among a more spiritual minority of the people of an opposing tendency to preserve the national heritage of religious ideals. The same records which portrayed the assimilation of the Yahweh cult to Canaanite beliefs and practices also showed the survival of Mosaic ideals of life and worship among such believers in ethical simplicity as the Nazirites and Rechabites and such champions of Yahweh, the one God of Israel, as Deborah, Samuel, Nathan, and Elijah. The critical school, by directing attention to the beliefs and practices of the common people, had emphasized those elements in Israel's religion which reflected a lower order of religious consciousness. To the extent that this was a partial interpretation, it gave a false picture of Israel's early religious development. Kittel and Sellin corrected it by showing how the cult of Yahweh had also been preserved upon a higher plane.

Equally illuminating was the identification of an intermediate stage of religious maturity: the official Yahwism of the great national shrines, such as Shiloh, and later of the royal court and the sanctuaries supported by it.[65] This national cult also centered in the worship of Yahweh as the one God of Israel; but its rituals

---

[64] See Kittel's *Geschichte des Volkes Israel, II: Das Volk in Kanaan* (2d rev. ed., Gotha, 1909) and Sellin's *Geschichte des israelitisch-jüdischen Volkes*, Vol. I (Leipzig, 1924).

[65] See Kittel, *op. cit.*, II, 120, 268–74.

had not escaped the influence of Canaanite practices, although it kept itself free from their grosser forms. Again, the thesis that the national cult emphasized the exclusive worship of Yahweh, in spite of the partial Canaanization of its ritual, counterbalanced the critical school's preoccupation with the Canaanite elements in it.

Thus Kittel and Sellin showed that the most basic feature of Israel's religion had remained the dominant element within it through all the centuries of assimilation to Canaanite beliefs and practices. The consciousness of loyalty to Yahweh had persisted, even though it was never very widely distributed and varied in purity among the different groups that sustained it. Eventually, it experienced a great resurgence and triumphed over the religion of the masses, through the work of the great prophets who refined the Mosaic conception of deity into strict monotheism.

The most important result of the work of these two scholars was a redistribution of emphasis among the various periods of Old Testament history. Without going to extremes like those members of the religio-historical school who were preoccupied with the problems of comparative analogies and external derivations, Kittel and Sellin supported the general viewpoint that the early Hebrew period had not been as primitive as the critics had assumed. They also reinterpreted the Mosaic era as a period of great significance, although they did not return completely to traditional views. Accepting the critical school's dating of the "Mosaic" law, they avoided the naïve assumption that the "Mosaic" institutions were all to be attributed to the founder himself. Neither law codes as such nor institutions in concrete form, but rather the basic spirit which later informed both laws and institutions was the great achievement of Moses. The Mosaic era was important because it laid the foundations for the high level of religious consciousness represented by the prophetic period. The latter period Wellhausen and his school had rightly emphasized as the climax of the history, but Kittel and Sellin no longer separated it so completely from what had gone before. Their accounts of Israel's spiritual growth were less schematic than Wellhausen's story of development from the simple to the complex but were probably more historical and true to life. Eventually, the treatment of Israel's religious history by the critical school began to show the effect of the new approach through comparative religious history. Gustav Hölscher,[66] who generally followed the method and point of view of historical criticism, even rejecting on critical grounds Gressmann's view that eschatology was an early development in Israel, gave much more space than was customary among the followers of Wellhausen to the early stages of the religion's history and took cognizance of the ancient oriental environment in a way that the early critical historians had never done.

The Most Recent Phase of Religio-Historical Research

As part of their survey of Old Testament religious history, Kittel and Sellin had given extensive consideration to the influences exerted upon Israel's spiritual development by the religious currents flowing through the Canaanite milieu. But even after a summary of all the available information in extrabiblical sources, it was difficult to establish the extent of Israel's assimilation to the cults of the Canaanites; for the true character of religious belief and practice among the Canaanites was not fully known. The chief source of information was still the Old Testament, which gave a good deal of indirect evidence—colored, however, by the bias of the writers against the practices they denounced. The very few inscriptions which had been found in Palestine and Syria (mostly Phoenician rather than Canaanite)[67] supplied some information on the funerary ritual and the sacrificial system of the western Semites but gave no comprehensive view of the conceptual background.

---

[66] *Geschichte der israelitisch-jüdischen Religion* (Giessen, 1922).
[67] See George A. Cooke, *North Semitic Inscriptions* (Oxford, 1903).

Some information about the latter could be gleaned from Baby-lonian and Egyptian references to the gods of Canaan and the allusions of late Greek and Roman writers (Lucian, Philo of Byblos, Plutarch) to the religious beliefs of the Phoenicians and Syrians.[68] But none of this information came from either the age or the geographical area in question, while the meager amount of really contemporary evidence made it difficult to evaluate the historical worth of these written sources. The archaeology of Palestine began to fill the gap in direct evidence during the early years of the twentieth century,[69] but the results of excavation in the land of Canaan before World War I were notoriously scant, not only in epigraphical finds but even in material remains.[70] The evidence discovered was related almost entirely to the practical side of religious worship (stone pillars, sacred places, and tombs); it did not provide an insight into the dominant conceptions under-lying ritual practice. Such interpretation as had been attempted was made largely in terms of the primitive religious beliefs made known by anthropology.[71] This helped to clarify the substructure of Canaanite religion but failed to provide enough concrete infor-mation for a study of the actual relationship between Canaanite and Israelite beliefs.

But, with the discovery of the Ras Shamra tablets in 1929 at the ancient Phoenician city of Ugarit on the Syrian coast, the haze which had obscured Canaanite culture and religion was dispelled. This discovery proved to be as important for the study of the Old Testament as the finding of the Amarna tablets forty years before

[68] See Wolf Wilhelm Graf von Baudissin, "Die Quellen für eine Darstellung der Religion der Phönizier und der Aramäer," *ARW*, XVI (1913), 389–422.

[69] See below, chap. VI.

[70] See Hugo Gressmann, *Die Ausgrabungen in Palästina und das Alte Testa-ment* (Tübingen, 1908).

[71] See, e.g., W. Carleton Wood, "The Religion of Canaan from the Earliest Times to the Hebrew Conquest," *JBL*, XXXV (1916), 1–133, 163–279; Stanley A. Cook, *The Religion of Ancient Palestine in the Second Millenium B.C.* (London, 1908).

had been for ancient oriental studies in general. For the Ras Shamra texts offered a wealth of pertinent information on the Canaanite background of Old Testament religion such as had not been available to earlier investigators.[72] The texts revealed a much less primitive stage of development in the Syro-Palestinian area than had once been pictured[73] and supplied that insight into the religious ideology of Phoenician-Canaanite culture without which the material remains uncovered by the spade had had little meaning.[74] Since the type of religious belief and practice indicated by the new documents seemed to be closely related to that denounced by the prophets of Israel in their struggle against Baalism, the new evidence offered an insight into those very elements in the Canaanite background which had influenced the popular religion of the Israelites. Now, whatever syncretism had taken place could be studied from original evidence of primary value.

Among other things, the Ras Shamra texts strongly suggested some connection between the sacrificial ritual of the Hebrews and that of the Canaanites. They revealed that the Phoenicians of Ugarit, in the period just before the Hebrews entered the Canaanite world, used the same technical expressions for some of their sacrifices and employed similar modes of slaughtering victims as the Israelites used later on.[75] Whether this meant that the Israelites had borrowed and adapted their sacrificial system from Canaanite prototypes was debatable, in view of the fact that both Phoenicians

---

[72] See R. de Vaux, "Les textes de Ras Shamra et l'Ancien Testament," *Revue biblique*, XLVI (1937), 526–55; A. Bea, "Ras Samra und das Alte Testament," *Biblica*, XIX (1938), 435–53; XX (1939), 436–53; C. F. A. Schaeffer, *Ugaritica: Etudes relatives aux découvertes de Ras Shamra*, Vol. I (Paris, 1939); René Dussaud, *Les découvertes de Ras Shamra et l'Ancien Testament* (Paris, 1937; 2d ed., 1941); Robert de Langhe, *Les textes de Ras Shamra-Ugarit et leurs rapports avec le milieu biblique de l'Ancien Testament* (2 vols., Gembloux, 1945).

[73] See Charles Virolleaud, "La civilisation phénicienne d'après les fouilles de Ras Shamra," *Annales de l'Université de Paris*, VIII (1933), 397–413.

[74] See Otto Eissfeldt, "Die religionsgeschichtliche Bedeutung der Funde von Ras Schamra," *ZDMG*, LXXXVIII (1934), 173–84.

[75] See James W. Jack, *The Ras Shamra Tablets* (Edinburgh, 1935), pp. 28–31; Samuel H. Hooke, *The Origins of Early Semitic Ritual* (London, 1938), pp. 66–67.

and Israelites, as members of the same Semitic race, may have inherited their ritual customs from a common source. At any rate, the similarity of the Ugaritic rituals to several aspects of the cultus described in the Priestly Code was the most striking fact discovered in the Ras Shamra texts. It gave strong support to the theory which had been gradually taking shape in critical circles[76] that not all the ritual prescriptions in the admittedly late Priestly Code were as late as Wellhausen had supposed. Wellhausen, recognizing "a distinction between traditional custom and formulated law," had granted that "at the restoration of Judaism old practices had been woven into a new system." [77] But he had maintained that the priestly spirit of minute regulation which animated the system was an entirely postexilic phenomenon without any roots in the Hebrew past. Now it appeared that this very spirit had been a dominant force throughout the evolution of the system. The priestly point of view was characteristic of the Ugaritic predecessor of Israel's cultus and may have been a part of early Israelite thinking after all. If so, the continuous development of a priestly tradition regarding ritual worship was historically more probable than its sudden appearance late in Israel's history.

The Ras Shamra texts also supported Rudolf Kittel's contention that the development of the conception of Yahweh toward the idea of a transcendent deity had started long before the prophetic period. The Canaanite god El, whom Kittel had dimly apprehended in the pre-Mosaic period, was frequently mentioned in the texts in such a way that his character was now more clearly known. He was revealed as the possessor of certain characteristics which the Israelites later ascribed to their own deity Yahweh. El was a remote and transcendent deity, a father and a king, pictured in Ugaritic sculpture as a bearded old man sitting upon a throne, and referred to in the Ras Shamra texts as "father of years" (cf. Daniel's

[76] See above, chap. I, pp. 32–33.
[77] Prolegomena (Berlin, 1883), pp. 388, 451.

"ancient of days").[78] Yet the differences between Canaanite theology and the religion of the Israelites were greater than the similarities. The former was polytheistic in nature, in spite of an apparent "tendency toward monotheism" in the worship of El at Ugarit.[79] The religion portrayed in the Ras Shamra texts was directed to the worship of a great pantheon of gods.[80] It was essentially a fertility cult, the rituals of which were designed to promote the productivity of the land. There was nothing here that indicated any direct influence upon the religion of Israel. What the Ras Shamra texts revealed was rather a clear picture of the kind of religion that had preceded Hebrew religion in the land of Canaan.[81] They showed, for example, that there was but one Baal in the Ugaritic pantheon. There could no longer be talk of an innumerable host of *baals,* as had been customary among the followers of Wellhausen. Moreover, the Ras Shamra texts showed the same conception of deity that Wolf Wilhelm von Baudissin had long ago pointed out as characteristic of the Semites generally, namely, that "the individual gods displayed not a monotheistic but a universal character from the beginning." [82] Data such as these helped to clarify the background of ideas against which the religion of Israel developed.

Additional insight into the background of Old Testament religion came from the mythology of the Ras Shamra texts. There

[78] See René Dussaud, "La mythologie phénicienne d'après les tablettes de Ras Shamra," *RHR,* CIV (1931), 358-59; J. Philip Hyatt, "The Ras Shamra Discoveries and the Interpretation of the Old Testament," *JBR,* X (1942), 72-73.

[79] See Otto Eissfeldt, *El im ugaritischen Pantheon* (Berlin, 1951).

[80] On the pantheon of Ugarit, see René Dussaud, *op. cit.,* pp. 353-77; James W. Jack, *op. cit.,* chap. III; Hans Bauer, "Die Gottheiten von Ras Schamra," *ZAW,* LI (1933), 81-101; LIII (1935), 54-59; James A. Montgomery, "Notes on the Mythological Epic Texts from Ras Shamra," *JAOS,* LIII (1933), 101-11; W. F. Albright, *Archaeology and the Religion of Israel* (Baltimore, 1942), pp. 71-84.

[81] See Walther Baumgartner, "Ugaritische Probleme und ihre Tragweite für das Alte Testament," *Theologische Zeitschrift,* III (1947), 81-100. Cf. Johannes Pedersen, "Canaanite and Israelite Cultus," *Acta Orientalia,* XVIII (1940), 1-14.

[82] "Zur Geschichte des Monotheismus bei semitischen Völkern," *DLZ,* XXXV (1914), 5-13. The quotation is from p. 8.

were numerous parallels in the literary epics of Ugarit to the occasional mythological terms and conceptions scattered through the Old Testament like the debris of ancient myths.[83] The Ras Shamra texts contained several variations on the theme of the slaying of a dragon, represented in the Old Testament by the fragmentary references to a primeval combat between Yahweh and the dragon Rahab or Leviathan. These traces of the legend had been attributed by Gunkel to the influence of the Babylonian myth of Marduk and Tiamat. Now a more direct influence from Canaanite mythology seemed likely, even if the latter was itself dependent upon Babylonian motifs ultimately.[84] The Ras Shamra texts, moreover, bolstered Sigmund Mowinckel's theory regarding the existence of a cult-myth in the liturgy for the New Year's festival celebrated at Jerusalem. From the tablets found at Ugarit it was evident that elaborate liturgies for a similar New Year's festival with a parallel mythological and conceptual background had existed in the very cultural milieu that had influenced the development of Hebrew ritual most directly.

Such similarities provided strong arguments for the belief that a common pattern of thought had existed among the Canaanites and Israelites. The basic elements of the pattern of belief and practice which the scholars of the "ritual myth" school supposed had overspread the ancient East were actually to be found in the religious texts of the Ras Shamra tablets. Significantly, the Ugaritic versions of the common vegetation myths were all associated with rituals performed at stated seasons for the promotion of fertility

[83] See Theodore H. Robinson, "Hebrew Myths," in Samuel H. Hooke (ed.), *Myth and Ritual* (London, 1933), pp. 172–96; Herbert G. May, "Pattern and Myth in the Old Testament," *Journal of Religion*, XXI (1941), 285–99.

[84] See Adolphe Lods, "Quelques remarques sur les poèmes mythologiques de Ras Chamra et leurs rapports avec l'Ancien Testament," *RHPR*, XVI (1936), 112–17; Charles Virolleaud, "Les poèmes de Ras Shamra," *Revue historique*, CLXXXV (1939), 1–22. Cf. Julian Obermann, *Ugaritic Mythology: A Study of Its Leading Motifs* (New Haven, 1948); Charles Virolleaud, *Légendes de Babylone et de Canaan* (Paris, 1949).

and material prosperity.[85] They offered direct evidence, therefore, to support the theory that the religious situation in Canaan just before the entrance of the Hebrews embodied the general pattern of thought common to the ancient Orient.[86] The probability that the Hebrews quickly adapted themselves to this pattern of belief and practice after their settlement in the land further altered the usual view of Old Testament religious history. There was nothing new, of course, in the idea that the religion of Israel had been influenced in its early stages by religious conditions prevalent in the Canaanite environment.[87] But the theory that the contemporary religion of Canaan was dominated by the ritual myth pattern of the ancient East put a different face upon the early character of Israel's religion. As Samuel H. Hooke declared, the preprophetic religion of the Israelites perhaps received more illumination from the pattern of contemporary religion than from primitive animistic survivals or from a hypothetical nomadic culture.[88]

Significantly, the new theory supported the changed view of the history of Old Testament religion set forth by Kittel and Sellin. Their thesis that there had been a sharp struggle between a prevalent form of popular religion and a strongly antagonistic form of prophetic religion seemed strengthened by the new evidence regarding the nature of religious belief and practice in Canaan. The likelihood that the Israelites, worshiping at the old Canaanite shrines, performed all the rituals of a magical fertility cult gave new meaning to the recorded denunciations of the prophets. The prophetic preaching now appeared as a protest against and a con-

[85] See René Dussaud, "La mythologie phénicienne d'après les tablettes de Ras Shamra," *RHR*, CIV (1931), 377–408.
[86] See Samuel H. Hooke, "Traces of the Myth and Ritual Pattern in Canaan," in *Myth and Ritual*, pp. 68–86.
[87] This point of view was expressed once more in terms of what was known before the discovery of the Ras Shamra tablets by Constant Toussaint in *Les origines de la religion d'Israël* (Paris, 1931).
[88] "Archaeology and the Old Testament," in H. Wheeler Robinson (ed.), *Record and Revelation* (Oxford, 1938), p. 358.

scious break with the implications of the Canaanite religious pattern to which the popular religion of the Israelites conformed.[89] Thus Sellin's emphasis on the interacting tension of two opposing forces as the chief characteristic of Israel's religious history was justified.[90] The development of Israel's religion was not a process of unilinear evolution but, periodically, of cultural mixture which the prophets tried to counteract by opposition.

The effect of such cultural mixture, however, seems to have been exaggerated by Samuel Hooke and his school. That ritual and myth were inseparably connected in the religious thinking of the ancient Orient they had established in a general way. But there was a disturbing tendency among these scholars, when explaining the significance of Hebrew rituals, to use their hypothesis to the exclusion of all other considerations. Hooke, for example, labored hard to show that the central conceptions of the ritual myth pattern had existed in the Hebrew New Year's ritual;[91] but he failed to inquire what meaning the rituals had for the Israelites themselves. He quite overlooked the fact that the New Year's festival as celebrated by the Israelites was primarily a thanksgiving festival, in which the worshipers shared with their God the fruits of his bounty. Instead of allowing the Old Testament to speak with its own voice, the advocates of the ritual myth theory listened to other voices coming from behind it. This attempt to interpret Old Testament religious practice exclusively in terms of external evidence was as one-sided as the attempt to follow only the conclusions of internal criticism had been.

[89] The contrast between Hebrew prophecy and the essentially magical type of religion common among the Semites was drawn in an illuminating manner by Alfred Guillaume, *Prophecy and Divination among the Hebrews and Other Semites* (London, 1938).

[90] In his latest history of Israel's religion, *Alttestamentliche Theologie auf religionsgeschichtliche Grundlage, I: Israelitisch-jüdische Religionsgeschichte* (Leipzig, 1933), Sellin described this interacting tension in greater detail than he had done in his previous works.

[91] *The Origins of Early Semitic Ritual*, pp. 51–56.

Undoubtedly, the sum total of the extrabiblical evidence gathered over the years indicated that Israel's participation in the cultural heritage of the ancient Orient was richer than had been supposed before comparative studies in this field began. The religio-historical school, having pushed the horizon of Old Testament history back beyond the age of Moses and outward to include the whole oriental world, had shown that the religion of Israel had not started in a primitive environment but in a milieu possessing religious conceptions more complex than those of nomadic belief. Hence the conclusion could be drawn that certain ideas once thought to have been late went back to much older prototypes and had their beginnings in conceptions extant in the oriental world. But the originality with which Israel had made use of the oriental heritage indicated that caution must be exercised in applying the new material to the interpretation of Israel's religious history. The religio-historical school had also shown that the distinctive features of Old Testament religion—specifically, its monotheistic conception of deity and the ethical implications of the covenant idea— were more important than those it had in common with other religions. Even derivative elements had been transformed into vehicles for these distinctive beliefs. Hence it was a mistake to exaggerate the importance of the external evidence.

The really significant aspect of Old Testament religious history was the long struggle by which Israel's distinctive achievement had been accomplished—the struggle between the popular religion of the masses, affected as they were by the beliefs and practices of their environment, and the higher level of religious thinking of their spiritual leaders, who sought to build upon the creative beginnings made by Moses in his conception of Yahweh and the idea of the convenant. This story could be understood better from the Old Testament records than from the extrabiblical evidence regarding the beliefs and practices prevailing in the contemporary environment. Each new discovery in the oriental field, of course, enlarged the total record of relevant cultural and religious experience by which to appraise the specific experience of the Israelites. But Israel's religious history had characteristic features of its own which could not be explained without primary attention to the biblical evidence. To have drawn from the latter—against the background of the external evidence—a picture of the true character of Israel's achievement was the most significant contribution of the religio-historical school to the interpretation of Old Testament religious history.

IV

Form Criticism
and the Old Testament

The Genesis of Form Criticism in Old Testament Studies

An important aspect of the work of the religio-historical school had been the examination of the popular ground from which religious ideas had sprung. It was based on the belief that significant aspects of religion were to be found not only in the teachings of great men but in the undercurrents of belief and fancy among the masses. Out of this concern with the religion of the people there came a new method for studying the literary history of the Old Testament. For one means of attaining an insight into the conceptual content of popular religion was an analysis of the various literary forms in which the people gave expression to their beliefs. The written forms of popular tradition were clues to the oral forms in which tradition originated, and only the oral traditions behind the written texts embodied the essence of popular beliefs. Hence, as a means of tracing the basic conceptions back to the oral traditions, Hermann Gunkel initiated the technique of analyzing the various types of literary composition in the Old Testament. Since he also sought to determine the specific situation in the life of the people with which each "literary type" was most closely associated, as an index to the kind of religious experience of which the literary type was a formal expression, his new methodology contributed greatly to an understanding of the popular origins of religious belief.

But, while Gunkel's method was chiefly auxiliary to the study of Old Testament religious history, he gave it an independent function also as a means of studying the literary history of the Old

Testament. There was a great need for some such means. With all the work that had been done on the Old Testament during the nineteenth century, there was, as Gunkel said, nothing that could properly be called a history of Hebrew literature.[1] Wellhausen's scheme of literary history was incidental to his history of Old Testament religion and was designed primarily to support the latter. His followers produced elaborate "introductions to Old Testament literature"; but, beyond substituting a chronological treatment according to the age of the source documents for the traditional arrangement according to the canonical order of the books, they contributed little toward the sort of organic history that would portray the actual growth of the literature. Gunkel maintained that literary history must show how the literature grew out of the history of the people and was the expression of their spiritual experience. That had been the goal of the critics also, but they had been too preoccupied with the technical problems of analysis ever to reach it. The only means of attaining the goal, according to Gunkel, was to study the literary types of religious expression and the "situations in life" from which they sprang.[2] Such an investigation would enable the historian to get behind the "documents" of critical analysis to the formative influences and the ultimate sources of the literature.

Gunkel's most instructive undertaking along this line was his manner of dealing with the genre of narrative literature. Believing that the literary genius of a primitive people first expressed itself in myths about the origins of things and legends about the exploits of folk heroes, he turned to the narratives of Genesis for the earliest

[1] In his survey of "Die Grundprobleme der israelitischen Literaturgeschichte," *DLZ*, XXVII (1906), 1797–1800, 1861–66; reprinted in his *Reden und Aufsätze* (Göttingen, 1913), pp. 29–38. An English translation was included in his *What Remains of the Old Testament? and Other Essays* (London, 1928), pp. 57–68.

[2] Cf. Gunkel's initial attempt to sketch the history of such literary types, "Die israelitische Literatur," in Paul Hinneberg (ed.), *Die Kultur der Gegenwart*, Div. I, Vol. VII (Berlin, 1906), pp. 51–102.

examples of popular tradition among the Hebrews.[3] Assuming, furthermore, that "popular legend by its very nature takes the form of the individual story" rather than extended narration,[4] Gunkel reduced the narratives of Genesis to separate literary units. These, he argued, had existed independently in recitation and in song long before they were written down in their present connected form. They were not the products of an author's workshop but examples of the storyteller's art from a time when literature was still in the unwritten stage. Even the grouping of these stories into story-cycles such as Genesis contained was first made in the preliterary stage. "Therefore, we must consider Genesis first of all in the form which it had as oral tradition."[5] It is true that Gunkel's work would not have been possible without the minute and patient analysis of the written sources by the critics, who had laid the foundations for his identification of the separate story-units. But he felt it was a mistake to approach them in the spirit of scientific historians analyzing the source materials of history. Myths and legends were folk-literature, to be studied for the qualities imparted to them by the spontaneous creative urge of the people.

Essentially, what Gunkel proposed was to substitute a broad literary approach for a coldly analytical one. Into a discipline which had sought to operate with strictly scientific methods he introduced an aesthetic sense of form in literature. He felt that "if beside critical insight, which until now has so often alone guided the scholar, discerning appreciation should be given a place," a better understanding of the narratives of Genesis would result.[6] Gunkel realized that a purely literary treatment of such narratives would be considered unscientific and subjective by the advocates

[3] *Die Genesis* ("Handkommentar zum Alten Testament," edited by Wilhelm Nowack, Div. I, Vol. I; Göttingen, 1901).
[4] *Ibid.*, pp. xix–xx.
[5] *Ibid.*, p. xviii.
[6] *Religionsgeschichte und die alttestamentliche Wissenschaft* (Berlin, 1910), p. 10.

of critical analysis.[7] The predominance of critical method in the study of the Old Testament had quite pushed aside any interest in the aesthetic evaluation of the Old Testament literature. But Gunkel felt strongly that the natural charm of the ancient Hebrew compositions was not sufficiently appreciated. The legends of Genesis were literary creations and could not be understood without a feeling for their characteristic beauty.

But more was involved here than literary appreciation. Gunkel thought there was a fundamental problem of interpretation to be considered. The critical approach to the Old Testament had not made the literature meaningful in any real sense to the modern generation of its readers, and the secularizing spirit of research into its background had obscured the Old Testament's significance, not merely as a part of the literary heritage of mankind, but as an expression of religious aspiration. Gunkel's new approach to the Old Testament was meant to provide the means for re-emphasizing the greatness of its literature and for pointing out the religious values in it. By treating the narratives of Genesis as a kind of "poetic composition" of the people, Gunkel believed he could show that they effectively conveyed significant ideas and communicated religious feelings.[8] For they were not a repository of historical data, but an expression of spiritual experience by and for the people. The approach to the Old Testament through literary appreciation was a way of apprehending its central value, the religious content, which otherwise threatened to become a lost heritage of the modern generation.[9]

The aesthetic appreciation of Old Testament literature and the attempt to understand it as the expression of a people's spiritual experience were, of course, nothing new. In the eighteenth century

---

[7] See *Reden und Aufsätze*, pp. 32–33.

[8] See *Die Genesis* (1901), p. ii.

[9] See Gunkel's popular essay, "Was haben wir am Alten Testament?," *Deutsche Rundschau*, CLXI (1914), 215–41; translated in *What Remains of the Old Testament? and Other Essays*, pp. 13–56.

Bishop Lowth had shown a purely literary appreciation of Hebrew poetry and had made a study of its various types and their literary structure.[10] His contemporary, the philosopher-critic Herder, had not only displayed a genuine feeling for the literary qualities of Hebrew poetry but showed a profound insight into its spiritual character as the product of a living religious experience. In this connection Herder advanced the significant theory that the poetic spirit expressed itself in specific "forms" suited to the purpose, which became conventional in the written stage of literary history.[11] Thus Gunkel's approach to the Old Testament, including the analysis of literary "forms" or types, had worthy antecedents.

Even his emphasis on the important part played by oral tradition in the formation of Old Testament literature had been anticipated. Alexander Geddes, an early English critic who appreciated better than most students of the written sources the vitality of oral tradition among the Hebrews, had clearly expressed the view that the Pentateuch was composed of separate literary units which had existed first in oral form.[12] But he had elaborated no new method of analysis on the basis of this view. Actually, the notion that Moses had learned all he knew about the beginnings of history from oral traditions was a very old one. In the seventeenth and eighteenth centuries it had been made the basis of a theory that the oral traditions had come down to Moses' time in fixed, unchanging form.[13] At the time, the theory was advanced only in the interests of orthodoxy to prove the authenticity of the traditions preserved by Moses. It might have generated a significant line of study, had

---

[10] *Praelectiones academicae de sacra poesi Hebraeorum* (Oxford, 1753); English translation by G. Gregory (2 vols., London, 1787; 3d ed., 1835).

[11] *Vom Geist der Ebräischen Poesie*, edited by J. G. Müller (Stuttgart, 1827), II, 107–13.

[12] *Critical Remarks on the Hebrew Scriptures* (London, 1800).

[13] See Adolphe Lods, "Le rôle de la tradition orale dans la formation des récits de l'Ancien Testament," *RHR*, LXXXVIII (1923), p. 51, and the references given there.

not the rival theory advanced by Astruc, that Moses had made use of written sources, wholly absorbed the attention of scholars. But Gunkel's realization that the written sources were largely compiled from oral traditions which had already been given a certain form through constant repetition by the people led to the modern attempt to reconstruct the history of Old Testament literature through a study of the forms of oral tradition. The principles of Gunkel's method were presented for the first time in the famous introduction to his commentary on Genesis,[14] in which he showed that by examining the varieties of literary form occurring in the written texts it was possible to reconstruct the history of legend in the oral stage, much as the architectural history of a cathedral could be reconstructed from the various styles in which it had been built. Taking a hint from Ferdinand Brunetière's theory that oral tradition always followed definite laws of development,[15] Gunkel not only classified the stories of Genesis according to types but tried to show how they had grown from the most primitive to the more complex literary forms. He distinguished three stages in the development of the genre: brief hero tales, extensive legends, and story-cycles.[16] Naturally, the transition from one stage to the next was a gradual one. But "even in the oldest legends of Genesis we do not have naive, crude stories, lightly dashed off; rather, a mature, accomplished, and highly animated artistry is manifest in them." [17]

Gunkel's analysis clearly implied that an attempt to garner much historical information from these narratives would be futile. "Legend," he said, "weaves a poetic web around historical memories

[14] See above, n. 3. The introduction was published separately as *Die Sagen der Genesis* (Göttingen, 1901), and in an English translation, *The Legends of Genesis* (Chicago, 1901).

[15] *L'évolution des genres dans l'histoire de la littérature* (Paris, 1890). Cf. Axel Olrik, "Die epischen Gesetze der Volksdichtung," *Zeitschrift für deutsches Altertum*, LI (1909), 1–12.

[16] See *Die Genesis* (1901), pp. xxi–xxxii, xxxvi–xl.

[17] *Ibid.*, p. xxxvi.

and hides the circumstances" of time and place.[18] As in the folk-literature of other peoples, the story-cycles of the early Hebrews consisted of kernels of historical fact embedded in enveloping layers of legend.[19] The conclusion that, during the years of oral transmission, legend had entered more prominently than historical reminiscence into the composition of the patriarchal narratives[20] confirmed Wellhausen's distrust of their value as history. But it gave them greater importance as a part of the literary heritage of Israel.

What Gunkel had done to illuminate the character of the narratives of Genesis, Gressmann tried to do with the stories about Moses scattered through the books of Exodus and Numbers.[21] Assuming that the stories had been taken up into the compositions of the Yahwist and the Elohist from the stock of popular tales current in the mouths of the people, Gressmann identified the individual units of narrative by diversities of type and sought to distinguish between those that were primitive and those that had received more or less elaboration. Fortunately, it was possible to achieve results in this direction, since the harmonizing tendency of the redactors had not obliterated the original features of the individual stories. Gressmann found that they still bore the marks of their origin in popular tradition: they had the literary form and the legendary character of "poetic" creations of the people. Genuine historical memories regarding the figure of Moses had been overlaid with elements of a supernatural or a marvelous nature, so that in

[18] *Ibid.*, p. x.
[19] Cf. Hugo Gressmann, "Sage und Geschichte in den Patriarchenerzählungen," *ZAW*, XXX (1910), 1-34.
[20] See Gunkel's essays, "Die Komposition der Joseph-Geschichte," *ZDMG*, LXXVI (1922), 55-71, and "Jakob," *Preussische Jahrbücher*, CLXXVI (1919), 339-62; the latter translated in *What Remains of the Old Testament? and Other Essays*, pp. 150-86. Cf. Gressmann's study, "Ursprung und Entwicklung der Josephsage," in Hans Schmidt (ed.), *Eucharisterion: Studien zur Religion und Literatur des Alten und Neuen Testaments* (Gunkel *Festschrift*; Göttingen, 1923), I, 1-55. See also W. F. Albright, "Historical and Mythical Elements in the Story of Joseph," *JBL*, XXXVII (1918), 111-43; and Herbert G. May, "The Evolution of the Joseph Story," *AJSL*, XLVII (1930-31), 83-93.
[21] *Mose und seine Zeit* (Göttingen, 1913).

their final form the stories often had the character of popular wonder tales. These narratives, in other words, were not so much historical as another important part of Israel's literary heritage.

Studies such as these by Gunkel and Gressmann greatly advanced the understanding of Old Testament narrative as a literary genre. Their identification of the various types of legends and tales and their clarification of the nature of the contents showed that the characteristic features of Old Testament narrative had been acquired during the oral stage of development, not in the process of assembling the traditions in written form. The general effect of this conclusion was to reduce the importance of the authors of the written narratives. The early critics had described the Yahwist and the Elohist as creative writers, who presented the early history of their people in literary compositions each of which was "masterful both in plan and execution." [22] But, when Gunkel drew attention to the literary qualities of the original materials, the contributions of the Yahwist and the Elohist no longer seemed so great. The variety of material to be found in one and the same document indicated to Gunkel that J and E were the work of mere compilers who had gathered and arranged the multifarious legacy of oral tradition "essentially in the form in which they found it." [23] Moreover, since its legendary and mythical elements indicated that it was primarily folk literature, "what each individual hand contributed to the whole is relatively unimportant." [24]

Gunkel's view that the qualities of Old Testament narrative were the product of the collective genius of the people rather than the achievement of individual authors reflected the influence of the sociological trend of thought in historical studies at the beginning of the twentieth century. This trend embodied the belief that the people, much more than individual leaders, were the important

[22] See, e.g., Rudolf Smend, *Die Erzählung des Hexateuch auf ihre Quellen untersucht* (Berlin, 1912), pp. 345–48, from which the quotation is taken (p. 348).
[23] *Die Genesis* (1901), p. lvi.
[24] *Ibid.*, p. lviii.

factor in cultural history.[25] Gunkel's approach to the Old Testament was in a very real sense his own; yet it was unconsciously affected by the intellectual currents of his day. "The form-critical method did not spring from the brain of the scholar but was suggested to him by the whole conceptual tendency which surrounded him." [26]

The Application of Form Criticism to the Old Testament

(1)

Gunkel's work on prose narrative was his first substantial contribution to that history of Old Testament literature which he felt needed to be written. But the desired goal was far from being attained. Before such a history could be written, special studies of other genres of Hebrew literature had to be undertaken. Next in importance among Gunkel's researches was his work on the genre of religious poetry. For a quarter of a century, in addition to his other labors, Gunkel studied the psalms of Israel, devoting his research to the problems of literary type, distinctive characteristics, and historical development.[27]

Starting with Herder's hint that the form of religious poetry was always suited to the purpose, Gunkel first classified the psalms according to the types suggested by their subject matter. Then, analyzing the literary characteristics of each classification, he discovered—as Herder had also suggested—that for each type of psalm there were conventions of literary form, fixed by long usage.[28] In classical studies, research on the various genres of literature had led to the conclusion that conventions of form were much more

[25] See below, chap. V, p. 158.
[26] Erich Fascher, *Die formgeschichtliche Methode: eine Darstellung und Kritik* (Giessen, 1924), p. 36.
[27] The milestones of his progress in this area of research were his *Ausgewählte Psalmen* (Göttingen, 1904; 4th rev. ed., 1917), *Die Psalmen* ("Handkommentar zum Alten Testament," edited by Wilhelm Nowack, Div. II, Vol. II; 4th ed., Göttingen, 1926), and *Einleitung in die Psalmen: Die Gattungen der religiösen Lyrik Israels* (in two parts, Göttingen, 1928-33).
[28] See his "Formen der Hymnen," *Theologische Rundschau*, XX (1917), 265-304.

binding upon an author in ancient times than they were in modern literature. Style was not a matter of individual artistry; an author usually adapted his technique of composition to the literary form traditional for the type of subject matter he was treating.[29] In the category of religious literature, the same formulas of expression could be traced for centuries.[30] This principle, Gunkel found, also applied to Hebrew poetry. Typical formulas, especially noticeable at the beginning and the end of a psalm, appeared repeatedly in each category. The fixity of form made it difficult to sketch the historical development of a literary type; but comparison with the numerous poetical compositions scattered through other books of the Old Testament provided a number of clues to the growth of poetical forms, while allusions in the psalms themselves sometimes suggested fixed points in Old Testament history to which the psalms could be related.[31]

The most important of Gunkel's conclusions in this connection was that religious poetry in Israel had a long history. He maintained that the typical forms had originated at a comparatively early date, in the oral stage, and had reached the height of their development before the Exile. The postexilic psalmists, he conceded, had composed most of the psalms in their present form; but he pointed out that many of the psalms showed a mixture of literary types which indicated that they had been composed from various older forms. Gunkel therefore assigned a great number to an earlier date than the critics had allowed, without questioning the late date for the compilation of the Psalter as a whole.[32]

[29] See Eduard Norden, *Die antike Kunstprosa* (Leipzig, 1898), I, 11–12; Theodor Birt, *Kritik und Hermeneutik* ("Handbuch der klassischen Altertumswissenschaft," Vol. I, Part III; 3d rev. ed., Munich, 1913), pp. 164–70.

[30] See Eduard Norden, *Agnostos Theos: Untersuchungen zur Formengeschichte religiöser Rede* (Leipzig, 1913).

[31] See "The Poetry of the Psalms: Its Literary History and Its Application to the Dating of the Psalms," in *Old Testament Essays* (London, 1927), pp. 118–42.

[32] See *Einleitung in die Psalmen*, pp. 415–33: "Die Geschichte der Psalmendichtung." For a review of recent theories on the dating of the psalms, see C. L. Feinberg, "The Date of the Psalms," *Bibliotheca Sacra*, CIV (1947), 426–40.

The antiquity of the most important literary types was supported by comparison with analogous forms of religious poetry in the literature of Babylonia and Egypt. Parallels could be found not only to the genre in general but to the structural composition of particular types of psalms.[33] The resemblance of the penitential hymns to those of the Babylonians had been noticed from the beginning by the scholars who deciphered the cuneiform tablets.[34] The similarity of the thanksgiving hymns to examples of the same in Egyptian literature strengthened the supposition that certain types of psalms were not original with the Israelites but were based on models provided by the other ancient peoples.[35]

After the discovery of the Ras Shamra tablets in 1929, it became evident that more significant parallels to the Hebrew psalms were to be found in the Ugaritic literature than in Babylonian or Egyptian literature. The Ugaritic epic texts showed striking resemblances in poetical form and language, as well as similar conceptions of the attributes of deity, to those occurring in the psalms.[36] The comparative study of these texts revealed a multitude of words, phrases, and stylistic features common to the psalms that could be paralleled in the Canaanite texts.[37] Some of the psalms

[33] See Friedrich Stummer, *Sumerisch-Akkadische Parallelen zum Aufbau alttestamentlicher Psalmen* (Paderborn, 1922), and "Die Psalmengattungen im Lichte der altorientalischen Hymenliteratur," *JSOR*, VIII (1924), 123–34; Hugo Gressmann, "The Development of Hebrew Psalmody," in D. C. Simpson (ed.), *The Psalmists* (Oxford, 1926), pp. 1–21; Charles G. Cumming, *The Assyrian and Hebrew Hymns of Praise* (New York, 1934).

[34] See G. R. Driver, "The Psalms in the Light of Babylonian Research," in D. C. Simpson (ed.), *The Psalmists*, pp. 109–75; George Widengren, *The Accadian and Hebrew Psalms of Lamentation as Religious Documents* (Uppsala, 1937).

[35] See Aylward M. Blackman, "The Psalms in the Light of Egyptian Research," in D. C. Simpson (ed.), *The Psalmists*, pp. 177–97; Hermann Gunkel, "Aegyptische Danklieder," in his *Reden und Aufsätze*, pp. 141–49.

[36] See the texts translated in Cyrus H. Gordon's *Ugaritic Literature* (Rome, 1949), or in James B. Pritchard (ed.), *Ancient Near Eastern Texts* (Princeton, 1950), pp. 129–55 (trans. by H. L. Ginsberg).

[37] See James Montgomery and Zellig Harris, *Ras Shamra Mythological Texts* (Philadelphia, 1935); C. F. A. Schaeffer, *The Cuneiform Texts of Ras Shamra* (London, 1939); John H. Patton, *Canaanite Parallels to the Psalms* (Baltimore, 1943); Joseph Coppens, "Parallèles du psautier avec les textes de Ras Shamra-Ougarit," *Muséon*, LIX (1946), 113–42.

showed a very strong influence from Canaanite patterns of composition, while one in particular (Ps. 29) seemed taken directly from the Ugaritic with only the substitution of Yahweh for Baal. This did not mean that the Israelites had borrowed all the features of their psalmody, but it showed how strongly Canaanite thought patterns had persisted into Israelite times. Even so, the Hebrew psalms showed a significant discrimination in their borrowing. Forms of expression repeatedly occurred, but all polytheistic and mythological elements had been trimmed away, except those which had been given a metaphorical significance.[38]

(2)

As Gunkel had applied the technique of form criticism to the narratives of Genesis and the poetry of the Psalms, his followers applied it to the other genres of Old Testament literature. Hugo Gressmann undertook a detailed investigation of the genre of historical writing, as it was found outside the Hexateuch.[39] He started with the assumption that whatever qualities of narrative style written history possessed could be traced directly to the living art of narration which had grown up in the oral stage. Hence, he devoted most of his attention to the literary form in which individual narratives were composed. Analysis of the structure and the documentary development of an entire book, while not to be ignored, seemed relatively unimportant beside the interesting and illuminating study of the single narrative as a literary type.

So fruitful did Gressmann's technique seem to be in clarifying the nature of historical composition, that it was applied with en-

[38] For a convenient review of the discovery, decipherment, interpretation, and comparative study of the Ras Shamra tablets, see W. F. Albright, "The Old Testament and Canaanite Language and Literature," *Catholic Biblical Quarterly,* VII (1945), 5–31. See also H. L. Ginsberg's popular summary of results, "Ugaritic Studies and the Bible," *Biblical Archaeologist,* VIII (1945), 41–58.

[39] *Die älteste Geschichtsschreibung und Prophetie Israels* ("Die Schriften des Alten Testaments in Auswahl neu übersetzt und für die Gegenwart erklärt," Div. II, Vol. I; Göttingen, 1910).

thusiasm by a number of other scholars to various portions of the historical literature. As a matter of fact, the technique was regarded by some as sufficient to solve all the problems in the historical books which criticism itself had left unanswered. They abandoned the attempt to trace the narrative documents of the Hexateuch into Judges and Samuel, in favor of a new analysis based on the hypothesis that there existed separate sources peculiar to these books. Leonhard Rost, for example, argued that the books of Samuel did not contain parallel narratives like the Hexateuch but a succession of originally independent materials, which stood out from the whole as self-contained units because of their peculiarities of style and form.[40] Gerhard von Rad later identified three such units of narrative material, which he considered the oldest examples of historical writing in Israel's literature.[41] Wilhelm Caspari subjected each of the narrative units in the books of Samuel to an exhaustive analysis of its peculiarities of style and its underlying thought content, in an effort to identify all the original units from which the present narrative texts had been built up.[42] Gressmann's method of evaluating the separate stories as individual literary creations was similarly applied to the book of Judges by Kurt Wiese.[43] The resulting tendency to fragmentize the historical books did not derive from any concerted effort to find a substitute for the document hypothesis; it sprang naturally from preoccupation with questions of form and content in relation to separate literary units.

Results such as these were useful contributions to the ultimate goal of rewriting the history of Old Testament literature. Also useful toward achieving that goal was the attempt to trace the historical development of particular units of tradition to be found

[40] *Die Ueberlieferung von der Thronnachfolge Davids* (Stuttgart, 1926).

[41] "Der Anfang der Geschichtsschreibung im Alten Testament," *Archiv für Kulturgeschichte*, XXXII (1944), 1–42.

[42] *Die Samuelbücher* ("Kommentar zum Alten Testament," edited by Ernst Sellin, Vol. VII; Leipzig, 1926).

[43] *Zur Literarkritik des Buches der Richter* (Stuttgart, 1926).

in the literature of the Old Testament. Where the first technique of analyzing literary form had been effective in reconstructing the development of the outward forms of literature, the second technique contributed a great deal toward the history of its conceptual content. The method consisted in collecting the existing variants of a tradition, arranging them in the order of development from primitive to complex, and reconstructing the original form of the tradition as far as it still showed through the existing texts. It was the method Gunkel had pioneered in his *Schöpfung und Chaos* in 1895, when he attempted to reconstruct the original nature of certain mythological motifs from the smallest hints in the surviving texts. Now, Anton Jirku applied the technique to the explanation of the various brief summaries of Israel's early history that were scattered through the Old Testament (e.g., Josh. 24, Ps. 78, Ps. 105, and Deut. 29).[44] These summaries, containing certain oft-used formal expressions, constituted a literary "type," which furnished an example of how oral tradition had become fixed before written history began. Jirku demonstrated that these brief, didactic passages, made for instructional purposes, contained a form of the tradition that antedated in conception the canonical history in the Pentateuch. He argued that this older form of the tradition stemmed from the "sermon" delivered by the priests in the worship service and had received its present form in the transition from the short didactic style of oral delivery to the more expansive style of written narration.

Martin Noth made a similar investigation of "the original form and further written elaboration" of a specific tradition in his study of the conception of "twelve tribes" in Israel.[45] He maintained that this tradition had originated in the period of the Judges, and that it was nothing more than the listing of the members of an early

---

[44] *Die älteste Geschichte Israels im Rahmen lehrhafter Darstellungen* (Leipzig, 1917).

[45] *Das System der zwölf Stämme Israels* (Stuttgart, 1930).

Israelitic league analogous to the "amphictyony" of early Greek history.[46] Although in its existing written form the tradition of twelve tribes in Israel stemmed almost exclusively from later times, when no such system any longer existed, Noth was convinced by his detailed analysis of each form of the tradition (Gen. 49, Num. 26, and Num. 1) that the notion of twelve tribes as a constitutional entity had existed from the very beginning of the settlement in Palestine. Noth's investigation was a good example of the effort being made, through techniques initiated by Gunkel, to bring to light the origin and significance of portions of Israel's historical traditions which literary criticism had declared unrepresentative of the facts.

The value of investigating the original nature of the historical traditions in the Old Testament is shown by Kurt Galling's study of the two different traditions regarding the manner in which Yahweh "chose" his people Israel.[47] Of the two—the call of Abraham and the deliverance from bondage in Egypt—Galling showed that the exodus tradition was the only one generally mentioned throughout Israel's history. It appeared frequently in various references down to the time of the Exile and was the basis for the ethically motivated appeal of the prophets for obedience to the will of God. The tradition of descent from Abraham, on the other hand, was referred to only rarely in pre-exilic literature (outside the patriarchal narratives). Even in the Psalms, Abraham was mentioned only twice as the father of his people, while the events of the exodus were repeatedly emphasized. Galling concluded that the exodus tradition had been a living tradition in Israel, while the other was an artificial construction, prefixed to the exodus tradition by the first Yahwistic historian for political and religious reasons.[48] Galling's investigation of these two traditions, like the preceding

[46] See, *ibid.*, pp. 39–60.
[47] *Die Erwählungstraditionen Israels* (Giessen, 1928).
[48] Cf. the theory of Gerhard von Rad, below, pp. 153–54.

studies of single units of tradition, revealed something of the nature of the materials that had contributed to the growth of Israel's historical literature.

(3)

The technique of studying small literary units also seemed to offer the key to a better understanding of the apparently amorphous literature contained in the prophetical books.[49] The process of breaking up the extensive "orations" into separate oracles and poetical compositions, begun by Bernhard Duhm and others of the critical school, appeared entirely justified in the light of the hypothesis that prophetic oracles, like other "literary types" in their original form, were always brief utterances confined to the statement of single ideas. Rarely, of course, did they stand alone in the existing written texts; they usually occurred in groups which contained a succession of units dealing with the same or similar subjects. But in the longer passages it was possible to determine the limits of the original oracles by the introductory and concluding phrases. Accordingly, the prophetic writings were to be regarded as compilations of small units—some stemming from the prophets themselves, others contributed by their disciples—rather than as "books" written entirely by the reputed authors.[50] Gunkel suggested that the prophets often added to their original short oracles after reflection,[51] but the old conception of "writing prophets" was given up in favor of the view that the prophets spoke their messages in brief form under the inspiration of an ecstatic experience,[52]

[49] See Hermann Gunkel, "Die Propheten als Schriftsteller und Dichter," in Hans Schmidt, *Die grossen Propheten* ("Die Schriften des Alten Testaments in Auswahl neu übersetzt und für die Gegenwart erklärt," Div. II, Vol. II; Göttingen, 1915), pp. xxxvi-lxxii.
[50] The classic exposition in English of this view is Theodore H. Robinson's *Prophecy and the Prophets in Ancient Israel* (New York, 1923; 2d ed., 1944).
[51] *Op. cit.*, p. xli.
[52] The ecstatic nature of prophecy, first expounded by Gustav Hölscher in *Die Profeten* (Leipzig, 1914), pp. 129-58, became a favorite principle of interpretation, although it was denied or limited by some, in the case of the great

and that these messages were current as oral tradition before they were collected into the present books.[53] According to Theodore H. Robinson, the process of collection itself was partially completed in the oral stage. As Gunkel had described the grouping of early legends into story-cycles before they were written down, Robinson suggested that the separate utterances of a prophet were collected by his disciples into a cycle of prophetic tradition, which later was amplified in a book.[54]

Research along these lines in the historical and prophetic literature showed how the methods of Gunkel could be extended to areas which he himself had not brought within his purview. As a matter of fact, a whole new school of criticism was generated from his principle that the original sources of written literature were to be found in oral literature. Gunkel's real heirs in recent times have been the group of young Scandinavian scholars who developed the special field of research called by them the "history of tradition." They undertook to investigate the formation and transmission of tradition in the preliterary oral stage, and ended with a view of Old Testament literary history quite different from that of the critical school. Taking seriously the suggestion that the books of the prophets grew out of the oral traditions preserved and amplified by their disciples,[55] the Scandinavian scholars not only studied the prophetic books intensively from this point of view[56] but extended

canonical prophets. For a review of the whole subject, see Adolphe Lods, "Recherches récentes sur le prophétisme israélite," *RHR*, CIV (1931), 279–316; and H. H. Rowley, "The Nature of Prophecy in the Light of Recent Study," *HTR*, XXXVIII (1945), 1–38.

[53] See Johannes Lindblom, "Ueber die literarische Gattung der prophetischen Literatur," *Uppsala Universitets Arsskrift* (1924), pp. 1–122; Harris Birkeland, *Zum hebräischen Traditionswesen: Die Komposition der prophetischen Bücher des Alten Testaments* (Oslo, 1938).

[54] See "Die prophetischen Bücher im Lichte neuer Entdeckungen," *ZAW*, XLV (1927), 3–9.

[55] The Scandinavian scholars derived this suggestion from H. S. Nyberg's *Studien zum Hoseabuche* (Uppsala, 1935), rather than from Robinson's paper.

[56] Besides Harris Birkeland's work, mentioned above (n. 53), see Sigmund Mowinckel, *Prophecy and Tradition* (Oslo, 1946), and George Widengren, *Literary and Psychological Aspects of the Hebrew Prophets* (Uppsala, 1948).

the theory of oral transmission to other books in the Old Testament. They explained the present text of the Hexateuch as the final fixation in written form of traditions which had been handed down orally until the postexilic period. The strata of literature usually designated as J, E, D, or P were not actually written "documents" that could be assigned to specific authors or particular periods; they were the literary crystallization of various bodies of oral tradition stemming from different circles or centers of tradition.[57] Moreover, these different bodies of tradition were not necessarily successive, but probably developed contemporaneously for long periods of time.[58] Since each "tradition" was a growing thing, supplemented, adapted, and even transformed by the circle which undertook its preservation, the attempt to distinguish what was early and what was late in the tradition could not succeed by the usual methods of literary criticism. The Old Testament scholar was dealing here, not with written "sources" and "redactors" of written materials, but with units of oral tradition and circles of traditionists. Hence his task was to go behind the written literature to find the origin, nature, and history of the blocks of oral tradition that had gone into the making of the written literature. This was the task to which the Scandinavian school of "tradition history" devoted itself.[59] In its hands, "form criticism" became not

[57] This theory has been developed chiefly by Ivan Engnell in a number of exegetical writings in Swedish, which the present writer has not seen. The above information is necessarily given at second hand (cf. the references in n. 59, below).

[58] Cf. the similar theory of Ezekiel Kaufmann, above, chap. I, pp. 33–34. Another history of religious thought in Israel by a Jewish scholar, written more strictly along the lines of "tradition history," is Martin Buber's *The Prophetic Faith*, translated from Hebrew by C. Witton-Davies (New York, 1949).

[59] See G. W. Anderson, "Some Aspects of the Uppsala School of Old Testament Study," *HTR*, XLIII (1950), 239–56; Aage Bentzen, "Skandinavische Literatur zum Alten Testament 1939–1948," *Theologische Rundschau*, XVII (1948–49), 272–328. For pertinent criticisms of the Uppsala school's general position, see Christopher R. North, "The Place of Oral Tradition in the Growth of the Old Testament," *Expository Times*, LXI (1949–50), 292–96; J. van der Ploeg, "Le rôle de la tradition orale dans la transmission du texte de l'Ancien Testament," *Revue biblique*, LIV (1947), 5–41. Cf. H. Ringgren, "Oral and Written Transmission in the Old Testament," *Studia theologica*, III (1937), 34–59.

merely the analysis of literary *form* but more specifically the study of the *formation* of literature from oral tradition.

In this connection, the most significant contribution of the school was its description of the milieu in which the prophetic literature originated and developed. The circles of disciples who preserved and transmitted the oral pronouncements of the prophets were described by Alfred Haldar as associations of cult-prophets attached to the various shrines in the monarchical period.[60] Making use of certain evidence presented by Ivan Engnell in his studies of ancient oriental materials,[61] Haldar maintained that associations of cult-prophets, attached to the popular shrines, were common throughout the ancient Near East. In Israel, they included even the great prophets, who had always been placed by critical scholars in a separate class distinct from the ordinary "sons of the prophets" of early times and the later "false prophets." But according to Haldar, the books of the prophets were the outcome of the care taken by such associations of prophets to preserve the oracles of their most illustrious members. This interpretation was an example of the search for the "situation in life" which produced a particular type of literature. It was one of the results of putting into practice Gunkel's suggestion that, if the nature of Old Testament literature was to be understood, the study of literary types must be supplemented with an investigation of the milieu from which each type had sprung.

The Search for the "Situation in Life" of Literary Forms

Gunkel had never been satisfied with a mere surface examination of literary form; he always emphasized the importance of also determining the situations in life which called forth the various forms. For he believed that every ancient literary type was originally related to some particular aspect of the national life, which

---

[60] *Associations of Cult Prophets among the Ancient Semites* (Uppsala, 1945).
[61] *Studies in Divine Kingship in the Ancient Near East* (Uppsala, 1943).

could be determined by studying the practical use to which each type of literature had been put. The psalms, for example, were obviously connected with the ritual of worship. But had they been used by the whole community worshiping together, or did they express the spiritual aspirations of pious individuals worshiping in private? It was difficult to specify their original uses except in very general terms; but because the great majority of them seemed to express an intensely personal religious feeling, the critical school had assigned them to the individualistic age of late postexilic Judaism. Gunkel, however, believing that the psalms went back to a much earlier time, was convinced that in their original form they were not expressions of personal piety but cultic hymns composed to be chanted as part of the rituals performed at the local shrines in pre-exilic days.[62]

This interpretation was applied in great detail by Sigmund Mowinckel, who went much farther than Gunkel along the road of searching out the cultic connections of the psalms. His series of studies, analyzing the various types and discussing the purpose for which each had been composed,[63] related each type to some specific act in the ritual of the pre-exilic sanctuary. His cultic interpretation of the hymns of supplication has already been discussed.[64] Although these psalms expressed the desires of the individual suppliant, Mowinckel regarded them, not as the work of pious individuals, but as typical psalms composed by the priests for use by any individual who felt the need of expressing himself in the manner indicated.[65] He also identified a type of didactic psalms (e.g., Pss. 15 and 24B) which he described as "instructions" pronounced by the priests at the entrance to the shrines before the

[62] See *Einleitung in die Psalmen*, pp. 10-19. Cf. Antonin Causse, *Les plus vieux chants de la Bible* (Paris, 1926), chap. III: "La poésie cultuelle" (pp. 79-134).

[63] *Psalmenstudien* ("Skrifter der Norske videnskaps-akademi: Hist.-fil. klasse," 1921, Nos. 4, 6; 1922, Nos. 1, 2; 1923, No. 3; 1924, No. 1; Kristiania, 1921–24).

[64] See above, chap. II, pp. 64–65.

[65] See *Psalmenstudien*, I, 138, 157.

worshipers were permitted to enter. Psalms which had the style of oracles (e.g., Ps. 60:6-8, Ps. 75, Ps. 82) Mowinckel described as responses spoken by the prophets attached to each shrine as cult-officials, whose duty it was to communicate the divine answers to the prayers of the worshipers.[66] Such interpretations revealed wholly new aspects of pre-exilic religious practice at the local shrines and provided some new insights into the "situation in life" of various types of psalms.[67] Mowinckel made clear that, whatever the date of their final redaction, the psalms were the product of centuries of liturgical use in the religious life of the community. Even more than Gunkel, he emphasized the social rather than the individual factor in the creation of Israel's religious hymns.[68]

But Mowinckel seems to have overshot the mark by assigning each category of psalm to one ritual occasion exclusively. His most debatable suggestion along this line was his description of the "accession psalms" as the liturgy for the ritual of "the enthronement of Yahweh" in connection with the New Year's festival.[69] The association of these psalms with a "cult drama" representing the enthronement of the Divine King was not supported by the contents of the psalms themselves. Mowinckel deduced it entirely from the analogy of the Babylonian New Year's ritual. But whether every psalm which mentioned Yahweh as king or referred to the Creation was to be related to the New Year's festival was

[66] *Psalmenstudien, III: Kultprophetie und prophetische Psalmen* (1922). Cf. Johannes Pedersen, *Israel*, Vol. II, pp. 115-17. See also Aubrey R. Johnson, *The Cultic Prophet in Ancient Israel* (Cardiff, 1944).

[67] Similar conclusions were expressed by John P. Peters, *The Psalms as Liturgies* (New York, 1922), and C. C. Keet, *A Liturgical Study of the Psalter* (London, 1928). See also W. O. E. Oesterley, *A Fresh Approach to the Psalms* (New York, 1937).

[68] A convenient summary in English of the theories of Gunkel and Mowinckel (among others) is now available in Elmer A. Leslie's *The Psalms Translated and Interpreted in the Light of Hebrew Life and Worship* (Nashville, Tenn., 1949). See also Aubrey R. Johnson, "The Psalms," in H. H. Rowley (ed.), *The Old Testament and Modern Study* (Oxford, 1951), pp. 162-207.

[69] See above, chap. II, pp. 66-67.

questionable.[70] Mowinckel failed to consider the possibility that the cultic situation to which these psalms applied was of a more general nature than the specific enthronement ritual.

While conjecture based on the ideological content of the psalms played too large a part in Mowinckel's method of investigation, his studies were valuable in that they did justice to the cultic factor in the religion of which the psalms were an expression. Nineteenth century scholarship had underrated the place of ritual in the religious life of the Israelites, attributing all that was vital and progressive in that religion to the teaching of the prophets. Ritual was "priestly" and therefore suffered the disparagement accorded to the priestly literature in the Old Testament. Mowinckel made it possible to understand more clearly that in the early periods of Israel's religious history the cultus itself expressed a genuinely religious spirit. It provided an opportunity for the worshiper to draw nigh to the deity and receive an assurance of divine favor from the lips of the priest or the cult-prophet, and it gave him the feeling of participating with the deity in ensuring prosperity for the coming year. The ceremonial elements in Israel's religion were not mere survivals of primitive practice to be outgrown; they embodied beliefs that were long significant in the religious life of the people.

This emphasis on the significance of the cultic factor in Israel's religion and the probable connection of prophets with the cult shrines bore fruit in a new view of the relation between priests and prophets. Critical scholars had usually set them in opposition to each other, emphasizing the polemic of the prophets against ritual worship.[71] Now there was a growing appreciation of the fact that the canonical prophets did not repudiate sacrifice as such

[70] See Gunkel's criticism in *Einleitung in die Psalmen*, pp. 100-16. Cf. Norman H. Snaith, *Studies in the Psalter* (London, 1934), and *The Jewish New Year Festival* (London, 1947). See also Hans Joachim Kraus, *Die Königsherrschaft Gottes im Alten Testament* (Tübingen, 1951).

[71] See, e.g., John Skinner, *Prophecy and Religion* (Cambridge, 1922); J. Philip Hyatt, *Prophetic Religion* (Nashville, 1947), chap. VII.

or regard the ritual forms of worship as necessarily bad. They laid more stress on a right attitude of mind, but they advocated no program that would dispense entirely with the established forms of worship. Not the cultus itself but ritual divorced from morality was the object of the prophets' attacks.[72] With this altered perspective on the prophetic function, it was possible to see the priest and prophet, each in his own sphere, working for the furtherance of religion without being continually at cross-purposes.[73] The priest had the help of the cult-prophet in teaching the significance of ritual actions; the canonical prophet added yet more by infusing religious worship with an ethical content.[74]

In spite of exaggeration in Mowinckel's theories, his emphasis on the cultic function of Hebrew religious poetry suggested a fresh approach to the Old Testament writings. Other literary categories were examined with a view to determining whether they too had once been "liturgies" read or recited in connection with some religious festival. Those who had followed Gunkel in studying individual narratives in the Old Testament turned from the popular hero tales which had been his first concern and devoted more attention to the cult legends, i.e., the narratives designed to explain the origin or the purpose of the sacred rituals. Gunkel himself had suggested that etiological stories which attempted to justify the sacred character of the popular shrines were originally told by the priests at religious festivals in the very shrines to which they referred.[75] Now, under the influence of Mowinckel's theo-

---

[72] See W. O. E. Oesterley, *Sacrifices in Ancient Israel* (London, 1937), chap. XII; H. Wheeler Robinson, "Hebrew Sacrifice and Prophetic Symbolism," *Journal of Theological Studies*, XLIII (1942), pp. 129–39.

[73] See Adam C. Welch, *Prophet and Priest in Old Israel* (London, 1936); Jacob Hoschander, *Priests and Prophets* (New York, 1938); N. W. Porteous, "Prophet and Priest in Israel," *Expository Times*, LXII (1950–51), 4–9.

[74] See Norman W. Porteous, "The Basis of the Ethical Teaching of the Prophets," in H. H. Rowley (ed.), *Studies in Old Testament Prophecy* (Edinburgh, 1950), pp. 143–56. For a review of the whole subject, see H. H. Rowley, "The Unity of the Old Testament," *BJRL*, XXIX (1945–46), 327–53.

[75] *Die Genesis* (1901), p. xv.

ries, this "liturgical" interpretation of cult legends received renewed emphasis. It was even extended to the myths regarding the origin of things in the early chapters of Genesis. On the analogy of the fact that the creation epic was recited at the Babylonian New Year's festival, Paul Humbert suggested that the creation ode of Genesis 1 was recited as part of the liturgy at the New Year's festival of the Israelites, pointing to the schematic arrangement and the rhythmic prose as evidence of liturgical form.[76]

An interesting variation of the new technique was its application to several Old Testament narratives which had usually been taken as "historical" but were now regarded as cult legends. Narratives such as those of the exodus from Egypt or the dramatic events at Sinai were interpreted as liturgical recitations which had accompanied dramatic presentations of the historical events commemorated in one or another religious festival. The exodus narrative, according to this interpretation, was a cult legend for the Passover festival;[77] while the stories of events at Sinai were a description "in the language of historical myth" of a New Year celebration at Jerusalem, which included the representation of a theophany, the sealing of a covenant, and the recitation of divine commands.[78] The latter interpretation was another of Mowinckel's brilliant conjectures, which sprang from the tendency to make his theory regarding the "cult drama" acted during the New Year's festival explain more than it was meant to when he first advanced it in connection with the "enthronement of Yahweh." [79]

Apparently, once the search for a cultic "situation in life" of Old Testament narrative had got under way, there was no portion

---

[76] "La relation de Genèse 1 et du Psaume 104 avec la liturgie du Nouvel-An israélite," *RHPR*, XV (1935), 1–27.

[77] Johannes Pedersen, "Passahfest und Passahlegende," *ZAW*, LII (1934), 161–75. Cf. his *Israel*, Vol. II, pp. 726–37. In order to make such an interpretation possible, Pedersen ignored the usual critical analysis of Exodus 1–15 and treated these chapters as an organic literary unit.

[78] Sigmund Mowinckel, *Le décalogue* (Paris, 1927), pp. 114–30.

[79] Cf. the more plausible interpretation of Gerhard von Rad, below, pp. 143–44.

of the literature which could escape such an interpretation.[80] The very "documents" of critical analysis were assigned a liturgical function. Ernst Sellin supplemented his theory of their literary development with the hypothesis that they had been composed to be read in connection with the cultus.[81] If this meant no more than that the priests of the local sanctuaries used the ancient narratives to instruct the people on the religious significance of the nation's past,[82] it was a plausible hypothesis. But where the liturgical recitation of specific stories was assumed to have taken place in connection with cult dramas, the hypothesis suffered the same disability as Mowinckel's theory regarding the "enthronement of Yahweh" liturgy, in that it failed to reckon with the fact that the biblical texts didn't even hint at the purpose implied by the theory.

A less radical interpretation was made by Gerhard von Rad,[83] who stayed somewhat closer to Gunkel's method of working with small literary units. He discovered within Galling's "exodus tradition"[84] two distinct bodies of historical tradition relating to events since the exodus from Egypt. The one, repeated a number of times in various parts of the Hexateuch,[85] was a succinct summary of the exodus itself and the subsequent entrance of the Israelites into Canaan, with no mention of events at Mt. Sinai. It emphasized the saving power of Israel's God in rescuing his people from bondage and bringing them into the promised land. Von Rad regarded it as a kind of "creed" recited as part of a religious ceremony, believing that the formal recitation of the chief facts in the history of the nation must have constituted a permanent feature of the ancient Israelitic cultus. The "situation in life" of this

[80] The members of the "Scandinavian school" of interpretation, in particular, carried this method to extremes. See, e.g., Aage Bentzen's treatment of "The Cultic Use of the Story of the Ark in Samuel," *JBL*, LXVII (1948), 37–53.

[81] *Einleitung in das Alte Testament* (5th ed., Leipzig, 1929), pp. 60–61.

[82] As maintained by Anton Jirku, *Die älteste Geschichte Israels im Rahmen lehrhafter Darstellungen* (Leipzig, 1917), p. 167.

[83] *Das formgeschichtliche Problem des Hexateuchs* (Stuttgart, 1938).

[84] See above, p. 133.

[85] Exod. 15:4–16, Deut. 26:5b–9, 6:20–24, Josh. 24:2b–13.

particular "creed" was the Feast of Weeks as celebrated at the old shrine of Gilgal, the first religious center of the Israelites after their entrance into Canaan. The other "tradition" embraced the stories regarding the events at Sinai (Exod. 19-24, 32-34) and emphasized the ruling power of Israel's God as demonstrated in the giving of the Law. Von Rad regarded this "tradition" as the cult legend which developed at the famous sanctuary of Shechem, the religious center of the Israelite amphictyony. The original "situation in life" of the tradition was the ancient festival of the Covenant celebrated by the tribes united at Shechem in the common worship of Yahweh. In later times it was associated with the Feast of Booths. The form-critical analysis by which von Rad identified the two "traditions" seems justified.[86] But his attempt to attach each to a particular sanctuary as a liturgical element in a particular ceremony overlooked the possibility that the same terseness or formalization of historical tradition could have been the result of a more general process of repetition from generation to generation. Anton Jirku's interpretation, already mentioned,[87] was probably nearer the truth. He regarded the various summaries of Israel's early history as old traditions handed down in more or less fixed form for the instruction of the people regarding God's guidance of the nation's destiny, but he did not attempt to relate them as specific sanctuaries or identify them as "liturgies" for particular festivals.

Gunkel had made the suggestion that "liturgies" to be read on special occasions could also be found among the collections of prophetic oracles.[88] After examining the longer composite passages of prophecy with a view to identifying the individual parts accord-

---

[86] For the larger significance of von Rad's work, see below, pp. 153-54.

[87] See above, p. 132.

[88] "Jesaja 33, eine prophetische Liturgie," *ZAW*, XLII (1924), 177-208; "Der Micha-Schluss," *Zeitschrift für Semitistik*, II (1924), 145-78; English translation: "The close of Micah: a Prophetic Liturgy," in *What Remains of the Old Testament? and Other Essays* (London, 1928), pp. 115-49.

ing to literary type, he came to the conclusion that certain prophetic compositions, complex in form but unified in thought, were
literary unities. The similarity of subject matter between the
various parts was evidence of a purposeful compilation, even
though the separate sections fell into different categories. This
literary phenomenon received a plausible explanation from the
subsequent theory of the Scandinavian scholars, Haldar and Engnell.[89] They explained such prophetic compositions as due to the
activity of the cult-prophets who collected the separate oral pronouncements of outstanding members of their associations and
fashioned them into unified compositions for liturgical use at the
shrines to which they were attached. Gunkel's use of the term
"liturgies" to describe such portions of the prophetic literature was
therefore entirely justified.

In line with Gunkel's original suggestion, several of the smaller
prophetic books were then interpreted as liturgies especially drawn
up for specific occasions. The little book of Nahum was described
by Paul Humbert as a liturgy composed for the New Year festival
of the year 612 to celebrate the fall of Nineveh.[90] He also saw in
the book of Habakkuk a liturgy written a few years before the
fall of Jerusalem to prepare the people to face the Chaldean
danger.[91] The Scandinavian scholars, especially, adopted this type
of interpretation and began to find "cultic liturgies" everywhere
in the prophetic books. Haldar, in his study of the associations of
cult-prophets, endeavored to connect various prophetic pronouncements with specific cultic situations, particularly the New Year's

[89] See above, p. 137.

[90] "Le problème du livre de Nahoum," *RHPR*, XII (1932), 1–15. Alfred Haldar
later interpreted this "liturgy" as the work of a cult-prophet who used the
imagery of the ritual myth concerning Yahweh's triumph over his enemies as a
vehicle for his prophecy of the fall of Nineveh two years before its destruction.
See his *Studies in the Book of Nahum* (Uppsala, 1947).

[91] Paul Humbert, *Problèmes du livre d'Habacuc* (Neuchatel, 1944). For a similar treatment of the book of Zephaniah, see Gillis Gerleman, *Zephanja textkritisch
und literarisch untersucht* (Lund, 1942).

rituals. Ivan Engnell carried the method so far as to pronounce the whole of Deutero-Isaiah a cultic liturgy for the New Year festival.[92] Both scholars tried to show how much the prophetic literature made use of the terminology of the ritual myth pattern of the ancient East.[93] Frequently, these studies showed greater zeal than judgment; but the attempt to identify a specific literary type under the term "liturgy" represented a healthy reaction against the former fragmentation of the prophetic books into small literary units. It could now be recognized that an appreciable amount of heterogeneity in literary form was not incompatible with conceptual unity.

The last branch of Old Testament literature to feel the influence of Gunkel's methods of research was the Pentateuchal law, but as applied to this category of literature his methods attained their most fruitful results. The classification of the laws according to form and content and the investigation of the life situations from which each type arose gave a clearer picture than critical analysis had given of the real beginnings of law in Israel and the history of its development. The history, in fact, could better be approached through a study of the law's "situation in life" than by analysis of the formal codes embedded in the written sources. For the creation of law was not essentially a literary process but a living growth from social experience.

The first attempts at a classification of Pentateuchal laws according to type were those of Anton Jirku and Alfred Jepsen, who made simultaneous but independent studies of the Book of the Covenant, the oldest of the Hebrew law codes.[94] Their classi-

[92] See "The Ebed Yahweh Songs and the Suffering Messiah in 'Deutero-Isaiah,'" *BJRL*, XXXI (1948), 54–93. Cf. Curt Lindhagen, *The Servant Motif in the Old Testament* (Uppsala, 1950), and Johannes Lindblom, *The Servant Songs in Deutero-Isaiah* (Lund, 1951).

[93] See especially Engnell's *The Call of Isaiah: An Exegetical and Comparative Study* (Uppsala, 1949).

[94] Anton Jirku, *Das weltliche Recht im Alten Testament* (Gütersloh, 1927); Alfred Jepsen, *Untersuchungen zum Bundesbuch* (Stuttgart, 1927).

fications differed in detail but agreed in a preliminary division of
the laws into two general groups: those which showed any affinity
with ancient oriental law and those which could be regarded
as specifically Israelite because they were unique in literary form.
This distinction was clarified by Albrecht Alt, who pointed out
that the first group were laws of the casuistic type, the second of
an apodictic nature.[95]

The first type, the Hebrew "judgments" or "decisions," comprising about half of the Book of the Covenant, closely resembled
the laws of the ancient codes (Babylonian, Assyrian, Hittite) in
formulation, in content, and in juristic approach. Like the Code
of Hammurabi, they had a thoroughly secular spirit and lacked the
religious and humanitarian basis characteristic of later Hebrew law.
Hence, they were probably the oldest element in the Book of the
Covenant and either had been borrowed directly from or had
been influenced in their formative stage by the casuistic jurisprudence of the contemporary milieu.[96] Since they presupposed
the activities of a settled population, Alt thought that most likely
they had originated among the predominantly Canaanite population of Palestine, at a time when it was subject to the influence
of ancient oriental legal principles, and then had been adopted
by the Israelites soon after their entrance into the land. His view
was supported by the fact that the most natural "situation in life"
of casuistic law was to be found in the normal judicial activity of
the popular courts of each locality, presided over by the elders of
the people.[97]

On the other hand, the native Hebrew element in the prescriptions of the Covenant Code consisted of adjurations and moral
precepts in the solemn and uncompromising tone of apodictic

[95] *Die Ursprünge des israelitischen Rechts* (Berlin, 1934), pp. 12-16.
[96] See, *ibid.*, pp. 17-19, 23-26. Cf. Henri Cazelles, *Etudes sur le Code de l'Alliance* (Paris, 1946).
[97] See Alt, *op. cit.*, pp. 16–17, 26–30.

statement. In contrast to casuistic law, it embodied generalized principles covering the most important aspects of ethical life rather than specific regulations dealing with a multitude of practical eventualities. The authoritative tone of the apodictic laws, forbidding and condemning in the name of Yahweh, suggested to Alt that they emanated from a religious source in the form of solemn promulgations by the priests. A clue to this source was the description in Deuteronomy 27 of a convocation of the whole people in the valley of Shechem, at which the priests pronounced a series of such condemnations and prohibitions. Apodictic law, like the casuistic, was rooted in the fundamental institutions of the early age of Israel. But in this case it was the religious congregation rather than the secular court that provided its "situation in life." [98]

How an individual group of laws might have been promulgated by the priests was explained by Mowinckel with reference to the literary type of the "decalogue." He maintained that a specific series of religious requirements grouped together in that form represented a kind of "sacred law," recited by the priests at the entrance to a shrine before the start of a cultic ritual, as a reminder to the participants of what constituted ritual purity.[99] It followed that originally there existed more than one decalogue and that they varied in content from shrine to shrine. As a matter of fact, critical analysis had identified a Yahwistic decalogue of an entirely ritualistic nature in Exodus 34 and traces of an Elohistic decalogue with the same general character in Exodus 21–23, both quite distinct from the traditional Decalogue in Exodus 20.[100] From Mowinckel's point of view, the two older "decalogues" were literary remnants

---

[98] See, *ibid.*, pp. 34–37, 61–65. Cf. Karlheinz Rabast, *Das apodiktische Recht im Deuteronomium und im Heiligkeitsgesetz* (Berlin, 1949).

[99] *Le décalogue* (Paris, 1927), p. 154. Compare his theory regarding certain psalms as "instructions" of the priests (above, pp. 138–39).

[100] See Mowinckel's own analysis, *op. cit.*, chap. I; and cf. his "Zur Geschichte der Dekaloge," *ZAW*, LV (1937), 218–35.

of the sort of pronouncements made by the priests at the local shrines. Like so many of his hypotheses, this attempt to identify the original "situation in life" of such independent groups of laws was based on conjecture. But it had the merit of freeing the laws in question from their literary context and placing them, as a part of the cultus, in living relationship to the religious life of the people. Here again, Mowinckel's tendency to emphasize the social origin of a literary category showed itself.

Concentration upon specific types of law had drawn attention away from the comprehensive codes in which they were included and turned it toward various small groups of laws, which were regarded as having been independent entities at one time. Otto Eissfeldt, whose treatment of such bodies of law in the Priestly Code has already been discussed,[101] maintained that the present codes of law had been preceded by smaller collections of regulations dealing with particular subjects. Implicit in this view of the history of Pentateuchal law was the conception that Israel's law had been a living, growing thing, developing in the hands of the elders or the priests in the environment of actual practice at the courts "within the gates" or in the sanctuaries of the local shrines.[102] The theory of the critical school that there were only a few creative epochs in Old Testament legal history—those marked by the great codifications—was thus significantly modified into a theory of gradual, continuous growth of the legal heritage of Israel. It could even be argued that the growth of the Pentateuchal law was essentially an oral development, like that of other forms of tradition. Joachim Begrich, for example, in his study of the concept of *Torah* (the Law), defined it as the legal tradition of the priests, handed down orally through successive generations, devel-

---

[101] See above, chap. I, pp. 32-33.

[102] On the origin and "situation in life" of Hebrew laws, see Martin Noth, *Die Gesetze im Pentateuch* (Halle, 1940).

oped and expanded in ever greater detail, but always in terms of its original basic conceptions.[103]

The Literary History of the Old Testament in Recent Research

The search for the "situation in life" of various categories of Old Testament literature had brought form criticism a long way since Gunkel's initial suggestion of a cultic milieu for the psalms. But the continual preoccupation with small units of material had so far prevented the attainment of Gunkel's goal of a "creative synthesis of literary history." Up to this point, research in the field had been analytical rather than constructive. Those who made use of Gunkel's techniques did, indeed, perform a valuable service in tracing back the "sources of sources" to the earliest forms of oral expression; but exclusive attention to the separate elements had obscured the fact that, in their written forms, the units of material were parts of complex literary works which had special characteristics of their own. "Literary history," to fulfill the promise of its name, must survey the history of the written literature as well as its origins in oral tradition. By failing to follow up the search for the genesis of the original oral materials with an investigation of the subsequent processes of literary composition, the heirs of Gunkel had so far produced only limited results.

A progressive step forward was made, however, when scholars began advocating that more attention be paid to the factors which had determined the selection and arrangement of the materials in written form.[104] As Otto Eissfeldt emphasized, the proper task of the literary historian was the identification of the various unifying

---

[103] Joachim Begrich, "Die priesterliche Tora," in Paul Volz (ed.), *Werden und Wesen des Alten Testaments* (Berlin, 1936), pp. 63–88. On the tenacity of oral tradition down to late times, see Solomon Gandz, "Oral Tradition in the Bible," *Jewish Studies in Memory of George A. Kohut* (New York, 1935), pp. 248–69; reprinted, with a few additional notes, as chap. XVI of his "The Dawn of Literature," *Osiris*, VII (1939), 415–38; H. W. Herzberg, "Tradition in Palästina," *Palästinajahrbuch*, XXII (1926), 84–104.

[104] See Willy Staerk, "Zur alttestamentlichen Literarkritik: Grundsätzliches und Methodisches," *ZAW*, XLII (1924), 34–74.

points of view which had brought together the separate elements; for the Old Testament documents were not simply casual compilations of diverse materials but historical works skilfully constructed according to a conscious plan.[105] Eissfeldt recognized, of course, that behind the documents lay a variety of literary productions; but he insisted that they had been made to serve various religious or historiographical purposes and were meant to be taken, in the first instance, as members of a whole. Even where materials had been combined without eliminating the original variations of literary form, they had been given a certain unity by the "redactor" who adapted them to his philosophy of history.[106]

In his own major work, Eissfeldt attempted to combine this point of view with the results of form criticism. His "Introduction to the Old Testament" [107] offered a comprehensive survey of the whole development of the Old Testament from the beginnings in oral tradition to the final stage of crystallization as an authoritative canon. Actually, the work was not cut to Gunkel's pattern of a literary history based on aesthetic appreciation of form; it was fundamentally a standard introduction to the books of the Old Testament based on critical analysis of their sources. But the essential achievements of form criticism and the worthwhile insights of "literary history" were taken up into the whole and presented in the relevant connections. A great variety of particular literary forms was described in a manner never before attempted in an Old Testament introduction,[108] and the book did full justice to the

---

[105] See "Die kleinste literarische Einheit in den Erzählungsbüchern des Alten Testament," *Theologische Blätter*, VI (1927), 333–37. English translation in *Old Testament Essays* (London, 1927), pp. 85–93.

[106] See "Text-, Stil-, und Literarkritik in den Samuelisbüchern," OLZ, XXXI (1928), 801–12.

[107] *Einleitung in das Alte Testament* (Tübingen, 1934).

[108] Another recent work that accomplishes the same task is Aage Bentzen's *Introduction to the Old Testament* (2 vols., Copenhagen, 1948–49), a translation of the Danish work (1941); see Vol. I, pp. 102–264; Vol. II, pp. 9–80. Artur Weiser added a treatment of the preliterary stage of Old Testament literature to the second edition of his *Einleitung in das Alte Testament* (Göttingen, 1949).

conclusion of the form critics that the origins of each literary type went back to the stage of oral tradition. But the main emphasis of the book was on the written stages of development, in which the "unifying points of view" of the authors had created masterpieces of religious literature from oral tradition and written record.

The closest approximation to a genuine history of Hebrew literature of the kind that Gunkel had indicated as the goal of Old Testament study was achieved by Johannes Hempel,[109] who applied all the resources made available by form criticism to his task. The chief conclusions of the critical school regarding the historical milieu of the major source documents were not abandoned, but the whole orientation of Hempel's work was different. The development of Hebrew literature from the smallest literary units of oral tradition through the increasingly complex forms of written material to the great literary works identified by criticism was described in panoramic sequence. Hempel gave due weight to the shaping influence of formal literary types in the early stages of composition, without neglecting the creative action of great literary personalities in the later stages. Most important of all, he brought out clearly how the literature—much of it secular in the beginning (consisting of saga, poetry, and proverb)—came to be dominated in its written form by a religious ideology, as the authors sought to adapt the materials to their theological philosophy of history.

In this respect, Hempel's book fulfilled the ultimate objective of Gunkel's program for "literary history": to make clear to the modern reader the significance of the religious content of the Old Testament. By showing how each stage in the development of the literature was progressively dominated by Israel's characteristic viewpoint that its history had been determined from the beginning

---

[109] *Die althebräische Literatur und ihr hellenistisch-jüdisches Nachleben* ("Handbuch der Literaturwissenschaft," Vol. XXI; Wildpark-Potsdam, 1930-34). The most comprehensive general history of Hebrew literature now available is Adolphe Lods, *Histoire de la littérature hébraïque et juive* (Paris, 1950).

in accordance with the will of the national deity, Hempel succeeded in communicating a sense of the vitality of religious thought
in the biblical writings. The fact that the authors of the narrative
documents regarded the task of writing history, not simply as a
factual recording of events, nor even as an explanation of the
political trends which governed them, but primarily as an effort
to understand and explain their religious significance, was the
important fact which gave their writings significance as a cultural
achievement. It was the fact which the higher critics had disregarded, thus missing the opportunity of giving their meticulous
dissection of the sources significant meaning. Hempel's chief accomplishment was that he showed how closely religious interpretation was identified with historical composition in the work of
the Old Testament writers.[110]

This recognition of the religious motivation of Hebrew historiography is the most important development in biblical criticism
of the last two decades. It has brought about a new appreciation
of the purposeful character of the Yahwistic history, the oldest
example of historical composition in Hebrew literature, and of the
literary achievement of its author. As Rudolf Smend had once
described the Yahwist as an easily identifiable literary personality,
who was the most important historical writer in the Old Testament,[111] others now began to give him great importance as a
creative writer. Gerhard von Rad, in a detailed study of the
manner in which the Hexateuch had been composed, showed how
the Yahwist had taken previously existing materials and welded
them together into a unified whole by supplying the basic viewpoint from which the history of Israel's beginnings was to be

---

[110] How the various writers dealt with tales, legends, and oral traditions in their
historical composition is described by E. Jacob, *La tradition historique en Israël*
(Montpellier, 1946).

[111] See above, n. 22.

regarded by loyal Israelites.[112] Taking as his basic theme the succinct summary of tradition regarding the exodus and the settlement in Canaan (the "creed" of Gilgal),[113] the Yahwist built around it a great history of Israel's origins, by combining with it the Sinai "tradition" and prefixing the patriarchal narratives and the legends of the origins of things. This expansion of the initial tradition with stories and legends, many of which were originally secular in spirit, the Yahwist organized into a consistent unity by presenting the whole as the story of the working out of God's purposes in history.[114] The ideological framework, far from being, as the critics had assumed, a postexilic product of priestly circles, was a basic feature from the beginning.

Von Rad's point of view on the achievement of the Yahwist was supported by Gustav Hölscher's re-examination of the basic unity of the Yahwistic literature,[115] and his view of the history and significance of the composition of the Hexateuch was confirmed by Martin Noth's study of its first four books.[116] Noth, however, analyzed in greater detail the original traditions that lay behind the Yahwist's history and the process whereby they were combined and supplemented with folk narratives originally lacking the unifying religious viewpoint impressed upon them by the Yahwist.

Another result of the new appreciation of the importance of studying the unifying viewpoints of the Old Testament's redactors

---

[112] *Das formgeschichtliche Problem des Hexateuchs* (Stuttgart, 1938), see esp. pp. 46–68. For a brief summary of the detailed argument there presented, see the introduction of his later work, *Das erste Buch Mose* (Göttingen, 1949). Cf. G. Ernest Wright, "Recent European Study in the Pentateuch," *JBR*, XVIII (1950), 216–20.

[113] See above, pp. 143–44.

[114] Cf. W. Norman Pittenger, "The Earliest Philosophy of History," *Anglican Theological Review*, XXIX (1947), 238–41. See also Gunnar Ostborn, *Yahweh's Words and Deeds: A Preliminary Study of the Old Testament Presentation of History* (Uppsala, 1951).

[115] *Die Anfänge der hebräischen Geschichtsschreibung* (Heidelberg, 1942).

[116] *Ueberlieferungsgeschichtliche Studien, II: Ueberlieferungsgeschichte des Pentateuch* (Stuttgart, 1948). Cf. Otto Eissfeldt, *Geschichtsschreibung im Alten Testament* (Berlin 1948), a discussion of the theories of von Rad, Hölscher, and Noth.

has been a similar insight into the significance of the "Deuteronomistic" history. Martin Noth's studies of the historical literature outside of the Pentateuch resulted in recognition of a second great block of historical material as significant, in its way, as the Yahwistic history.[117] Rejecting the critical view that the books from Joshua to II Kings were simply a redaction of J and E by a supposed Deuteronomic school, Noth regarded all the literature from Deuteronomy to II Kings as the work of a single author, who had assembled and reinterpreted materials from J and E and other sources in terms of his "Deuteronomic" philosophy of history. These books, which presented a comprehensive account of Israel's history from the Conquest to the fall of the state, interpreted from a single theological perspective, thus bore a unity which had not been recognized by the critical school. They constituted the second great example of religious historiography in Israel's literature.

These latest studies of Old Testament literature illustrate the contemporary reaction against fragmentation of the literature and the new appreciation of its unity of purpose. Whereas form criticism had started with the study of literary types and the attempt to trace them back to the earliest forms of oral expression, so that the analysis of the structure and the documentary development of an entire book had come to seem relatively unimportant, there was now a new emphasis on the processes of literary composition, with special attention to the purposes which had guided the selection and combination of the various materials. Originally, the variety of literary types had led the form critic to treat the units of material as independent entities; now, as Gunkel had first realized with reference to the prophetic literature, an appreciable amount of heterogeneity in literary form was not incompatible with conceptual unity. The latter was more significant than the literary form. Hence the new emphasis on the basic philosophy of history

---

[117] *Ueberlieferungsgeschichtliche Studien, I: Die sammelnden und bearbeitenden Geschichtswerke im Alten Testament* (Halle, 1943).

by means of which creative writers imposed unity on their materials. The literary study of the Bible, which had started with aesthetic appreciation of the various categories of literature, thus ended with a deeper insight into the shaping influence of religious ideology upon the more extensive compositions contained in the Old Testament.

V

The Sociological Approach to the
Old Testament

The Nature of Sociological Studies in the Field of Religion

In the preceding chapters there was occasion to refer from time to time to attempts to explain the origin of religious institutions in terms of the social milieu. Both Wellhausen and Robertson Smith had recognized that religion is an integral part of the social order. The anthropologists had come to recognize the force of social compulsion in determining the form of religious institutions. Not only had the "history of religions" school been concerned with the cultural context in which religious ideas had sprung up, but its off-shoot, form criticism, had endeavored to identify the actual situations in the life of the social group which had generated specific forms of religious tradition. This occasional interest in the social background of religion, on the part of investigators whose researches were basically otherwise motivated, testifies to the importance of the social factor in the history of religion. But reference to this factor in the work of these scholars was incidental, not determinative. There was need of an investigation devoted primarily to the social background of Old Testament religion—a need that could be filled only by consciously adopting the method and approach of the science of sociology.

Books were not lacking which described the social customs of the ancient Hebrews;[1] but little effort had been expended on studying the formative elements of Hebrew social life or on deter-

---

[1] See, e.g., John Fenton, *Early Hebrew Life: A Study in Sociology* (London, 1880); Frantz Buhl, *Die sozialen Verhältnisse der Israeliten* (Berlin, 1899).

mining how, in comparison with the surrounding cultures, these elements had made Hebrew culture peculiarly fitted to produce the religious ideas characteristic of it. John Fenton's early work, little noticed when it appeared, made a beginning toward supplementing the predominant literary criticism of the time with a sociological analysis of the data. But this first attempt to interpret the data of the Old Testament in the light of social structure had little to say about the relationship between the social organization of the Hebrew people and the development of their religion.[2]

It was the relationship between religion and social organization that became the primary subject matter of religious sociology. Fundamental to the sociological viewpoint was the proposition that every religion arose in a particular social milieu and was subject to its influence; and the correlative proposition that the religion, in turn, exerted an influence upon the formation of the social structure. Investigation of this interaction between religion and society was the distinctive task of the sociology of religion.[3]

Also characteristic of the sociological approach was the study of religion in its relation to the group rather than the individual. Since religion, to the sociologist, was a social phenomenon, he emphasized collective factors rather than personal experience as the essential element in religion. Accordingly, the sociologist did not deal with great religious leaders except as members of a social group. By preference, he investigated the religious life of the common people who made up the mass of the social group.

This approach to the study of religion, with respect to the Old Testament, meant that a study of its social origins was the key to the important developments in Israel's religion. Such a study was

[2] Cf. R. H. Kennett's more recent survey, *Ancient Hebrew Social Life and Custom as Indicated in Law, Narrative, and Metaphor* (London, 1933).

[3] See Joachim Wach, "Religionssoziologie," in Alfred Vierkandt (ed.), *Handwörterbuch der Soziologie* (Stuttgart, 1931), pp. 479-94. Cf. his fuller exposition of the scope of the new science, *Einführung in die Religionssoziologie* (Tübingen, 1931); English edition in greatly expanded form: *The Sociology of Religion* (Chicago, 1944; London, 1947).

first undertaken, not by an Old Testament scholar, but by the real founder of religious sociology, Max Weber.[4]

Max Weber's Contribution to the Sociology of Old Testament Religion

Max Weber's interest in the relation between religion and society had been aroused by the subordination of the "spiritual" factor in human history, by Marxian historians, to the economic factors. The thesis that all institutional and ideological aspects of the social order were determined by the material basis of a society and by the character of its "relations of production" persuaded Weber of the urgent need for an investigation into the relative importance of the economic and "spiritual" factors.

In the course of such an investigation, Weber discovered that in Western capitalistic society—the prime example of economic determinism in the eyes of the "materialistic" school—the religious side of life was not a secondary factor of little importance, but rather the original mainspring of economic activity. The capitalistic spirit, Weber explained, had been generated by the Protestant ethic, which emphasized the virtues of frugality and tireless industry.[5] Whereas the ancient, pagan motive for amassing wealth had been enjoyment of the good things of this world, the modern system of accumulating capital was an outgrowth of the idea that wealth was not to be enjoyed but saved and put to work. This "ascetic rationalization" of pecuniary gain, Weber believed, was the root of the extraordinary capacity for economic enterprise that developed in the Protestant countries of the West. In this case, the religious beliefs which a particular society had elaborated in order to give meaning to its life had inevitably affected the

[4] See Talcott Parsons, "The Theoretical Development of the Sociology of Religion," *Journal of the History of Ideas*, V (1944), 176-90.

[5] "Die protestantische Ethik und der Geist des Kapitalismus," first published in *Archiv für Sozialwissenschaft und Sozialpolitik* (1904-05), reprinted with extensive additional footnotes in *Gesammelte Aufsätze zur Religionssoziologie* (3 vols., Tübingen, 1920-21), I, 17-206; English translation by Talcott Parsons, *The Protestant Ethic and the Spirit of Capitalism* (London, 1930).

development of its economic activities. Religion had determined the economic life, not the reverse.[6]

Weber was too careful a historian, however, immediately to raise his conclusion to the status of a general principle. He had directly contradicted the materialistic conception of history in a single instance. But only thorough investigation of the facts in other areas would permit a final conclusion that the religious attitude of a society always exercised a determinative influence upon its economic philosophy. Accordingly, Weber turned from the Protestant world of the West to the religious systems of the East, in order to find out if they too had generated an "ethic of economic activity" which would explain the economic institutions of the oriental societies. He found that none of the religions of China or India had given rise to any positive ethical impulses which could direct the activities of the people toward the development of a purposeful type of economic life. These religions were rather characterized by certain negative motivations which acted as restraining forces on the development of the indigenous forms of economic activity. It was not possible to say that religion "determined" the economic life, as the Protestant ethic had shaped it in the West. But neither did economics dominate the other aspects of social life, as the theory of economic determinism required. There was no simple formula, apparently, that covered the relationship between the religious and the economic factors in society everywhere and at all times.

Only in the case of ancient Judaism[7] did Weber find the situation at all analogous to that which he had found obtaining in the

[6] See the incisive critique of Weber's conclusions by Richard H. Tawney, *Religion and the Rise of Capitalism* (New York, 1926; 2d ed., 1937), pp. 316-17; and cf. Lujo Brentano, *Die Anfänge des modernen Kapitalismus* (Munich, 1916), pp. 117-57.

[7] See *Die Wirtschaftsethik der Weltreligionen: Das antike Judentum* ("Gesammelte Aufsätze zur Religionssoziologie," Vol. III; Tübingen, 1921). An English translation, *Ancient Judaism*, ed. H. H. Gerth and D. Martindale (Glencoe, Ill., 1952; London, 1953).

Protestant West. The similarity was only natural, after all, since the one was the historical progenitor of the other. In Judaism there was an element (the prophetic element), lacking in the other oriental religions, which had generated a powerful impulse toward the development of an ethical basis for the economic life. At first, Israel's economic life had been motivated by entirely secular interests, but from the beginning its social organization had been shaped by certain religious ideas. It was from the latter that the stimulus eventually came, through the prophets, for reconstructing the economic life upon an ethical basis. Since "this ethical system in large measure still lies at the basis of the present-day European . . . religious ethics," ancient Judaism, through its connection with Christianity, had "a special historical significance for the development of the modern ethics of economic activity in the West." [8]

Weber, by his own admission,[9] was dependent upon the critical school for the use that he made of the Old Testament sources. The result was that his discussion of Israel's religious history made the heritage of ideas with which Israel began seem less complex than it probably was. But his sociological approach to the material resulted in a number of new insights into the economic and social conditions of successive epochs, as reflected in the sources.[10]

He began his interpretation of the economic life of the early Israelites by emphasizing the distinction between seminomadic and settled agricultural clans.[11] The important fact, however, from the point of view of social history, was that these two basically different groups united on occasion for military purposes; and the force that brought them together was a religious idea which proved to be stronger, in times of crisis, than the separate economic inter-

---

[8] *Gesammelte Aufsätze zur Religionssoziologie*, III, 6; I, 238.
[9] See the lengthy footnote, *ibid.*, III, 1–6.
[10] See the comprehensive summary of his theories by Julius Guttmann, "Max Webers Soziologie des antiken Judentums," *MGWJ*, LXIX (1925), 195–223.
[11] See *Religionssoziologie*, III, 10–13, 44–49.

ests of each group. It was the idea of the covenant, which Old Testament scholars had often discussed from the standpoint of its religious significance,[12] but seldom in terms of its effect upon the social and political organization of early Israel. Weber maintained that the covenant not only defined Israel's relation to its God but also established the political unity of the tribes in the premonarchical period. The confederation of tribes was "a military league united under and with Yahweh, the warrior god of the league, the guarantor of its social institutions, and provider of its material needs." [13]

Weber's most original contribution to the interpretation of the premonarchical conditions was his description of the "charismatic" type of leadership which functioned at the head of the Israelite confederacy.[14] The covenant league, so far as the records showed, did not have any permanent political institutions, but in time of war "a God-inspired warrior hero" temporarily exercised authority over the combination of tribes whose only tie in peace time was the consciousness of being united in the worship of the same God.[15] Even after the establishment of the kingship and the rise of autocratic rulers, the belief that the basis of the king's authority was an agreement between him and the people, under a religious

[12] Most recently by Joachim Begrich, "*Berit*: Ein Beitrag zur Erfassung einer alttestamentlichen Denkform," *ZAW*, LX (1944), 1–11.

[13] See *Religionssoziologie*, III, 82–90 (the quotation is from p. 90). Wilhelm Caspari, who examined Weber's conclusions critically and gave a somewhat different interpretation to several matters which Weber had discussed, did not think it possible to regard a military league as the cradle of Yahwism. He upheld the traditional view that the covenant idea had originated in a religious league existing before the settlement in Canaan. See *Die Gottesgemeinde von Sinai und das nachmalige Volk Israel* (Gütersloh, 1922), pp. 15-20, 137-38. Martin Noth made the covenant idea the basis for the amphictyonic organization of early Israel which he described in *Das System der zwölf Stämme Israels* (Stuttgart, 1930); see above, chap. IV, pp. 132–33.

[14] Cf. his general discussion of *charisma* as a religious phenomenon, in his *Wirtschaft und Gesellschaft* ("Grundriss der Sozialökonomik," III; Tübingen, 1922), pp. 140-48.

[15] See *Religionssoziologie*, III, 92. Albrecht Alt also made the charismatic type of leadership the basis of the political organization of early Israel, in *Die Staatenbildung der Israeliten in Palästina* (Leipzig, 1930), pp. 7-12, 16-26.

sanction, was never entirely given up. Later generations looked back to the original religious confederacy under its charismatic leaders as the ideal form of social organization. In the beginning at least, there had been a close tie between Israel's religion and its social organization.

The keystone of Weber's interpretation of Israel's history was the thesis that the further development of its religion, in the prophetic movement, was the result of a crisis in the socioeconomic development of the nation. It was not so much the threat of syncretism with Canaanite religion that called forth the protest of the prophets as the gradual submersion of Israel's original social system under new forms imitated from the Canaanites. The religiously motivated social organization of the old confederacy retained its significance as an ideal, but it practically disappeared from actual existence as the rise of new economic conditions broke down the old feeling of solidarity between the various groups within Israel. The growth of a landowning aristocracy, which subjected the formerly independent farmers and sheepraisers of Israel to economic servitude, divided the people into a small urban nobility and a large mass of debt-ridden or entirely landless peasants. The significance of this development was that it contradicted the basic principle of equality implicit in the covenant which had formerly governed the socioeconomic life of the tribes. The displacement of effective power toward the top of the social scale introduced a conflict that had not previously existed between the religious ideals of Israel and its socioeconomic organization.[16]

This was the situation that called forth the social criticism of the prophets. It would have been easy for Weber to explain their agitation in terms of "the class struggle," as if they had taken sides with the small farmers against the great landowners.[17] But Weber

[16] See *Religionssoziologie*, III, 63–66.

[17] Such an application of Marxist principles to ancient Hebrew social history was actually made by M. Lurje in his *Studien zur Geschichte der wirtschaftlichen und sozialen Verhältnisse im israelitisch-jüdischen Reiche* (Giessen, 1927).

ascribed no "populist" motives to the prophets. He stated bluntly
that "no prophet was an advocate of 'democratic' ideals. . . . No
prophet proclaimed any kind of 'natural rights,' still less any right
to revolution or self-help on the part of the masses oppressed by
the great." [18] They made their pronouncements not from political
or economic interest but from ethical convictions that went far
beyond the immediate social problems of the time. The prophets
took it for granted that the people needed rulers. It was the misuse
of power and position by the people's rulers that they criticized.
Their emphasis was on the need for justice and humanity in the
ruling classes' treatment of the economically weak and the politi-
cally helpless. The absence of these ethical virtues in the upper
strata of society, not the necessity for social reform, explains why
"the prophets passionately proclaimed socio-ethical principles . . .
in favor of the little people and hurled their angry denunciations
particularly against the great and the rich." [19]

Thus, through the prophets, the ethical element in Israel's religion—once a reality embodied in the covenant relationship—was
re-emphasized as the central element which should govern the
sociopolitical relations of the people. Weber's study of ancient
Judaism remained uncompleted at the time of his death. But
enough of the trend of his thought had been indicated to show
what he meant to emphasize—that, of the two contradictory systems of social morality competing for acceptance in ancient Israel,
the significant one was that which survived the political catastrophe
of the nation's downfall. It was the teaching of the prophets, with
its emphasis on the obligation of doing the will of the Lord, as a
demonstration of the "chosen" status implied by the covenant,[20]
which lived on in the Calvinistic faith that work was a worthwhile end in itself, if only because diligence and attention to the
task in hand were a sign that one belonged among those predestined

[18] *Religionssoziologie*, III, 292.
[19] *Ibid.*, III, 291. See, in general, *ibid.*, pp. 120–26.
[20] See, *ibid.*, III, 310–11.

for salvation. It was this faith that provided the basis for the Protestant ethic of economic activity.

This summary of Weber's survey of ancient Judaism embraces only those points in his discussion which have a bearing on the problem with which he had begun. Weber frequently dropped his main theme to discuss other aspects of Hebrew history and did it in such a way as to throw light upon many a problem broached by other scholars. His discussion of the "rationalization" of the Hebrew conception of God[21] introduced into the interpretation of Old Testament religious history one of the more important elements of his general system of religious sociology[22] and had some bearing on the problem of how and when Israel outgrew the "prelogical" type of thinking characteristic of primitive peoples. His comments on the Levites,[23] whose nature and functions have been perennially debated problems, contributed a new insight by emphasizing the part played by the Levites in preparing the way for the prophets through the ethical teaching they did as upholders of the Law. Inasmuch as Weber's interpretation counteracted the thesis of the critical school that priests and prophets were opposed in objectives and methods, it was significant. But these special features of his discussion, perhaps because of the lack of final revision, were not always well integrated with the main theme. Nevertheless, Weber's study of the relationship between social conditions and the development of religious ideas in Israel's history stimulated an entirely new approach to the subject matter, which shifted the major emphasis from the political to the social and economic trends as the background of religious history.

The Application of Weber's Principles to the Old Testament

A number of Old Testament scholars, who were not concerned with the origins of the capitalistic spirit, nevertheless found that

[21] See, *ibid.*, III, 137–48, 224–35, 239–42.
[22] See *Wirtschaft und Gesellschaft*, pp. 227–41.
[23] See *Religionssoziologie*, III, 181–94, 250–59.

Weber's sociological method of dealing with the interpretation of the Old Testament greatly illuminated this or that aspect of Israel's religious history. In general, it was his emphasis on the problem created by the settlement of a people organized on a family, clan, and tribal basis among a people whose way of life and social organization were essentially urban that provided the chief stimulus to new ways of looking at the spiritual history of Israel.

Adolphe Lods rewrote the history of Israel[24] in terms of the tension, resulting from the above situation, between the desire of the Israelites to preserve old ways peculiar to themselves and the tendency to follow new ways learned from the Canaanites. He first described how Israel's original economic and social order had been radically affected by the necessity of adjustment to new conditions in Palestine. On the economic side, the principle of the common tribal domain was supplanted by the principle of individual ownership of land.[25] On the social side, the principle of equality between the members of the clan was lost as the difference between the rich new landowners and the poor landless remnants of the old social order became more and more accentuated. Then remarking that "we can understand the bitterness which was aroused in the mass of the people by such a complete reversal of the old equality of nomad times," [26] Lods went on to describe how the bitterness found expression in the decision of Jonadab and the Rechabites to repudiate all that the new way of life represented and to live in tents, owning neither fields nor vineyards. They saw the salvation of society only in returning to the condi-

---

[24] *Israël des origines au milieu du VIIIe siècle* (Paris, 1930); English translation by S. H. Hooke: *Israel from its Beginnings to the Middle of the Eighth Century* ("History of Civilization"; New York: Alfred A. Knopf, 1932); *Les prophètes d'Israël et les débuts du judaisme* (Paris, 1935); English translation by S. H. Hooke: *The Prophets of Israel* (New York: E. P. Dutton and Co., Inc., 1937). All quotations are made from the English translations with the kind permission of the respective publishers.

[25] Cf. Frantz Buhl, *Die sozialen Verhältnisse der Israeliten* (Berlin, 1899), pp. 55-64.

[26] *Israel*, p. 398.

tions of nomadic life as known by their fathers.[27] This protest symbolized the nature of the struggle as a conflict between the "nomadic ideal" and the agricultural way of life.[28]

Lods' countryman, Antonin Causse, in a study devoted more specifically to the religious history of Israel,[29] described how the crisis confronting the Israelites eventually broke the tie between their social organization and their religion. It was the close relationship between the two which had been the chief virtue of the nomadic way of life. But after the settlement in Palestine, as private ownership of land took the place of tribal ownership, the solidarity of the clans relaxed and the spirit of community gave way to private interest. The result was that the individual was cut loose from the obligations to which the social group had held him, and the principle of collective responsibility tended to be forgotten. Thus, when Israel set its foot on the road to a higher culture by accommodation to the ways of the new land, a split developed in the national conscience. For the first time in Israel's experience "culture and religion were not integrated." [30]

In discussing the role of the prophets in relation to this crisis, both Lods and Causse emphasized their opposition to the corrupting influence of urban civilization and their attempt to restore the former solidarity of the family and the tribe by advocating a return to ancient principles. Characterizing the prophets, Lods said that, "from the social point of view, they, too, are reactionaries. . . . They even frequently speak as if they shared the 'nomadic ideal' of a Jonadab. For Amos, for Hosea, for Jeremiah, the time of the sojourn in the desert was the ideal time, as far as relations

[27] See, ibid., p. 399; cf. The Prophets of Israel, p. 64.

[28] The term, "nomadic ideal," was first suggested by Karl Budde, "The Nomadic Ideal in the Old Testament," New World, IV (1895), 726–45; German version: "Das nomadische Ideal im Alten Testament," Preussische Jahrbücher, LXXXV (1896), 57–79. Cf. Eduard Meyer, Die Israeliten und ihre Nachbarstämme, pp. 82-89, 129-41; John W. Flight, "The Nomadic Idea and Ideal in the Old Testament," JBL, XLII (1923), 158–226.

[29] Du groupe ethnique à la communauté religieuse (Paris, 1937).

[30] Ibid., p. 55.

between Israel and Yahweh were concerned."[31] Causse gave a more strictly sociological interpretation of the "nomadic ideal" by pointing out that "it was not romanticism concerning the desert which played the decisive role in the social aspirations of the prophets . . ., but simply the conservatism of the Israelite peasants who sought to maintain their primitive culture and their patriarchal organization" in the face of the disruptive influence of Canaanite civilization.[32] In making the prophets the spokesmen of this opposition to "civilization," Causse was following Max Weber. But Lods disagreed with the view that their "tendency to react against Canaanite civilization" was sufficient to explain their uncompromising attitude toward the political and social life of their times.[33] He made the prophets the spokesmen for an ideal of simplicity, derived from the tradition of the desert, which, he believed, had remained alive among the lower classes. The fact that such an ideal was not based on any actual historical situation existing in the patriarchal period did not lessen the effectiveness of their propaganda against the corruptions of contemporary society.

However, Lods did not claim that the prophets were simply defenders of the "nomadic ideal." He realized that, "though the prophets shared to a great extent the sympathies and antipathies of Jonadab, they saw much farther than he did; they could not overlook the superficiality and inadequacy underlying the facile solution of a return to nomadic existence."[34] Hence, in spite of the fact that "the reaction against Canaanite civilization was one of the special watchwords of the prophetic movement, . . . like many reform movements it aimed at and achieved something very different from the mere restoration of the past."[35] Lods believed that

[31] *The Prophets of Israel*, p. 65.
[32] *Du groupe ethnique*, p. 75.
[33] As had been claimed by Causse in *Les prophètes contre la civilisation* (Alençon, 1913) and in *Les "Pauvres" d'Israël* (Strasbourg, 1922), pp. 1-80.
[34] *The Prophets of Israel*, p. 65.
[35] *Israel*, p. 411.

"the great prophets were responsible for a new conception of religion"; they demanded "not merely certain social reforms, but moral reformation," a new "general attitude, to describe which they made use of such general terms as righteousness"; and, as Max Weber had made clear, they "placed the demands of righteousness above everything, even above the existence of their nation." [36] Lods described the resulting effect on Israel's religion in that detail which Max Weber had not been able to carry through. Weber had succeeded at least in showing how much the prophets depended on the ancient social principles of the Covenant for the content of their message; Lods went on to analyze the new religious principles which they taught. He showed how their ideal of piety became more and more personal in its bearing and found its highest expression in Jeremiah's announcement of the new covenant which Yahweh would make with each individual (Jer. 31:31).

The same point of view affected even more strongly the remainder of Causse's study. As Lods had ascribed a "new concept of religion" to the prophets, so Causse maintained that "the prophets prepared the way for an individualistic conception of religion and the social order" which produced a very significant change in the relationship between religion and the structure of society. "The decisive moment in the religious evolution was the appearance of that essentially personal element in the relations between God and the faithful." The ancient notion of the collective responsibility of the group was left behind and the individual now acted on his own responsibility. With the prophets, "the transition from primitive collectivism to moral individualism was accomplished." [37]

This emphasis on the element of individual piety as the end-product of Israel's long religious development was essentially a Protestant interpretation. It was not directly concerned with providing an explanation of the ultimate sources of the Protestant ethic,

---

[36] *The Prophets of Israel*, pp. 62, 66, 120; *Israel*, p. 423.
[37] *Du groupe ethnique*, pp. 106, 110, 112.

as Max Weber's study had been; but its unconscious tendency to make paramount the very aspect of Old Testament religion which became the chief element in the Protestant tradition made this sociological interpretation seem equally significant. Both Lods and Causse, however, overlooked another important aspect of the heritage of prophetic teaching when they left out of consideration the solidarity of postexilic Judaism and the strong sense of community feeling which has characterized the religion of the Jewish people down to the present time.

These general works were the more important products of the fertilizing effect which Max Weber's theories had on the study of Israel's religious history. In addition there were a number of specialized studies of specific aspects of Old Testament history which also profited from attention to the relationship between social and religious factors.

Albrecht Alt found the sociological approach useful in elucidating the nature of religion among the earliest Hebrews.[38] Believing that a religion must be explicable in terms of the social organization of the people who professed it, he rejected the view that the religion of the Hebrew tribes before their adoption of the Yahweh cult was the El-religion of the Canaanites, since the latter had no relation to tribal organization.[39] Examining the patriarchal narratives for traces of the tribal religion which the Hebrews must have had before they were united, Alt found a clue in the distinctive epithets applied to the "god of the fathers." Such occasional phrases as the "God of Abraham," the "Fear of Isaac," and the "Mighty One of Jacob" indicated to Alt the original nature of religious belief among the tribal groups represented by the patriarchs. The several tribes, in the beginning, had distinct deities who were always referred to as the gods of the tribal leaders. Alt supported his theory by appealing to external data which seemed to prove

[38] *Der Gott der Väter* (Stuttgart, 1929).
[39] See, *ibid.*, p. 7.

the existence of the same conception of deity in the religion of other tribal societies. Certain inscriptions left behind by the Nabateans and Palmyrenes contained examples of the practice of naming gods after the tribal leaders who had founded the cults.[40] In view of "the displacement of the deity's association with a specific locality in favor of his relation to the social group," and in view of "the limitation of this special form of religion to tribes which still stood outside the circle of the ancient civilized peoples," [41] Alt concluded that this form of religion was typical of primitive tribal societies.[42]

His theory, Alt believed, was more consistent with the later development of a cult of Yahweh among the united Hebrew tribes than the theory of primitive polydemonism or a more highly developed El-worship. For the cults of the tribal gods more certainly carried the seeds of specifically Israelite beliefs. "A religion with a preponderant emphasis on the relation between God and man, especially on that between God and human society, without close attachment to any particular locality," was a more logical preparation for the bond which later united the Hebrew tribes in a cult with ethical and universal implications.[43] From its patriarchal heritage Israel derived that conception of a close relationship between God and the people which was the fundamental basis of its religion, as expressed in the doctrine of the Covenant.

In like manner, Abraham Menes found the sociological approach useful in explaining the history of law among the Israelites.[44] Studying the two pre-exilic law codes (the Book of the Covenant and the Deuteronomic Code) in the light of the sociopolitical and the economic data, Menes decided that the chief purpose of each

[40] See, *ibid.*, pp. 32–48.
[41] *Ibid.*, p. 33.
[42] But see the criticism by Herbert G. May, "The God of My Father: a Study of Patriarchal Religion," *JBR*, IX (1941), 155–58; cf. his article, "The Patriarchal Idea of God," *JBL*, LX (1941), 113–28.
[43] *Op. cit.*, p. 67. See, in general, pp. 62–68.
[44] *Die vorexilischen Gesetze Israels* (Giessen, 1928).

had been social rather than religious reform. In each code he saw primarily a democratic protest against the growing economic power of the upper classes. The Book of the Covenant was not simply a deposit of customary law adapted to new humanitarian principles, but the program of a social movement for checking the progressive enslavement of the free yeomanry of the land. The Deuteronomic Code was the manifesto of a similar social movement, not written under priestly-prophetic inspiration but elaborated by the party of "the people of the land" (the proletariat). Both movements were called forth by the rise of a money economy and the gradual proletarianization of the masses. Menes, therefore, found the historical origin of the law codes in sociopolitical revolutions initiated to improve the economic position of the lower classes. The Book of the Covenant was the program of the revolution under Jehu; the Deuteronomic Code, the charter of reform adopted when Josiah was placed on the throne by "the people of the land." Thus, events which historical criticism had interpreted as chiefly religious in motivation—the Jehu revolution as instigated by the prophetic party in violent protest against Baal worship, and the Deuteronomic reform as intended primarily to centralize the cult of Yahweh in Jerusalem—Menes interpreted as springing from the socioeconomic life of the people.

But Menes sometimes carried his interpretation to extremes. He frequently gave a sociopolitical explanation to matters which could better be understood in terms of religious history. The religiously motivated demand for the centralization of the cultus at Jerusalem Menes interpreted as an attempt by the revolutionary party to break down opposition to the political centralization of power for the defense of the rights of the people.[45] The pilgrimages instituted by Deuteronomy at the chief festivals he explained as intended to facilitate the holding of general assemblies of the people.[46] In spite

[45] See, *ibid.*, p. 99.
[46] See, *ibid.*, p. 100.

of many a useful observation on individual points, Menes' attempt to interpret the history of the law entirely in terms of social factors was too narrow an approach even to the limited data with which he dealt.

The sociological approach, however, provided genuine insight whenever it addressed itself to the broader problem raised by Max Weber's definition of the relationship between the social and religious factors in the history of Israel—the problem of explaining the significance of the tension between the secular pull toward adaptation to existing social conditions and the struggle to maintain and develop Israel's own spiritual and ethical ideals. This tension was the chief problem in sociological discussions of the Old Testament by American scholars.

Biblical Sociology as Interpreted by American Scholars
(1)

The first American scholar—and for a long time almost the only one—who approached Hebrew history from a sociological standpoint was Louis Wallis. As early as 1912, at a time when interest in the social aspects of Old Testament religion was confined to the search for quotable precepts on ethics, divorced from any real appreciation of the forces which had been at work to create such precepts, Wallis published his first sociological study of the Bible.[47] He was the pioneer in America of the attempt to work out the relationship between the social development of the Hebrew people and their religious and ethical thinking. Without once mentioning or referring to Max Weber, Wallis reproduced a number of Weber's ideas, while developing a particular interpretation of his own.[48]

---

[47] A Sociological Study of the Bible (Chicago, 1912).

[48] Years later Wallis published an amplification of the specifically Old Testament portion of his early work in God and the Social Process (Chicago, 1935). He covered the same ground again, with greater emphasis on his own special thesis, in The Bible Is Human (New York, 1942).

Conscious of the limited nature of literary and historical criticism, and believing that "the still unfinished historical interpretation of the Bible can be completed only in terms of sociology," [49] Wallis sought to elaborate the "social process" by which the religion of the Old Testament had come into being. He started with the thesis that the dominant factor in Old Testament history was the long struggle for supremacy between the original nomadic way of life of the Israelites and the civilized urban institutions of the Canaanites, and tried to show, in the light of this thesis, that "monotheism is a byproduct of a utopian struggle to impose migratory clan ethics upon a territorial state." [50]

According to Wallis, the historical situation out of which the monotheistic conception of Yahweh eventually grew was the uneasy coalescence of the wandering Israelite tribes, with a nomadic code of ethics that recognized the brotherhood of all men in the clan, and the settled Canaanites, whose code of ethics recognized class distinctions and gave few or no rights to peasant classes. Inevitably, "a great struggle arose between the standpoints of the two races that united in the development of the Hebrew nation." [51] The Israelite elements in the new nation attempted to preserve and bring to realization the ideals inherited from their nomadic ancestors. They succeeded in outlining in the law codes a utopian social system based on the proposition that all members of the social group had obligations to each other. But they found themselves in competition with the established property system of the Canaanite elements in their midst, which gave a small proprietary class a monopoly over the economic sources of well-being in the social group. Eventually, the struggle to maintain the clan ethics of the nomad against the class ethics of the city dwellers was defeated, but out of the frustration of the struggle came a new idealism which

[49] *Sociological Study of the Bible*, p. xxiii.
[50] *God and the Social Process*, p. 7.
[51] *Sociological Study of the Bible*, p. xxvi; cf. pp. 88–91.

rose "into a realm of spiritual truths and values transcending the original economic and social experiences" of the people.[52]

The struggle between the equalitarian ethics of the clan group and the socioeconomic system of the settled groups was really a struggle, Wallis argued, to determine the proper meaning of "justice." To the original nomadic worshipers of Yahweh it had meant equality through the common ownership of land. But when Yahweh came to be worshiped as "lord" of the land, the ideal ran the danger of becoming perverted into a defense of the landowning rights of a special class. Eventually, however, in the prophetic struggle against "civilized" society, a higher meaning was hammered out for the equalitarian ethics of nomadic society, with the important consequence that "the evolution of Yahweh . . . into a god of 'civilization' was obstructed." [53] The prophets taught that only Yahweh, the patron of the nomadic ideal of brotherly justice and equal opportunity, not the Baals who protected the rights of a proprietary class, could assure the ultimate triumph of justice for the common man. This emphasis on dependence upon the one true God of Israel led to monotheism.

It is not true, as some of Wallis' critics have asserted,[54] that he interpreted the whole course of Hebrew history as an economic conflict between two rival theories of land tenure. The question of land ownership was, indeed, emphasized more strongly in each succeeding volume which he wrote, but only as part of the larger social struggle for social justice. However, Wallis' main thesis that Hebrew monotheism was the byproduct of a social struggle involving ethical considerations can fairly be called an over-simplification. Like other attempts to discover a simple key to a complex historical process it ran the danger of neglecting certain aspects of the actual historical situation. The nomadic ideal could

[52] *God and the Social Process*, p. 15.
[53] *Sociological Study of the Bible*, p. 96.
[54] See the reviews by Shirley Jackson Case in the New York *Herald-Tribune*, December 6, 1942, and by Clarence T. Craig in *Christendom*, VIII (1943), 124–25.

not have been so exclusive a factor in the development of Israel's religious principles. In making the prophetic denunciations of the oppression of the poor grow out of the competition between nomadic equalitarian ethics and proprietary rights, Wallis overlooked the larger humanitarian motives which inspired the prophets' defense of the poor. Moreover, Wallis treated the religious developments entirely without reference to the light which archaeology and comparative religion threw upon the nature of religious belief in pre-Israelite Canaan. His assumption that the gods of Canaan included a large number of local Baals was a common one among scholars who depended exclusively on the Old Testament sources. But the Ras Shamra tablets had made it plain that there was but one Baal in the Canaanite pantheon and that he was a cosmic deity. Wallis failed to accommodate his theories to the evidence supplied by such extrabiblical sources.[55]

(2)

Fortunately, Louis Wallis did not remain a lone pioneer in the sociological study of the Bible. An adequate consideration of the extrabiblical evidence regarding the cultural background of social history enabled William C. Graham to give a more substantial interpretation of the social process through which Old Testament religion had progressed to the stage of ethical monotheism. Graham suggested a reconsideration of the relationship between Canaanite culture and Hebrew religion in view of the possibility that the Canaanite environment had more than a negative influence upon the development of the Hebrew religion.[56] The prevailing sociological theory that Yahwism was a unique religious culture expressing the "nomadic ideal," born in the desert through the establishment of a covenant with the tribal deity, and that it was

[55] Cf. the critique of Wallis' three volumes by Herbert G. May, "A Sociological Approach to Hebrew Religion," *JBR*, XII (1944), 98–106.
[56] "Recent Light on the Cultural Origins of the Hebrews," *Journal of Religion*, XIV (1934), 306–29.

an intrusion into the cultural situation in Canaan, where it fought
a struggle to maintain itself as a distinctive way of life against the
encroachments of the environing culture, Graham considered an
essentially false picture. Believing that the roots of a culture must
be sought in the social milieu of "the environing world," he explored "the possibility of genetic relationship between the religion-
culture of the Hebrews and that which prevailed in the environment into which they intruded," [57] and came to the conclusion
that the distinctive Hebrew religious culture had grown out of the
best in the environing culture, through opposition to the degradation of that culture. For he found "the distinctive result emerging
. . . from the constant though never entirely victorious struggle of
a deviating minority [the prophets] to shape the dominant, indigenous culture pattern for the fulfillment of higher social
functions." [58]

This strikingly different interpretation of the origins of Israel's
religious achievement Graham presented in a small but thoughtful
and thought-provoking book.[59] Describing the dominant cultural
pattern which formed the starting point for Hebrew culture, he
emphasized the importance of fertility cults in the ancient Near
East as giving expression to the materialistic values at the basis of
culture throughout the area. He also emphasized the important
role played by political leaders in shaping the social structure toward the more efficient satisfaction of the material needs of man.
Graham pointed out that, by the time the Hebrews entered Palestine, these two features of the ancient oriental pattern were already
predominating there. The Baalism which so exercised the prophets
was like the fertility cults of Mesopotamia, Egypt, and Syria; and
the kingship of the Canaanite city-states was also associated with
the function of maintaining the material prosperity of the state.[60]

[57] *Ibid.*, p. 311.
[58] *Ibid.*, pp. 318–19.
[59] *The Prophets and Israel's Culture* (Chicago, 1934).
[60] See, in general, *ibid.*, chaps. I–II.

But, as Samuel H. Hooke had found with regard to the ritual-myth pattern of the ancient East, Graham discovered disintegration and degradation occurring in the general culture pattern of Palestine at the time of the Hebrew monarchy. "This pattern began to break up, not so much because it was fundamentally wrong, as because it was contemporaneously inadequate." Since its "philosophy could not rise above a pragmatic empiricism which easily degenerated into mere opportunism," it "tended too much to hold the range of values at the physical level and so lent itself to the exploitation of the many by the few." [61] The individual in the social group found himself more and more at the mercy of his leaders, who proceeded "to regiment his desires, his ideas, and his conduct for the perpetuation of the prerogatives thus reposed in themselves." [62] The old cultural pattern which had once given significance to both social organization and religious practice had lost its meaning for the masses, who found religion being used as a justification for social inequality and exploitation.

This situation gave the prophets their opportunity. But Graham did not describe the work of the prophets, as his predecessors in biblical sociology had done, in terms of mere opposition to the social and economic evils of the day or in terms of a "return to the past." He described it as "a process of regeneration" of the disintegrating culture pattern. The prophets, said Graham,

did not seek the solution of the problem by any confinement of the productive activities of the people. Their insight was not that the satisfaction of the physical is, in itself, wrong, but that such satisfactions are never adequate to the whole human need. . . . The words which they used in connection with these concrete economic and social situations, words such as justice, . . . honor, . . . faithfulness, . . . and so on, are words which signify spiritual relationships which arise from the disciplining of the desire for material things.[63]

[61] *Journal of Religion*, XIV (1934), 329.
[62] *The Prophets and Israel's Culture*, p. 10.
[63] *Ibid.*, pp. 64–65.

In other words, the prophets sought to give their people a new social ideal divorced from the exploitative pattern of the contemporary world, one in which the individual would again hold a significant place as a member of the group. Thus, Graham believed, the prophets "were able to contribute to the revitalization of the society into which they were born. . . . They did something to the current range of values; and, after they did what they did, the dominant pattern of culture was never quite the same as it had been before." [64]

The chief characteristic of the prophets' new social ideal, according to Graham, was its emphasis upon personal values; and the ultimate significance of their teaching was that it freed the human spirit for individual growth. "Israel must develop persons capable of using the material goods of life for the promotion of the sense of freedom, happiness, and well-being in the hearts of all members of the fellowship," instead of following "a way of life which . . . cows and breaks the spirit of the common people by treating them as though they were of no significance save to do the pleasure of the domineering few." [65] Again, this was an essentially Protestant interpretation of the significance of the prophetic teaching. It was an appreciation of the prophets' achievement from the standpoint of their ultimate contribution to modern Western culture. For "what has come down to the modern world by intricate channels as the democratic ideal" was this very emphasis upon "the inalienable right of every individual to be a person—not just an instrument." [66] There is no question that this emphasis was an important part of the teaching of the prophets, nor that it was their greatest contribution to modern social thought. But one senses that Graham was interpreting the prophetic message for modern readers rather than describing what the prophets had

[64] Ibid., pp. 63–64.
[65] Ibid., pp. 86, 88.
[66] Ibid., pp. 88–89.

emphasized to their own contemporaries. He saw similarities in the situation with which the prophets dealt to conditions in present-day society, and so he emphasized that part of their teaching which had the most direct bearing upon the modern situation. His little book thus became a tract for the times rather than an objective analysis of the actual core of prophetic teaching.

What concerned the prophets was not simply the inadequacy of a pattern of life which stunted the development of personality. It was the necessity of understanding the ultimate meaning of events, the meaning that gave significance not only to progress toward personal values but also to suffering and even catastrophe. Graham had failed to see that the real achievement of the prophets did not consist in "regenerating" the world's way of thinking but in breaking with it completely and creating a new "philosophy of history" to serve as the basis for belief and practice. The deeper substance of their teaching was to be grasped, not by reading them in the light of modern circumstances, but by closer attention to their own interpretation of history, as expressed in their writings and in such compositions, written under prophetic inspiration, as the Yahwistic and Deuteronomistic histories. Scholars such as Hempel, von Rad, and Noth, with their new appreciation of the significance of the Yahwist and the Deuteronomist, were working in the right direction.[67]

(3)

The most successful re-creation of the prophetic philosophy of history was that presented by Salo W. Baron in the relevant chapters of his socioreligious history of the Jews.[68] With a fine feeling for the significance of the religious philosophy of the Old Testament writers, Baron showed that "the Jewish religion has been

[67] See above, chap. IV, pp. 152–55.
[68] *A Social and Religious History of the Jews* (3 vols., New York, 1937; 2d rev. ed., Vols. I-II, New York, 1952). All references are to the revised edition.

from the beginning, and in the progress of time has increasingly become, an *historical* religion, in permanent contrast to all *natural* religions." [69] That is, the leaders of religious thought in ancient Israel succeeded in keeping their religion separate from the bond with nature and the tie to a specific locality which characterized the other religions of the ancient Orient. They developed instead a strong sense of the historical role of their religion and a sense of destiny for their people. The God that Israel worshiped was not a nature deity but the controlling power that guided history toward a specific end.[70] To accomplish his purpose, he had chosen this people and had laid upon it the obligation to rise above "nature" (the natural way of the world) and to find its significance in "history" (the working out of God's plan) by adhering to a way of life that transcended preoccupation with the things that other peoples usually considered necessary to successful living.

In line with this "philosophy of history," the writers of the Old Testament interpreted the past and the future of their nation. They made the exodus from Egypt (which had drawn no special notice from contemporaries) "the point of departure for a new era of mankind," a tremendous act of God setting in motion the divine plan for all subsequent history. The vicissitudes which Israel suffered in its attempt to lead the life of a political state were reduced to insignificance in the light of its ultimate mission. Its destiny as a people chosen by God to transcend "nature" through "history" lifted the aspirations of the Jewish people above the political concerns of other national groups. Neither the possession of a national territory nor the circumstance of political independence was important in the long view. After the Exile, when both state and territory had been lost, Jewish nationality became identified with ethnic solidarity rather than territorial status. "Common descent,

---

[69] *Ibid.*, I, 4. See, in general, the opening chapter.
[70] Cf. A. F. Puukko's exposition of the same theme, "Gott und Geschichte im Alten Testament," in the Bulmerincq *Festschrift* (Riga, 1938), pp. 166–74.

common destiny and culture—including religion—became the unit-ing forces." [71] As a matter of fact, "exilic existence was frequently hailed as a necessary instrument of the divine government of the world. Only as dispersed people could the Jews serve as 'the light' of many nations." [72]

This interpretation of the ultimate meaning of Jewish history, more expressive of the true "genius" of the people than Graham's cultural-historical interpretation, derived its cogency from the at-tempt to take into account the Old Testament's own philosophy of history. The resources of other approaches to the Old Testa-ment were not neglected; but here was shown the value of not stopping with the recovery of the history of the documents or the primitive basis of religious belief or the nature of the contemporary environment, but of going on to consider what the writers of the documents made out of the multiform heritage which was theirs to shape. Here was not only the actual "history behind the histor-ical documents" which the critics had sought to uncover, but the significance which that history had for its participants—or for those of them who were observant enough and thoughtful enough to attempt to read its meaning.

Baron called this philosophy of history "historical monotheism" and ascribed its original formulation to Moses himself, asserting that

Moses, reflecting the varied experiences of the people in the period be-tween the Egyptian bondage and the conquest of Canaan, set up and exalted the Jewish people as against a Jewish territory, their movement through time as against their occupancy of space, the course of history rather than the contours of nature.[73]

In the depths of the great founder's consciousness, Israel's religion achieved its essential character at the very beginning. Subsequent religious developments Baron described in terms of "a prolonged

[71] *Op. cit.*, I, 17.
[72] *Ibid.*, I, 19.
[73] *Ibid.*, I, 53.

struggle between . . . the 'essential' Mosaic religion and the so-called 'popular religion' of ancient Israel," emphasizing that, "regardless of how few the votaries of the former, how many the adherents of the latter, Judaism in its Mosaic formulation remained the main stream in Jewish history." [74] Whether "historical monotheism" was achieved at the beginning of Israel's religious history, or whether this "philosophy of history" was not rather the gradual achievement of Israel's thinkers through a long process of considering the meaning of history as they were living through it, the importance of Baron's exposition was to have called attention to the nature of this achievement. For it is this philosophy of history, implicit in the biblical writings, which gives them their meaning and provides the key to an interpretation of the Old Testament which has not only a basis in scientific method but substance as an exposition of the supreme attempt of the mind of man to understand his place in the world and in history.

Baron's exposition of the social and religious history of the Jews also presented the essential insights of the sociological approach to the Old Testament in a comprehensive synthesis. The importance of the social factor in the history of religion was amply illustrated by the interaction between the socioeconomic conditions of each epoch and the development of religious ideas. Sometimes the former were decisive enough to condition the forms in which religion was expressed, as when the "economic evolution from nomadic or seminomadic cattle raising to settled agriculture" resulted in "moves to reintroduce the local deities, the various 'Baalim,' [and] the idea of a god-father [of the clan] gradually was supplanted by the conception of a god-lord of a territory." [75] But, basically, religion was not "determined" by the socioeconomic conditions; it was itself a force working toward the improvement of the ultimate purposes of socioeconomic organization. In the

[74] *Ibid.*, I, 4.
[75] *Ibid.*, I, 55–57.

beginning, Israel's social organization had been shaped by certain religious ideas: the Covenant and "charisma"; and from the tradition of the Covenant, kept alive in those small circles which remained true to the original Yahwistic tradition, eventually came the stimulus for reconstructing the socioeconomic life of the nation upon an ethical basis. As the new economic conditions broke down the former solidarity of the Israelites, an "abnormal social situation" arose which called forth "those lofty and intense prophetic utterances" in which the prophets re-emphasized the basic principle of equality in the Covenant and the need for justice and humanity in all social relations.[76] Since man's only duty was submission to God's will by observing the ethical obligations of the Covenant, "social justice came to be regarded as one of the root essentials of the religion of Israel." [77] Thus it was the prophetic philosophy of history, which saw the ruling hand of God over the actions of men as the most important fact of human history, that gave Israel's religion its fundamental character.

[76] See, *ibid.*, I, 67–72, 77–79, 84–91.
[77] *Ibid.*, I, 88.

Archaeology and the Old Testament

The Scope and Purpose of Archaeological Research

In the study of Israel's religious history and of the literary development of the Old Testament, biblical scholars were largely dependent on archaeology for the extrabiblical sources which they made use of in their comparative studies. The written materials which had provided the basis for judging the relative maturity of Israel's culture and the degree of originality displayed in its religious literature were first discovered by excavators at the cultural sites of the ancient Near East. But, for the study of cultural history, archaeology offered another type of evidence in the form of non-literary, material remains. The excavated remnants of towns and villages, with a multitude of artifacts long buried in them, threw light upon some aspects of ancient civilization not adequately covered in the literary sources. Aside from the information such physical remains provided regarding the material culture and daily life of ancient peoples, considerable illumination was cast upon the religious aspects of oriental culture by the remains of temples, altars, and cultic objects.

Each type of evidence, written and material, had its own particular value. The epigraphic finds were a most valuable addition to the literary sources surviving from ancient times, sometimes supplying details which corroborated or corrected the information given there,[1] more often filling gaps in the history of the ancient oriental countries about which the literary works of antiquity said

[1] The annals of Assyrian kings, for example, supplement the historical data of the Old Testament regarding such events as the conquest of Samaria and Sennacherib's invasion of Judah. See George A. Barton, *Archaeology and the Bible* (7th ed., Philadelphia, 1937), pp. 471–75.

nothing.[2] As a result, much more is now known about the history and culture of Egypt and Mesopotamia than could be gathered from the classical and biblical literatures; and whole cultures and peoples whose history was unknown or all but forgotten—the Sumerians, the Hittites, Mitannians, and Hurrians—have been brought to life and set on the stage of Near Eastern history. The anepigraphic materials, on the other hand, provided firsthand testimony to the material aspects of ancient civilization and supplied concrete evidence regarding the cultic practices of ancient oriental religions. Archaeology, as a historical discipline, makes use of both the written and the material remains of antiquity in reconstructing the cultural background of biblical history.

Excavations in Palestine for the recovery of archaeological evidence during the early years of the twentieth century were disappointingly meager in their results. Whereas Egypt and Mesopotamia supplied the archaeologist with copious quantities of written material on stone, papyrus, and clay, Palestine and Syria yielded remains almost entirely of the anepigraphic variety. Even so, as compared with Egypt or Mesopotamia, very little in the way of monumental buildings or sculpture had been brought to light. The general public, which looked for spectacular finds and showy "museum pieces," was disappointed in its expectations; and biblical scholars, who looked for confirmation of the Old Testament records, were discouraged by the paucity of written materials among the finds. The vague and inconclusive nature of the inferences which could be drawn from the meager material remains led to some disillusionment with archaeology's contribution to the history of the land most directly related to biblical studies.

Some part of the disillusionment was probably the result of a

[2] In Old Testament history, for example, the fact that Ahab took an important part in the battle of Qarqar (853 B.C.) against Shalmaneser III and the fact that Jehu paid tribute to the same king, neither of which is mentioned in the Bible, have been revealed by the annals and the famous Black Obelisk of the Assyrian king. See Barton, *op. cit.*, pp. 457–59.

lack of clarity as to the proper objectives of archaeological research. The chief motive of investigation—and the paramount justification for subsidies—had been the corroboration of biblical tradition which archaeology was expected to furnish. When, therefore, scientific reports of the excavations provided little in the way of "confirmation" of particular passages in the Old Testament, but much general information on the cultural background of the whole, there was inevitable disappointment among those who expected archaeology to support the accuracy of the narratives of the Old Testament. However, the real function of archaeology in relation to biblical studies is not confirmation, but illumination. The goal is to understand the Bible, not to defend it. Archaeology best fulfills its function when it enlarges our knowledge of the background of history and cultural life against which the biblical story was played.[3]

This wider and more objective goal, which requires the patient accumulation of all data regarding the outstanding historical movements and cultural developments in the ancient Near East, irrespective of their immediate bearing on the Old Testament, constitutes the modern, scientific approach in archaeology. With more precise methods of excavation and a more disinterested and open-minded attitude toward new knowledge, the period of renewed excavations which began with the end of World War I was the most fruitful era in biblical archaeology. Quantities of remains, both written and unwritten, were recovered from mounds all over the Near East. But just because of the fulness and comprehensiveness of the results, archaeological research had not lost its relevance to the purpose of enriching the understanding of the Old Testament.[4]

[3] Cf. the remarks of Samuel R. Driver, *Modern Research as Illustrating the Bible* (London, 1909), p. 16.
[4] See W. F. Albright, "The Old Testament and the Archaeology of the Ancient East," in H. H. Rowley (ed.), *The Old Testament and Modern Study* (Oxford, 1951), pp. 27-47.

In Palestine itself, far more valuable results for the study of the Old Testament background were obtained than the previous period of excavation had produced. The re-excavation of mounds already worked upon during the prewar period (notably Megiddo, Jericho, and Samaria) and a restudy of the evidence assembled at that time brought clarification of the initial confusion of results, as well as an increase in the sum-total of knowledge. The excavation of previously untouched mounds in Palestine, each yielding its own kind of archaeological evidence, also greatly amplified the growing stock of information.[5]

The most notable feature of the new era of archaeological investigation was the vast improvement in the techniques of excavation and recording of results. Detailed maps of every stratum were made; photographs of every stage of the excavation were taken; and all objects discovered were carefully registered according to the location where each was found.[6] This careful attention to technical detail, with its faith in the value of empirical and statistical method, reflected the pragmatic attitude of American enterprise. For it was American excavators and their institutional sponsors who were chiefly responsible for the introduction of the modern techniques into archaeological exploration. They made archaeology a scientific discipline, operating with concrete data and marshaling evidence with objective care.

It often seemed, however, that the assembling, classification, and correlation of the data were more important than analysis and interpretation. It is a habit of the scientific worker to think that when phenomena have been described they have been explained. A technique for demonstrating facts with physical proof is prefer-

---

[5] See W. F. Albright, "The Old Testament and the Archaeology of Palestine," *ibid.*, pp. 1–26.

[6] For an informative description of how archaeologists work, see the first five chapters of Cyrus H. Gordon, *The Living Past* (New York, 1941). A brief but thoroughly readable chapter on how excavations in Palestine have been conducted is included in Chester C. McCown's *The Ladder of Progress in Palestine* (New York, 1943), chap. I.

able to the imaginative reconstruction of their meaning. Archaeologists, of course, did not neglect to discuss the bearing of their finds upon the Old Testament. Reports on the results of each excavation were followed by numerous articles and monographs on special features of archaeological discovery regarding the historical background of the Old Testament or the cultural life of its people. But, by and large, the interwar period was one of accumulation of materials rather than one of interpretation.[7] Partly this was due to the fact that the material results of excavation were accumulating faster than they could be studied and digested. Partly, however, it was the result of the belief that the increase of knowledge, based on verifiable data, was a sufficiently important undertaking to absorb the full attention of the scholar. A thorough discussion of the theoretical implications of archaeological discoveries for the history of culture and religion in the ancient Near East had to wait until the coming of World War II called a halt in the physical operations of archaeology.

Nevertheless, the accumulation of factual knowledge was of great importance in itself, for it copiously supplemented the meager information of the Old Testament with regard to the history of Palestine and the nature of its cultural development.

BIBLIOGRAPHICAL NOTE

For a general review of the history of archaeological investigations in Palestine during the nineteenth century, see Frederick J. Bliss, *The Development of Palestine Exploration* (New York, 1906). Another, which carries the survey through the prewar period, is R. A. S. Macalister, *A Century of Excavations in Palestine* (London, 1925). For an expert summary of the results of the early excavations, see Hugues Vincent, *Canaan d'après l'exploration récente* (Paris, 1907).

The old-fashioned type of archaeological compendium, which embraced

---

[7] The one exception was the pioneer effort to rewrite the history of religion in Palestine from an archaeological point of view, made by William C. Graham and Herbert G. May in *Culture and Conscience: An Archaeological Study of the New Religious Past in Ancient Palestine* (Chicago, 1936). This book is discussed below, pp. 209–12.

no more than a descriptive survey of the "antiquities" or *realia* of ancient Hebrew life, is best exemplified by Wilhelm Nowack's *Lehrbuch der hebräischen Archäologie* (2 vols., Leipzig, 1894), and Immanuel Benzinger's *Hebräische Archäologie* (Freiburg, 1894; 3d rev. ed., Leipzig, 1927). Among more recent compilations of archaeological information, George A. Barton's *Archaeology and the Bible* (7th ed., Philadelphia, 1937) is a general compendium of materials arranged in two parts: the first surveying in topical fashion the material results of excavation; the second presenting, in English translations made by the author himself, the most important written materials bearing upon the interpretation of the Bible. A masterly presentation of the chief discoveries of Palestinian archaeology, arranged by historical periods, is Carl Watzinger's *Denkmäler Palästinas* (2 vols., Leipzig, 1933–35). The most thorough and competent exposition of archaeological results, discussing their bearing upon biblical studies, is A. G. Barrois' *Manuel d'archéologie biblique*, Vol. I (Paris, 1939). A more popular, but entirely scholarly work of the same sort is Millar Burrows' *What Mean These Stones?* (New Haven, 1941). William F. Albright's *Archaeology of Palestine and the Bible* (New York, 1932; rev. ed., 1935) also treated the bearing of archaeological finds upon the Old Testament but has now been superseded by his subsequent works, *From the Stone Age to Christianity* (Baltimore, 1940; 2d ed., 1946), and *Archaeology and the Religion of Israel* (Baltimore, 1942; 2d ed., 1946). Albright's popular summary in the Pelican Books, *The Archaeology of Palestine* (1949), provides a convenient survey. Chester C. McCown's *The Ladder of Progress in Palestine* (New York, 1943) summarizes the new information available for both the Old and New Testament fields, in the course of describing the most typical excavations undertaken in Palestine. *The Haverford Symposium on Archeology and the Bible*, edited by Elihu Grant (New Haven, 1938), contains a series of survey articles summarizing the bearing of archaeological results on various aspects of biblical studies. The textual portion of G. Ernest Wright and Floyd V. Filson, *The Westminster Historical Atlas to the Bible* (Philadelphia, 1945), gives an excellent summary, the equivalent of a fair-sized book, of the historical background of biblical history from the vantage point of the new archaeological knowledge.

The New Archaeological Background of Old Testament History

The great amount of new material made available by excavation and the resulting increase in knowledge about the ancient Near East have made it possible to reconstruct all periods of Old Testament history in greater fulness than ever before. Whole chapters that were previously unknown have been added to the history of Palestine. Other periods that were imperfectly understood have been filled in from the wealth of new information. Particular problems of Old Testament history in relation to general historical movements or with reference to cultural evolution have been clarified.

Archaeology has supplied the previously missing prehistory of Palestine, stretching back to include the earliest men of the Old Stone Age.[8] It has also thrown a flood of light on the little known connections of the country with the surrounding world in historical times.[9] Much more precise information is now available regarding the correlation between the cultural history of Palestine and that of the two great centers of civilization in Egypt and Mesopotamia. Unfortunately, there is no room here to survey the effects of this information on the reconstruction of Palestine's general history. Our attention must be directed to specifically Old Testament problems.

The earliest of the periods of Old Testament history that have been placed in a new light is the period of the patriarchs, which has been considerably illuminated by the archaeological picture of the Middle Bronze Age in Palestine. No evidence has been found to prove the existence of any of the patriarchs themselves, but the background of the patriarchal narratives has been so clearly authenticated as to remove the implication of historical criticism that these were purely imaginative tales reflecting the conditions of the age in which they were written. Authentication of the background does not prove that the narratives themselves are historical, but it shows that the life which they portray is a faithful representation

[8] See Dorothy A. E. Garrod, "The Stone Age of Palestine," *Antiquity*, VIII (1934), 133–50.

[9] See W. F. Albright, "Palestine in the Earliest Historical Period," *JPOS*, XV (1935), 193–234.

of conditions in the times to which they refer.[10] The patriarchal narratives fit into the Western Semitic world of the first part of the second millennium (specifically 2000–1700 B.C.)

What has been learned about Western Semitic or Amorite culture in this period makes quite plausible the patriarchal picture of a pacific, pastoral mode of life. The simplicity of this way of life was formerly regarded as the idealization of remote antiquity by a later age, but it corresponds to conditions in Palestine during the early Amorite period as revealed by archaeological research. Eduard Meyer's conclusion, based on internal evidence, that patriarchal life as described in Genesis was not truly nomadic but seminomadic,[11] has now been confirmed by external evidence. The Egyptian Tale of Sinuhe, written c. 1900 B.C., vividly describes the conditions of life among the Amorites of eastern Syria in the early twentieth century B.C.[12] It is the same type of life as the patriarchs lived, sometimes tending flocks and herds, sometimes engaging in simple agriculture. The fact that scholars now accept the "local color" of this tale as genuine reflects the new respect for literary materials which archaeologists have generated, when such materials agree with other types of archaeological evidence. So it has been with the biblical tales which show the patriarchs moving back and forth between the hill country of central Palestine and the steppes of the south country, as their mode of living changed with the seasons. Because this picture fits the archaeological evidence for the fact that the hill country of Palestine was sparsely settled at the beginning of the second millennium and there was

[10] See H. H. Rowley, "Recent Discovery and the Patriarchal Age," *BJRL*, XXXII (1949–50), 44–79.

[11] See above, chap. I, p. 24.

[12] A translation is given in James B. Pritchard (ed.), *Ancient Near Eastern Texts* (Princeton, 1950), pp. 18–22 (by John A. Wilson); an illustrative excerpt by S. A. B. Mercer, *Extra-Biblical Sources for Hebrew and Jewish History* (New York, 1913), pp. 92–95. The most recent, and best, translation (in German) is that of Elmar Edel, in Kurt Galling (ed.), *Textbuch zur Geschichte Israels* (Tübingen, 1950), pp. 1–12.

plenty of room between the fortified towns of the Amorites for seminomadic groups to move about in, these tales are also accepted now as portraying a mode of life as it actually existed.[13]

A remarkable link between the patriarchal narratives and the cultural milieu of the early Middle Bronze Age has been provided by the discovery of close parallels between some of the customs of the patriarchs and those of a hitherto unknown people, the Hurrians,[14] who formed the basic ethnic stock of the very region from which the ancestors of Israel were traditionally supposed to have come—Harran in northwestern Mesopotamia. Certain enigmatic episodes and obscure details in the stories of the patriarchs which had not seemed to fit into the general Semitic background of Palestine received their explanation from the customs of this non-Semitic people who lived in the homeland of Abraham and Laban. Rachel's theft of her father's "gods" (Gen. 31:19-35) had never been satisfactorily explained; now it was understood to have been motivated by the desire to ensure title to her father's property for her husband Jacob. According to Hurrian law, possession of the household gods constituted title to a chief share in the inheritance.[15] The hitherto obscure adoption of Eliezer by Abraham before the birth of Isaac (Gen. 15:2) was explained by the numerous adoption contracts among the Hurrian texts found at Nuzu. Since land could not be alienated, adoption was a common practice to keep the family estate in the hands of a legal heir.[16] Esau's renunciation of his birthright for a consideration had no parallel in Semitic practice, but the custom occurred on occasion among the

[13] See W. F. Albright, *The Archaeology of Palestine* (Pelican Books), pp. 205-6.

[14] See Edward Chiera, "A New Factor in the History of the Ancient Near East," *AASOR*, VI (1926), 75-92; E. A. Speiser, "Ethnic Movements in the Near East in the Second Millennium B.C.," *ibid.*, XIII (1933), 13-54; Benjamin Maisler, *Untersuchungen zur alten Geschichte und Ethnographie Syriens und Palästinas* (Giessen, 1930), I, 33-36.

[15] See Cyrus H. Gordon, "The Story of Jacob and Laban in the Light of the Nuzi Tablets," *BASOR*, LXVI (1937), 25-27.

[16] See W. F. Albright, *Archaeology of Palestine and the Bible*, pp. 137-39.

Hurrians. Other parallels in the tablets from Nuzu illustrated Hagar's right to be included in Abraham's family and showed that Sarah's expulsion of her (Gen. 21:10) was illegal.[17] Thus, Hurrian laws and customs provided contemporary evidence from an external source to the authenticity of the social customs indicated in the patriarchal narratives. The details are demonstrably in keeping with the cultural background of the age, but are out of place in any later age.[18]

Finally, the background of the patriarchal narratives is authenticated by certain negative considerations. They contain no reference to the fertility cult which became dominant in Palestine during the next age; and they never mention horses, which were not brought into Palestine until c. 1700 B.C. by the Hyksos. Thus, all general conditions reflected in these narratives fit the period of about 2000–1700 B.C.[19]

But archaeology has not only clarified problems in early Hebrew history; it has sometimes raised problems which it could not solve satisfactorily. One of these is the identity and the place in history of the Habiru. When the existence of this people was first disclosed by the Amarna letters, their name was equated with "Hebrew" and the circumstantial account of their incursions into Palestine, as given in the letters of Abdi-Hepa of Jerusalem,[20] was assumed to represent the invasion of the Hebrews under Joshua. Further evidence in

[17] See E. A. Speiser, *op. cit.*, p. 44; James W. Jack, "Recent Biblical Archaeology," *Expository Times*, XLVI (1934–35), 376.

[18] See Cyrus H. Gordon, "Biblical Customs and the Nuzu Tablets," *Biblical Archaeologist*, III (1940), 1–9; *The Living Past* (New York, 1941), chap. VIII: "Private and Public Life in Nuzu."

[19] See R. de Vaux, "Les patriarches hébreux et les découvertes modernes," *Revue biblique*, LIII (1946), 321–48; LV (1948), 321–47; LVI (1949), 5–36. Cf. the earlier treatments by Edouard Dhorme, "Abraham dans le cadre de l'histoire," *ibid.*, XXXVII (1928), 367–85, 481–511; XL (1931), 364–74, 503–18; and F. M. T. Böhl, *Das Zeitalter Abrahams* ("Der alte Orient," Vol. XXIX, No. 1; Leipzig, 1930).

[20] Standard (German) translation in J. A. Knudtzon, *Die el-Amarna Tafeln* (2 vols., Leipzig, 1907–14), Nos. 285–90; English translations in Percy Handcock, *Selections from the Tell-el-Amarna Letters* (London, 1920), pp. 3–16; and George A. Barton, *Archaeology and the Bible* (7th ed., 1937), pp. 442–45.

texts from all parts of the Near East has made it plain, however, that the term "Habiru" was applied much more widely over several centuries to various groups in different places.[21] In the older sources it seemed to connote "wanderer" (hence its philological equivalence to "Hebrew"), or sometimes "foreign brigand," and was applied to unsettled groups that continually harassed the borders of the whole Fertile Crescent. In the later sources it seemed to imply an inferior social status, being applied to foreigners serving as laborers. If, therefore, the Habiru who invaded Palestine in the fourteenth century B.C. were the Hebrews of biblical tradition, they must be regarded as having formed a small part of a much larger group of peoples existent in the ancient oriental world.[22] However, the close similarity between the situation described in the letters of Abdi-Hepa and that indicated in the biblical account of the invasion under Joshua has kept the theory of equivalence alive to the present day.[23] Olmstead even identified a certain Yashuia in the Amarna letters with the biblical Joshua. But, if that was the case, then Joshua crossed the Jordan at least a century before the time of Moses[24]—an outcome of the problem which made this theory unacceptable to the majority of biblical scholars. More reasonable is the conclusion of W. F. Albright that the Habiru invasion was a pre-

---

[21] See W. F. Albright, "Western Asia in the Twentieth Century B.C.: The Archives of Mari," *BASOR*, LXVII (1937), 26–30; John A. Wilson, "The 'Eperu of the Egyptian Inscriptions," *AJSL*, XLIX (1932–33), 275–80; R. de Vaux, "La Palestine et la Transjordanie au IIe millénaire et les origines israélites," *ZAW*, LVI (1938), 229–31.

[22] See Martin Noth, "Erwägungen zur Hebräerfrage," in *Festschrift Otto Procksch* (Leipzig, 1934), pp. 99–112; Julius Lewy, "Habiru and Hebrews," *HUCA*, XIV (1939), 587–623; cf. *ibid.*, XV (1940), 47–58; Edouard Dhorme, "La question des Habiri," *RHR*, CXVIII (1938), 170–87; James W. Jack, "New Light on the Habiru-Hebrew Question," *PEQ*, 1940, pp. 95–115; H. H. Rowley, "Habiru and Hebrews," *ibid.*, 1942, pp. 41–53.

[23] See T. J. Meek, *Hebrew Origins* (rev. ed., New York, 1950), pp. 21–23; A. T. Olmstead, *History of Palestine and Syria* (New York, 1931), pp. 196–97.

[24] Meek (*op. cit.*, pp. 44–46) and Olmstead (*op. cit.*, pp. 197, 248) accept this drastic revision of biblical history.

Israelite phase of the occupation of Palestine by the "Hebrews" (in the wider sense).[25]

The knottiest problem in Hebrew history with which archaeology has attempted to deal is the problem of dating the Exodus from Egypt.[26] It is a particularly difficult problem because of the confusing, conflicting, and sometimes contradictory nature of the evidence. Biblical and extrabiblical data alike give grounds for placing the Exodus and the subsequent settlement in Canaan at more than one point in history. There is no doubt that the ancestors of Israel, or some part of them at least,[27] had sojourned in Egypt for several centuries. The question is when they left. Various theories have been propounded at different times to answer this question. The oldest, which stems from Josephus, is that the biblical account of the Exodus was the Hebrew version of the Hyksos expulsion from Egypt.[28] This theory has now been generally abandoned, for it is contradicted by all the archaeological evidence. Inscriptions of Seti I and Rameses II (the one ruling just before, the other after 1300 B.C.) represent the Hebrews ("Apiru") as engaged in heavy work on public buildings nearly three centuries after the expulsion of the Hyksos. Moreover, excavations which have confirmed the biblical tradition that the Hebrews built Pithom and Raamses as store-cities for Pharaoh (Exod. 1:11) have proved that the pharaoh in question was the same Rameses II. The dominant view of scholarship, therefore, became that Rameses II was the pharaoh of the oppression and Merneptah, his successor, the pharaoh of the Exodus, which, accordingly, took place c. 1230 B.C.[29]

---

[25] *From the Stone Age to Christianity*, p. 211. Cf. H. H. Rowley's similar conclusion in *The Rediscovery of the Old Testament* (London, 1946), pp. 62–63.

[26] As an example of the complicated nature of the problem, but not as a final solution of it, James W. Jack's *The Date of the Exodus* (Edinburgh, 1925) may be mentioned.

[27] For the theory that some of the tribes had never left Palestine, see Eduard Meyer, *Die Israeliten und ihre Nachbarstämme*, pp. 104, 204–5, 433.

[28] Still maintained in modern times by H. R. Hall, *The Ancient History of the Near East* (6th ed., London, 1924), pp. 403–9.

But the discovery of the "Israel stele," set up by Merneptah to celebrate his victories in Palestine,[30] brought forth the conflicting evidence that Israel was already in the land in 1230 B.C., where it had suffered a defeat at the hands of the pharaoh. An attempt to resolve the conflict was made with the hypothesis that the stele referred to that part of the Hebrew tribes which had never left Palestine. However, archaeological evidence discovered more recently, showing that Canaanite cities such as Bethel, Lachish, and Kirjath-sepher were destroyed by conquest c. 1250-1230 B.C.,[31] makes it necessary to conclude that practically all the Hebrews were already in Canaan before 1230 B.C., for the biblical record attributes the destruction of these cities to the invading army under Joshua.

Excavation has been responsible for a third theory regarding the date of the Exodus, namely, Garstang's view that it occurred about 1440 B.C.[32] His conclusion was based almost entirely on the fact that, according to his excavations at Jericho, that city fell c. 1400 B.C.,[33] presumably to the Hebrews invading the land (Josh. 6). The fact that this date for the fall of Jericho, plus the traditional forty years for the wilderness wanderings, coincided with the biblical statement (I Kings 6:1) that the Exodus took place 480 years before Solomon began to build the Temple convinced Gar-

---

[29] The most recent presentation of this view is by H. H. Rowley, "Israel's Sojourn in Egypt," *BJRL*, XXII (1938), 243-90—a review of the different theories regarding the Exodus, with full bibliographical references.

[30] A translation is given by George A. Barton, *Archaeology and the Bible* (7th ed., 1937), p. 376; and by John A. Wilson, in J. B. Pritchard (ed.), *Ancient Near Eastern Texts* (Princeton, 1950), pp. 376-78.

[31] See W. F. Albright, "The Kyle Memorial Excavations at Bethel," *BASOR*, LVI (1934), 2-15; "Further Light on the History of Israel from Lachish and Megiddo," *ibid.*, LXVIII (1937), 23-24; and *Archaeology of Palestine and the Bible*, pp. 100-1.

[32] John Garstang, *Foundations of Bible History: Joshua-Judges* (London, 1931), pp. 51-66; *The Story of Jericho* (London, 1940), pp. 129-31.

[33] *Foundations of Bible History*, pp. 61-62, 146-47; "The Fall of Bronze Age Jericho," *PEFQS*, 1935, pp. 61-68; "The Story of Jericho," *AJSL*, LVIII (1941), 368-72.

stang of the accuracy of his date for the Exodus. He therefore identified the Habiru invasion, which was taking place about the same time as the fall of Jericho, with the Hebrew conquest under Joshua and attributed to the Habiru-Hebrews the destruction of the city at the beginning of the fourteenth century.

Garstang's theory has been challenged, however, on the basis of other considerations.[34] That the identification of the Hebrews under Joshua with the Habiru is doubtful has already been indicated. The further fact that the other cities conquered by Joshua (Bethel, Lachish, Kirjath-sepher) did not fall until the second half of the thirteenth century also militates against it. Moreover, Nelson Glueck's explorations in Transjordan, which showed that the kingdoms of Edom and Moab did not exist before the thirteenth century,[35] make it impossible to assume that the tribes under Joshua appeared across the Jordan opposite Jericho as early as the beginning of the fourteenth century—unless the biblical tradition of a circuit around Edom and a hard-fought passage through Moab is to be questioned.

In order to avoid throwing any archaeological evidence out of court—even though it dated the fall of Jericho long before the Hebrew tribes could have made their circuit around Edom—W. F. Albright proposed still another theory, in an effort to harmonize as much of the conflicting evidence as possible without violating biblical tradition in any important particular.[36] He suggested that there had been two exoduses from Egypt, in the first of which the Joseph tribes left Egypt some time in the fifteenth century and during the disturbed conditions of the fourteenth century conquered Jericho. They settled in the sparsely populated hill country of Ephraim,

---

[34] See Albrecht Alt's criticisms in his review of Garstang's *Foundations of Bible History*, in *JPOS*, XII (1932), 172–80.

[35] *The Other Side of the Jordan* (New Haven, 1940), pp. 125–47.

[36] "Archaeology and the Date of the Hebrew Conquest of Palestine," *BASOR*, LVIII (1935), 10–18; "The Israelite Conquest of Canaan in the Light of Archaeology," *ibid.*, LXXIV (1939), 11–23.

where they continued to live a seminomadic life for some time without attempting to occupy the cities of the Canaanites. In the second exodus, the main body of Hebrews left Egypt under Moses' leadership c. 1290 B.C., made the circuit of Edom and Moab, and then under Joshua's leadership conquered Bethel c. 1250 B.C. and Lachish and Kirjath-sepher c. 1230 B.C. Thus, Albright's date for the (second) Exodus leaves adequate time for the circuit of Edom, fits the archaeological dates for the destruction of Bethel and the cities in the south, and agrees with the testimony of the "Israel stele" that by 1230 B.C. Israel was already in Palestine in force but had not yet settled down.[37] But his view that the conquest of Canaan was accomplished in two waves by separate but related groups is pure hypothesis.

One other theory touching the date of the Exodus has been advanced in recent years: the theory of T. J. Meek that only a small group of Hebrews (chiefly the tribe of Levi) had been involved in the events of the Exodus, leaving Egypt under Moses some time after 1200 B.C.;[38] that this group then amalgamated with the tribe of Judah, already settled in the south country since the days of the patriarchs, and with Simeonites, Kenites, and Calebites, to form a confederacy at Kadesh; and that this confederacy later pushed northward into southern Canaan without making the circuit round the Dead Sea. Only the tribe of Reuben, according to Meek, went around Edom and Moab to the east country, after its expulsion from the confederacy.[39] This limited interpretation of the Exodus was part of a comprehensive and intricate reconstruction of early Hebrew history,[40] which balanced the invasion across the

[37] Cf. *From the Stone Age to Christianity*, pp. 194-95.

[38] See *Hebrew Origins* (rev. ed., 1950), pp. 29, 31-33. Cf. pp. 35-36, 43-44, for Meek's reasons for placing the Exodus so late.

[39] See, *ibid.*, pp. 38-42.

[40] T. J. Meek, "A Suggested Reconstruction of Early Hebrew History," *American Journal of Theology*, XXIV (1920), 209-16; "Some Religious Origins of the Hebrews," *AJSL*, XXXVII (1920-21), 101-31; "The Israelite Conquest of Ephraim," *BASOR*, LXI (1936), 17-19; *Hebrew Origins*, chap. I.

Jordan of the Joseph tribes under Joshua (in the time of the Habiru) and the organization of an Israelite confederacy at Shechem, under a code of laws largely borrowed from the Canaanites,[41] with the later "invasion" from the south by the Judahite clans, organized into a southern confederacy with a code of laws of its own, Mosaic in origin. This clear-cut division of the Hebrew conquest into two quite distinct phases was based largely on historical criticism of the literary sources;[42] although Meek tried, wherever possible, to fit the archaeological data into his scheme.

The ultimate purpose of Meek's reconstruction was to account for the considerable ethnic and religious differences between the northern tribes known as Israel and the southern tribes known as Judah, which Meek considered "in their origin two separate and distinct peoples, as separate and distinct as the Babylonians and Assyrians." [43] He believed that

to put the settlement of Israel in the north some two hundred years before that of Judah in the south seems best to account for the cultural superiority of the north over the south. Two hundred years' earlier settlement in agricultural life and close contact with the more cultured Canaanites would give the northerners no little advantage over their kinsmen to the south.[44]

The differences between Israel and Judah are well known to Bible scholars, as well as the fact that these differences influenced the whole course of Hebrew history.[45] The hypothesis of separate origin for the Judahite clans, which partially explains the differ-

---

[41] See *Hebrew Origins* (rev. ed., 1950), pp. 25–26; cf. A. T. Olmstead, *History of Palestine and Syria*, p. 107.

[42] Cf. J. M. P. Smith, "Some Problems in the Early History of Hebrew Religion," *AJSL*, XXXII (1915–16), 81–97; D. D. Luckenbill, "On Israel's Origins," *American Journal of Theology*, XXII (1918), 24–53.

[43] *Hebrew Origins* (rev. ed., 1950), p. 82.

[44] *Ibid.*, p. 46.

[45] Albrecht Alt, however, in his *Staatenbildung der Israeliten in Palästina* (Leipzig, 1930), maintained that the distinction between northern and southern tribes did not become historically significant until the time of the monarchy.

ences, has been generally accepted on literary-critical grounds.[46] But in following out the implications of the archaeological evidence Meek's theory reversed the traditional order of Moses and Joshua, putting the latter at least a century and a half before the former. This radical revision of the tradition pointed up the apparently irreconcilable conflict between the literary and archaeological data.

None of these theories succeeded in accounting for all the facts in the biblical records and meeting the requirements of the archaeological data at the same time. As a recent writer has said, "Archaeology has not simplified the problem of the date of the conquest but has rather introduced new complications. Perhaps we should say rather that it has uncovered the original complexity which was obscured by the apparent simplicity of the records." [47]

Finally, there is the problem of the character of the Conquest itself. Archaeology at first confused the matter by depriving Joshua of his capture of Jericho, but with regard to the rest of his career it has tended to confirm the tradition of a swift and violent conquest by an organized army which exterminated the inhabitants. The long dominant view of critical scholarship was that the "conquest" had been a gradual process of infiltration by separate tribes and clans, who slowly assimilated the Canaanite population by adapting themselves to Canaanite culture. The critical view was based on the fact that the account of the conquest in the book of Joshua conflicts with the summary of the course of events given in the first chapter of the book of Judges. Literary criticism had determined that the latter is the older of the two accounts. Being

[46] See *Hebrew Origins* (rev. ed., 1950), pp. 40-41, 125-27, for Meek's restatement of these grounds. Cf. Martin Noth, "Die Ansiedlung des Stammes Juda auf dem Boden Palästinas," *Palästinajahrbuch*, XXX (1934), 31-47.

[47] Millar Burrows, *What Mean These Stones?* (New Haven, 1941), p. 79. The most recent general survey of the archaeological and literary evidence bearing on the problem of the date of the Exodus is H. H. Rowley, *From Joseph to Joshua* (London, 1950).

closer to the actual events, it was presumably the more authentic.[48]
The first excavations in Palestine during the early years of the
twentieth century seemed to support the view that the "conquest"
was neither swift nor complete. The results were generally interpreted as showing that there was no sharp break in Canaanite culture after the coming of the Hebrews.[49] Because the book of
Joshua (chaps. 1–11) painted a different picture, describing the
conquest of the whole country in a few swift campaigns within
the lifetime of the great leader himself, it was generally considered
to be a late "epic of conquest" which could not be taken literally.
Its clear implication that Joshua conquered, not only the central
highlands of Ephraim, but southern and northern Palestine as well,
and the detailed itinerary of his southern campaign (chap. 10) were
considered unhistorical. This "epic of conquest," it was assumed,
had been written, on the basis of materials taken from J and E,[50]
partly as nationalistic propaganda to emphasize that the people of
Israel was united from the beginning;[51] partly to show that, by
completely exterminating the native population, it had faithfully
carried out the Deuteronomic principle of not compromising with
Canaanite culture.[52]

But the results of archaeological excavation, especially at
Bethel, Lachish, and Kirjath-sepher, have forced some revision in
the critical view. The evidence of the violent and complete destruction of these cities suggests that the principle of the *herem* ("devo-

[48] Besides the usual handbooks of introduction to the Old Testament, see Elias
Auerbach, "Die Einwanderung der Israeliten: Jdc. 1," *ZAW*, XLVIII ((1930),
286–95.
[49] See, e.g., S. R. Driver, *Modern Research as Illustrating the Bible*, p. 87;
Hugues Vincent, *Canaan d'après l'exploration récente*, pp. 463–64.
[50] But how much less J and E had ascribed to Joshua in the way of actual con-
quests is shown by the analysis of these chapters in W. O. E. Oesterley and Theodore H. Robinson, *An Introduction to the Books of the Old Testament* (London,
1934), pp. 72–73.
[51] See Meek, *Hebrew Origins* (rev. ed., 1950), p. 42; Charles F. Burney, *Israel's
Settlement in Canaan* (London, 1918), pp. 1–58.
[52] See Julius A. Bewer, *The Literature of the Old Testament* (rev. ed., New
York, 1933), p. 228; Oesterley and Robinson, *op. cit.*, pp. 73–74.

tion" of the conquered population to the Lord) was not simply a late Deuteronomic principle invented to support the prophetic campaign against syncretism with Baal-worship, but an actual practice at the time of the invasions.[53] Moreover, the evidence that these towns were destroyed in the second half of the thirteenth century supports the tradition of Joshua 10 that there actually was a southern campaign led by Joshua himself.[54] Archaeologists do not deny that the picture of a complete conquest of Palestine within Joshua's lifetime is an exaggeration.[55] But the archaeological evidence which has steadily accumulated since the early excavations in Palestine makes it plain that there was not only an abrupt break in the continuity of culture at certain sites but a marked decline in the general level of culture in all Canaan between the Late Bronze (Canaanite) Age and the Early Iron (Hebrew) Age. Houses and fortifications built by the Hebrews at Bethel and Debir (Kirjath-sepher) were not so well constructed as those they had destroyed,[56] and pottery throughout Early Iron Age settlements shows a great deterioration in quality.[57] In the light of these facts, the theory that the Hebrews took over the country by gradual assimilation of Canaanite culture has had to be modified. "We must take seriously," says G. Ernest Wright, "the biblical claims for a storming of at least central and southern Palestine with such violence and such contempt for the inhabitants that there was small opportunity or desire for amalgamation on a large

[53] See W. F. Albright, *From the Stone Age to Christianity*, pp. 213–14; G. Ernest Wright, "Epic of Conquest," *Biblical Archaeologist*, III (1940), 25–40.

[54] See G. Ernest Wright, "The Literary and Historical Problem of Joshua 10 and Judges 1," *JNES*, V (1946), 105–14; cf. K. Elliger, "Josua in Judäa," *Palästinajahrbuch*, XXX (1934), 47–71.

[55] Cf. Albright's remarks, *op. cit.*, p. 210.

[56] See W. F. Albright, *Archaeology of Palestine and the Bible*, pp. 101–2; G. Ernest Wright, "Archaeological Observations on the Period of the Judges and the Early Monarchy," *JBL*, LX (1941), 27–42.

[57] See Millar Burrows, *What Mean These Stones?*, pp. 166–68.

scale." [58] This modification of critical theory does not require calling into question the historical data of the older sources; it is still possible to regard, for example, Othniel's "conquest" of Debir (Josh. 15:15-17; Judg. 1:11-13) as the occupation and rebuilding of the site after the destruction by Joshua's army. The main point is, as in the case of the patriarchal narratives, that archaeology has brought about a new respect for the general picture, if not the details, of the conquest given in the book of Joshua.[59]

This new respect for the historical value of the data presented in Joshua extends to the middle portions of the book also (chaps. 13-19), in which the territorial boundaries of the twelve tribes are given in detail. Critical scholars had tended to regard practically all the data of these chapters as ideal inventions of late priestly writers (D and P). But, as the result of a new approach to the criticism of this book, which its originator, Albrecht Alt, called "territorial history," considerable progress has been made toward establishing the view that these chapters rest on a basis of authentic tradition.[60] Alt's method of analysis was a combination of historical criticism (supplemented by some of the insights of Gunkel's studies of literary tradition) and topographical research based upon archaeological data. In general, Alt and his followers have demonstrated that the lists of cities and tribal boundaries in Joshua were not postexilic priestly fictions but reliable documents in the form of official memoranda from the pre-exilic period. The detailed description of tribal borders in chapters 13-14, for example, was identified as an early premonarchical document (no longer in complete form) dealing with the geographical distribution of the various tribal groups in the land at the time (toward

[58] "The Present State of Biblical Archaeology," in Harold R. Willoughby (ed.), *The Study of the Bible Today and Tomorrow* (Chicago, 1947), p. 83.
[59] See, in general, Albrecht Alt's "Erwägungen über die Landnahme der Israeliten in Palästina," *Palästinajahrbuch*, XXXV (1939), 8-63, in which he gives (*inter alia*) reasons for caution regarding too thorough abandonment of the theory of a gradual penetration into Palestine.
[60] See especially Alt's *Die Landnahme der Israeliten in Palästina* (Leipzig, 1925).

the end of the eleventh century B.C.).[61] In like manner, various other pieces of source material in the books of the Old Testament, on which the critics had placed no reliance, have been evaluated and exploited for their contribution to the clarification of Israel's history. The school of Alt emphasized the substantial historicity of the early traditions of Israel, in view of the tenacity of oral tradition and the concurrence of the topographical details with archaeological data.[62]

Archaeology's Contribution to the History of Israel's Religion

In the early decades of the twentieth century, when excavations in Palestine seemed to be showing that there had been no major break in the continuity of Canaanite culture attending the Hebrew conquest, it was widely believed that the religion of Israel had been strongly affected by the surviving religion of Canaan and that the so-called "popular religion" of the Israelite masses was largely indistinguishable from that of the Canaanites. The spade had uncovered a paraphernalia of religious worship which seemed to confirm the severest denunciations of the prophets against the people for worshiping in the ways of the Canaanites. "High places" with their sacred stones, rock altars, Astarte figurines, child sacrifices (evidenced by infants buried in jars), and offerings laid in the tombs of the dead not only revealed something of the nature of Canaanite religion but illuminated the sort of cultic practices which the prophets condemned.[63]

---

[61] See Albrecht Alt, "Das System der Stammesgrenzen im Buche Josua," in *Sellin Festschrift: Beiträge zur Religionsgeschichte und Archäologie Palästinas* (Leipzig, 1927), pp. 13–24; Martin Noth, *Das Buch Josua* ("Handbuch zum Alten Testament," edited by Otto Eissfeldt; Tübingen, 1938), pp. ix–xv.

[62] For a summary of results and conclusions, see Alt, "Josua," in Paul Volz (ed.), *Werden und Wesen des Alten Testaments* (Berlin, 1936), pp. 13–29; Noth, *Die Welt des Alten Testaments* (Berlin, 1940), pp. 50–74, 97–99.

[63] The state of knowledge at that time was summarized by Stanley A. Cook, *The Religion of Ancient Palestine in the Second Millennium B.C.* (London, 1908); cf. his "Notes on the Old Canaanite Religion," *Expositor*, X (1910), 111–27.

Interest in recovering the material evidences of Canaanite religion was so great that in the beginning much more "evidence" was found than later proved authentic. In almost every excavation of the early years in Palestine—Tell el-Hesi, Gezer, Taanach, and Megiddo—"high places" were discovered, complete with sacred pillars, which were identified as coming from Israelite as well as early Canaanite times.[64] The most famous of these "high places," that which Macalister unearthed at Gezer,[65] is still recognized as a genuine example of a Canaanite shrine, since it was a true open-air sanctuary without any buildings associated with it. But many other groups of standing stones, originally identified as sacred pillars or as the columns of a Canaanite temple,[66] are now known to have served a secular purpose. When continued excavation showed that a large number of the houses in Israelite towns of the Middle Iron Age had rows of three or four stone pillars to support the second story, it was evident that the phenomenon simply represented the revival of a type of house construction which had first appeared in the Middle Bronze Age. The absence of cultic objects in most of these pillared buildings strengthened the view that they were simply commodious private houses of the wealthier element in the population.[67]

Similarly, the early archaeologists had confidently recognized the altars of Canaanite "high places" wherever they came upon large, flat rocks with round depressions in their surfaces ("cup-marks"). The fact that rocks with these characteristic markings were often found situated over natural caves, as at Gezer, Megiddo, and Jerusalem, led to the theory that sacrifices to chthonic deities

[64] But C. C. McCown has recently shown that there never were any Israelite "high places," in "Hebrew High Places and Cult Remains," *JBL*, LXIX (1950), 205–19.

[65] See R. A. S. Macalister, *The Excavation of Gezer* (3 vols., London, 1912), I, 105–7; II, 381–404.

[66] See, e.g., Gottlieb Schumacher, *Tell el-Mutesellim* (Leipzig, 1908), pp. 110–24.

[67] See Carl Watzinger, *Denkmäler Palästinas*, I, 101–2; W. F. Albright, "The Excavation of Tell Beit Mirsim, III," *AASOR*, XXI–II (1943), 54–55.

were offered here, the blood of the sacrificial victims being allowed to flow down through cracks in the rock or grooves cut for the purpose.[68] Doubtless some of the roughly shaped rocks found at various sites, including the great rock on the temple hill of Jerusalem, were actually used as altars in the Middle or Late Bronze Age. But most of the natural slabs of stone containing "cupmarks" and grooves in their surfaces are now known to have been pressing tables for extracting oil from olives or wine from grapes.[69]

Thus, the early excavations in Palestine were actually less informative regarding the material equipment of Canaanite worship than had been supposed. The significance of most of the "cultic objects" identified was secularized by later interpretation. In the same way, the practice of burying infants in jars under the corners of houses was eventually reinterpreted. At first such burials were regarded as "foundation sacrifices" to the "spirits of the place," made at the time the houses were built to secure the welfare of the inhabitants.[70] But later excavators came to regard them simply as the pathetic evidence of a high rate of infant mortality; burial under the floors of the houses was the easiest method of disposal.[71] However, a sufficient number of infant burials has been found underneath the floors of Canaanite "high places" [72] and Phoenician shrines in Palestine and Syria to lend weight to the tradition preserved by literary sources regarding the practice of sacrificing a first-born child to

[68] See R. A. S. Macalister, *The Excavation of Gezer*, II, 378–80; Gottlieb Schumacher, *Tell el-Mutesellim*, pp. 156–58; George A. Barton, *Archaeology and the Bible* (7th ed., 1937), pp. 211–13.

[69] See George A. Barton, *ibid.*, p. 178; Millar Burrows, *What Mean These Stones?*, p. 173.

[70] See S. R. Driver, *Modern Research as Illustrating the Bible*, p. 88; Gottlieb Schumacher, *Tell el-Mutesellim*, pp. 45, 54; Ernst Sellin, *Tell Ta'annek* (Vienna, 1904), p. 61.

[71] See P. L. O. Guy and Robert M. Engberg, *Megiddo Tombs* ("Oriental Institute Publications," XXXIII; Chicago, 1938), p. 57.

[72] As, e.g., at Gezer; see R. A. S. Macalister, *The Excavation of Gezer*, II, 431–37.

"Moloch" (cf. II Kings 23:10; Jer. 32:35; Lev. 18:21; 20:2-5).[73]

The one type of material evidence from the excavations which has definitely thrown some light upon the nature of Canaanite belief and the "popular religion" of the Israelites is the ubiquitous figurine of the fertility goddess. Such figurines began to appear in Palestine during the Middle Bronze Age and remained popular in various forms down through the Middle Iron Age or until the end of the Israelite period. The characteristic Canaanite type of the Bronze Ages was a clay plaque showing the nude goddess in relief. It illustrates the important place in popular belief taken by the new fertility cult introduced from Mesopotamia, where such plaques have been found in great numbers. Significantly, this type of figurine was not found in Israelite sites of the Early Iron Age (period of the Judges), although it continued to be popular in the Canaanite cities of the same age. The Israelites had not yet succumbed to the allurements of the fertility cult of their neighbors. In the succeeding period of the monarchy (Middle Iron Age), however, several types of fertility goddess figurines became common in all the cities of Israel.[74] Because they were usually found in the ruins of houses rather than at sanctuaries, it was assumed that they had no specific cultic significance but simply represented the popular faith in talismans which stimulated the reproductive processes. But the fact that every Israelite house apparently had one or more of these representations shows how far the Israelite masses had gone in adopting the popular superstitions of their environment.

The material evidence of archaeology thus provided some glimpse into certain aspects of popular belief among the Canaanites of which the Old Testament contained no hint. It is true that none of the "fertility goddess" figurines ever bore the name of any goddess inscribed upon it, so that the common notion such figurines

---

[73] Cf. Otto Eissfeldt's study of this type of sacrifice, *Molk als Opferbegriff im Punischen und Hebräischen* (Halle, 1935).

[74] See W. F. Albright, *Archaeology of Palestine and the Bible*, pp. 121-22.

represented the goddess Astarte is simply an assumption.[75] Yet the popularity of the figurines, as attested by the archaeological remains, suggests the possibility that the cult of the Mother Goddess, the personification of fertility in nature, was widespread among the Canaanite masses of the day.[76]

That this interpretation is closer to an accurate description of the popular religion of Canaan than the former interpretation of standing stones and "cup-marks" has been confidently assumed. Of course, any attempt to go beyond external description of archaeological remains immediately introduces a subjective element into the interpretation. But whether the subjective element distorts or illuminates the concrete data depends upon the degree to which the result corresponds to the conceptual background of the data— and that can be determined only from written sources. The former interpretation of Canaanite religion in terms of animistic polytheism was made, in the absence of any written materials except the Old Testament, on the basis of anthropological data regarding the religious beliefs of primitive peoples. It therefore had as much weight as any argument from analogy—and no more. The later interpretation in terms of the fertility cult was drawn from the written religious texts of the ancient East, and so carried with it the greater probability of reflecting the conceptual background with reasonable accuracy.

The first attempt to interpret the material remains of cultic life in Palestine in terms of conceptual backgrounds was Graham and May's *Culture and Conscience.*[77] The authors used the wealth of material uncovered by archaeological research to survey the rise and growth of religious ideas in Canaan throughout its long history.

---

[75] See James B. Pritchard, *Palestinian Figurines in Relation to Certain Goddesses Known Through Literature* (New Haven, 1943).

[76] On the possibility of Mother Goddess worship among the Hebrews as well, see L. B. Paton, "The Cult of the Mother-Goddess in Ancient Palestine," *Biblical World*, XXXVI (1910), 26–38.

[77] See above, n. 7.

They painted a broad canvas depicting the sweep of religious history through successive cultural stages, while filling in the outlines of the picture with a multitude of specific details. Their ultimate purpose was to provide a background for understanding Israel's achievement in the religious sphere. But the chief significance of their book was its pioneering effort to convey some sense of the spiritual significance of the material remains uncovered by archaeology.

From the fact that no cultic objects occurred in Palestinian deposits earlier than the New Stone Age, and from the evidence of deliberate interment of the dead even in the earliest times, Graham and May judged that the oldest religion of Palestine had been "the cult of the dead." This term did not mean the worship of departed spirits but belief in some sort of after-life.[78] According to Graham and May, the beliefs associated with this cult had dominated the thinking and actions of men through all the early archaeological ages down to the Middle Bronze Age, when the radically different set of beliefs associated with the fertility cult were introduced into Palestine.

The authors devoted much space to the impact upon Palestine of the world-view of Mesopotamia which the Hyksos brought with them into the land, causing the inhabitants to turn from a cult "which tended to concentrate on death as the outstanding fact of experience" to a new cult which emphasized the promotion of "prosperity in this world." [79] The introduction of the fertility cult, according to Graham and May, had a fortunate effect on Canaanite culture. Its emphasis on increasing the productivity of fields and flocks not only led to a great improvement in the material basis of life but stimulated the "intellectual and executive capacities" of the people, by requiring them to work out the institutional side of life in ways that would contribute to the material ends of society.

[78] See *Culture and Conscience*, pp. 24–25.
[79] *Ibid.*, pp. 42, 67.

As a result,

[there] were inculcated in the masses two dispositions which were of themselves not without social value. One of these was the disposition toward
preoccupation with the production of material goods. The other was the
disposition to submit to authority as manifested in dominating individuals.
They were not evil dispositions, but only partially good. They were not
wrong, but only partially right. The spiritual aspects of life rise from the
use of material things, and a satisfying social order can only exist through
humanly mediated authority.[80]

It was necessary to the major thesis of the book to emphasize
in this way the values in Canaanite culture, while recognizing the
limits beyond which they did not reach. The point of view which
Graham had elaborated in his earlier work, *The Prophets and
Israel's Culture*,[81] was here made the climax of the authors' interpretation of the course of religious history in Palestine. That is,
they regarded the prophetic protest against the ways of the Canaanites, not as a rejection of the pattern of culture which had
grown up in Canaan, but as an attempt to reinterpret the best in
its world-view in terms that shifted the major emphasis from
materialistic to spiritual values. The achievement of Israel in the
sphere of religion, according to Graham and May, was that it
sublimated the materialistic philosophy which had dominated the
ancient Near East for two or more millenniums into a new world-
view, in which the conception of deity was lifted above nature and
completely spiritualized and the motivation of human activity was
ethicized. The challenge of the prophets ushered in the final,
climactic chapter of Palestine's religious history, which ended with
the "regeneration" of ancient culture by the prophetic spirit.

Obviously, this history of the rise, development, decadence,
and regeneration of religious culture in Palestine was based on
more than interpretation of the material remains uncovered by

---

[80] *Ibid.*, pp. 217–18.
[81] See above, chap. V, pp. 177–80.

archaeology. With all the minute detail in which the objective evidence is presented, the book has a philosophic sweep which could only come from a dominating point of view. Borrowing a theme from James H. Breasted, [82] the authors attempted to demonstrate that "in the human evolution the dawn of culture preceded the dawn of conscience," [83] that is, the sense of what the authors called "sociality" preceded any sense of individual responsibility. Their whole interpretation of the history of religion in Palestine was guided by this basic theme.

One can only admire the consistency with which the authors applied their leading idea to the material. But the basic theme seems not so much to have grown out of the archaeological evidence as to have provided a framework into which the archaeological data were fitted. Graham and May very properly drew their insight into the conceptual background of the fertility cult from the religious texts of Mesopotamia and Ras Shamra, and they made extensive use of the Old Testament texts in presenting the ideology of the prophets. But their general "frame of reference" seemed to go beyond the inferences that could legitimately be drawn from the written and the material archaeological evidence of which they made use.

Thus, in attempting the first interpretative synthesis of the results of archaeological research, Graham and May went to the other extreme from the merely technical analysis of archaeological remains which satisfied their contemporaries. They allowed their personal views of the meaning of cultural history to influence their exposition of the significance of the data. How to enter imaginatively and sympathetically, yet without preconception, into the thought-world of ancient times is the chief problem of archaeological research in its present interpretative phase.

[82] *The Dawn of Conscience* (New York, 1933)
[83] *Culture and Conscience*, p. 16.

The Interpretative Phase of Archaeological Research

When the advent of World War II ended the further accumulation of archaeological materials and forced scholars to turn their attention to the evaluation of the materials already accumulated, archaeological studies entered upon a new phase. Whereas the earliest phases had been concerned with the task of unearthing material remains, and the interwar period had assumed the additional task of reconstructing the cultural history of the ancient Orient, the latest phase of archaeological research has devoted the major portion of its attention to the attempt to penetrate and comprehend the conceptual life of ancient man.

The first major work of this sort was William F. Albright's comprehensive survey of the history of religious thought in the ancient Near East from its beginnings in primitive mentality down to the origin of Christianity.[84] Sketching the important conceptual developments in prehistoric ages and the significant intellectual achievements of the early historical periods, as a background for the advance of human thinking toward the attainment of a monotheistic faith in the Judeo-Christian thought-world, the book presented a complete archaeological and historical background for its reconstruction of Old Testament religious history. Without intending to be a handbook either of archaeology or of ancient history, it was a veritable storehouse of information on both. After two years it was followed by a somewhat more restricted presentation of the archaeological material with more specific reference to the history of Israel's religion.[85] Albright's purpose was to provide a foundation for "the ultimate reconstruction, as far as possible, of the route which our cultural ancestors traversed in order to reach Judeo-Christian heights of spiritual insight," [86] by systematizing

[84] *From the Stone Age to Christianity* (Baltimore, 1940).
[85] *Archaeology and the Religion of Israel* (Baltimore, 1942).
[86] *Ibid.*, p. 4.

and analyzing the conceptual data which Near Eastern archaeology provided.[87]

While these two complementary works provided a comprehensive survey of the cultural history of the ancient Near East, the most significant portion of Albright's presentation was his analysis of the intellectual development of ancient man. Accepting "in principle" Lévy-Bruhl's distinction between prelogical and logical thought, Albright suggested an intermediate phase of "empirico-logical" thought to designate that type of thinking, based on direct sensory experience, which governed a large part of the intellectual life of the ancient Orient.[88] In the intellectual history of Egypt and Mesopotamia, Albright found that

men start . . . with a prelogical, corporative tradition [but] after the late third millennium progressively discard prelogical thought and enter the empirical stage of logical thinking, where the highest thought is quite logical as a rule, but draws its sanctions from the results of experience and not from formal canons of thinking.[89]

Strictly logical thinking was not achieved until the Greeks in the fifth century B.C. had worked out the "formal canons of thinking." This expansion of Lévy-Bruhl's theory proved to be highly useful in explaining the thought-world of the ancient Orient.[90]

The most important result of Albright's interest in the intellectual background of Near Eastern cultural history was the insight it produced into the nature of religious belief in the ancient Orient. His major conclusion in this connection was that each of the great polytheistic systems of Egypt, Mesopotamia, and Canaan was a cosmic system, the gods of which were personified forces of nature exercising their functions throughout the universe without geo-

[87] Cf., *ibid.*, pp. 37–44, for Albright's survey of the available written and un-written materials.

[88] See *From the Stone Age to Christianity* (2d ed., 1946), p. 365.

[89] *Ibid.*, p. 84.

[90] See, especially, *Archaeology and the Religion of Israel*, pp. 30–33.

graphical limitation.[91] Quoting passages from the literature of the second millennium B.C. which illustrated the cosmic character of these gods,[92] Albright affirmed that "belief in the universal dominion of a high god was the natural result of the slightest reflection about his cosmic function and was facilitated by the general identification of gods with similar functions."[93] Albright also emphasized the tendency toward henotheism in Mesopotamia, "where the worshiper concentrated his adoration on a single deity, with whom he identified all other gods of the same type."[94] But he found no evidence for "tribal or national henotheism," that is, monolatry, the worship of one god exclusively as lord of a particular area or nation. "On the contrary," said Albright, "the cosmic gods of Mesopotamia were naively and unquestioningly believed to rule the entire world, each in his own designated sphere or function."[95] This conclusion had a bearing on Albright's view of Hebrew monotheism, to which we must return later.

Another comprehensive survey of the thought-world of the ancient Orient, which supplemented Albright's exposition with a still deeper penetration into the nature of thinking in the ancient Near East, was presented by Henri Frankfort and his collaborators in *The Intellectual Adventure of Ancient Man*. They characterized the ancient mode of thinking as "mythopoeic," that is, as an emotional rather than intellectual response to the impact of the universe upon the human consciousness, which expressed itself in myths. Man felt himself a part of a living cosmos which confronted him as a "Thou," not an "It," and so conceived of it as full of living forces which he personified (mythicized) as cosmic powers. Since

[91] See "The Ancient Near East and the Religion of Israel," *JBL*, LIX (1940), 102–10.
[92] *From the Stone Age to Christianity*, pp. 161–63, and (2d ed., 1946), p. 365.
[93] *Ibid.*, p. 161. Cf. Alfred Bertholet, *Götterspaltung und Göttervereinigung* (Tübingen, 1933).
[94] *From the Stone Age to Christianity*, p. 143.
[95] *Ibid.*, p. 143.

"all experience of 'Thou' is highly individual, and early man does, in fact, view happenings as individual events, . . . an account of such events and also their explanation can be conceived only as action and necessarily take the form of a story. In other words, the ancients told myths instead of presenting an analysis or conclusions." [96]

This explanation threw considerable light upon the "pattern of thinking" discussed by S. H. Hooke and the ritual myth school of interpretation. Since, according to Professor and Mrs. Frankfort, "the life of man . . . [is] for mythopoeic thought imbedded in nature, . . . the natural processes are affected by the acts of man no less than man's life depends on his harmonious integration with nature." A ritual act which symbolized a process of nature also influenced its outcome. Hence, dramatic presentations of cosmic myths in ritual form "are not merely symbolical; they are part and parcel of the cosmic events; they are man's share in these events." The most important role in establishing the connection was played by the king, and in ancient oriental thought the "divine kingship" was the integrating link between human society and the world of cosmic forces in nature.[97]

The upshot of these interpretations of the conceptual world of the ancient Orient was to emphasize anew the distinctiveness and uniqueness of the Old Testament's basic viewpoints. In the naturalistic religions of the ancient world, the chief emphasis was upon the continuity of deity, nature, and man, and on the necessity for maintaining a natural harmony among them in order to preserve the prosperity and well-being of human society. The biblical point of view was radically dissimilar. In contrast to the ancient oriental

[96] See H. and H. A. Frankfort, "Myth and Reality," the initial essay in *The Intellectual Adventure of Ancient Man* (Chicago, 1946), pp. 3–26. (The quotation is from p. 6.)

[97] See, *ibid.*, pp. 7–8, 24–26. Cf. H. Frankfort, *Kingship and the Gods: A Study of Ancient Near Eastern Religion as the Integration of Society and Nature* (Chicago, 1948).

conception that gods and men were "in nature," the dominant tenet of Hebrew thought was the absolute transcendence of God.[98] Hence, the relationship of deity to human society was conceived in distinctly different terms. Whereas, in Egypt and Mesopotamia, "the mainspring of the acts, thoughts, and feelings of man was the conviction that the divine was immanent in nature, and nature intimately connected with society," so that the object of fertility cults and ritual myth patterns was to harmonize human society with the order of the universe; among the Hebrews, "the doctrine of a single, unconditioned, transcendent God rejected [these] time-honored values, proclaimed new ones, and postulated a metaphysical significance for history and for man's actions." [99]

The Frankforts' exposition of Israel's religious ideology and the discussions of Egyptian and Mesopotamian religion in the same volume create quite a different impression of the thought-world in each area from that made familiar by previous approaches to the data. Frankfort and his collaborators deal with large abstractions, which succeed in penetrating farther beneath the surface of religious ideology in the ancient Orient than the theories of the anthropologists or the historians of religion had done. Yet, because of this abstractness, the total picture is at fault in one important respect. It lacks historical movement; it communicates little sense of development in time. For the most part, the sections of this volume present the product of religious experience and thought as a static whole. The authors accentuate "man's awareness of his essential involvement in nature" as "the basic conception of ancient Near Eastern thought," and, while they recognize "within the scope of mythopoeic thought a great variety of attitudes and outlooks," they treat this variety, not as the product of successive changes in outlook, but as a characteristic "richness and diversity" within the

---

[98] See H. and H. A. Frankfort, "The Emancipation of Thought from Myth," the final essay in *The Intellectual Adventure of Ancient Man*, pp. 363-87.

[99] *Ibid.*, pp. 363, 373.

whole.[100] The exposition is not untrue to the spirit of what it expounds, but a feeling for the historical development of attitudes and conceptions is largely lacking.

The same was true of Albright's discussion of the unique Hebrew conception of deity—except that he did not merely neglect the developmental interpretation; he consciously rejected it. Finding the distinctiveness of the Hebrew conception of deity in its monotheistic character, and believing that this character had already been imparted to the conception by Moses himself, Albright described the Mosaic teaching as "a living tradition . . . which did not change in fundamentals from the time of Moses until the time of Christ." [101] He objected to the evolutionary interpretation of Israel's religion, since the "unilinear scheme" of development from the simple to the complex seemed to him to be "a bed of Procrustes" in the hands of the critics. "If a phenomenon seems too advanced for its traditional phase, it is assigned 'on internal evidence' to a later stage; if it appears too primitive, it is pushed back into an earlier phase, regardless of extrinsic evidence or lack of evidence." [102] Monotheism had been transferred by the critics from the Mosaic to the prophetic age "on internal evidence." Albright believed that "extrinsic evidence" made the monotheistic conception of deity quite at home in the age of Moses.

In view of the fact that "tendencies toward monotheism," such as the identification of lesser gods with the chief god in the pantheon, the ascription of universal functions to the chief gods, and the mass identification of the gods of one pantheon with those of another, were part and parcel of the intellectual atmosphere of the Near East in the second millennium B.C., it seemed entirely possible to Albright that one endowed with religious genius should

[100] *Ibid.*, p. 364.
[101] *From the Stone Age to Christianity*, p. 309.
[102] *Ibid.*, p. 50.

have drawn the "empirically logical" conclusion that all the phenomena of nature were governed by one universal God.

We should expect [he said] that Israelite monotheism would come into existence in an age when monotheistic tendencies were evident in other parts of the ancient world, and not at a time [such as the eighth century] when no such movements can be traced. Now, it is precisely between 1500 and 1200 B.C., i.e., in the Mosaic age, that we find the closest approach to monotheism in the ancient Gentile world.[103]

Albright acknowledged that "all of the monotheistic tendencies so far described remained partial or ineffective"; [104] but he maintained—and most scholars agree—that monotheism was attained by the fourteenth century in Egypt in the cult associated with the name of the heretic king, Akhenaten. "In its full, though brief, development it appears as a true solar monotheism. . . . In the famous Hymn to the Aten . . . we find that the Aten is explicitly addressed as 'the only god, beside whom there is no other,' . . . as creator of everything, lord of the universe, including the most distant lands." [105]

Albright did not mean to imply that Moses borrowed his monotheism directly from Egypt or any other oriental source. He argued that Moses created his own monotheism under the stimulus of suggestive ideas tending in that direction, which were "in the air," so to speak, throughout the ancient Orient. "Owing to the absence of direct documentation," it was impossible to determine just what Moses learned in Egypt; but ideas which he "may well have" acquired there included "the concept of the god who is sole creator of everything . . . ; the concept of a single god . . .; recognition of the necessarily international, cosmic dominion of the reigning deity." [106] These ideas had added up to "monotheism" in the cult

---

[103] *Archaeology of Palestine and the Bible,* (New York, 1932, rev. ed., 1935) p. 163. Cf. *From the Stone Age to Christianity,* pp. 164-65.

[104] *Ibid.,* p. 165.

[105] *Ibid.,* p. 167.

[106] *Ibid.,* p. 206.

of Akhenaten—ephemerally; they did so again, Albright believed, in the cult established by Moses. But the particular combination which Moses made of these ideas was so far superior to anything that had gone before, that it was essentially a new creation. Albright called it a "mutation," an "abrupt break with the past," similar to the new beginnings that were made in Christianity, Islam, and Buddhism.[107]

That Albright had demonstrated the general possibility of Mosaic monotheism can be granted. He encountered difficulties, however, in attempting to describe the specific content of Moses' teaching.[108] As he himself recognized, "we are handicapped in dealing with this subject by the fact that all our literary sources are relatively late, . . . we must therefore depend upon a tradition which was long transmitted orally." [109] But, taking seriously the idea that the literary sources frequently preserved authentic traditions from much earlier times, he proceeded to derive the content of "the religion of Moses" from the character of early Yahwism as indicated in the oldest documents. He found evidence that the Israelites had always regarded their God as creator of all; that they believed his power to be universal, not restricted to their nation or territory; that their conception of God was thoroughly and consistently anthropomorphic,[110] in contrast to the bewildering variety of forms in which Egyptian and Mesopotamian gods were conceived and the "disconcerting fashion" in which they changed their forms; and that, finally, the worship of Yahweh was completely aniconic, images or representations of the deity in visual and

---

[107] See, ibid., p. 86. Albright's conception of an abrupt break with the past has been echoed by G. Ernest Wright, The Old Testament against Its Environment (Chicago, 1950).

[108] See op. cit., pp. 196–207.

[109] Ibid., p. 196.

[110] But see Johannes Hempel's study of "Die Grenzen des Anthropomorphismus Jahwes im Alten Testament," ZAW, LVII (1939), 75–85.

tangible form being "foreign to its spirit from the beginning." [111] This "rough picture of what Yahwism was like in the eleventh century B.C." Albright believed gave the clue to the essential elements which Moses had imparted to the religion of Israel. True, as T. J. Meek asserted, "there is no assurance that Moses taught any of them . . . because we do not have enough verifiable information about Moses to know exactly what he did teach";[112] but because the "tradition" was "so well attested by different pentateuchal documents, and so congruent with our independent knowledge of the religious development of the Near East in the late second millennium B.C.," Albright was convinced of "its essential historicity." [113]

With Albright's judgment that Moses was the real founder of Israel's religion no one will quarrel. Moreover, for his description of the essential content of the Mosaic conception of deity one can only be grateful, for it brought out a richness and depth in the founder's conception which had not been apparent in critical estimates of his role in the history of religion. But Albright's characterization of Mosaic religion as "monotheistic" has been questioned by others at its most essential point: the belief in "the existence of only one God." It is the one term in his definition which the critics believe was not "well attested" by "tradition." From this point of view it was not enough to have shown that Mosaic monotheism was possible in the Late Bronze Age; what was required was a demonstration that Moses had actually taught the doctrine. Albright was not able to show that Moses ever stated the doctrine as explicitly as the Hymn to the Aten stated it. "Thou shalt have no other gods before me" is not quite the equivalent of "the only god beside whom there is no other."

---

[111] Cf. Robert H. Pfeiffer's detailed study, "Images of Yahweh," *JBL*, XLV (1926), 211–22, which came to the conclusion that no images of Yahweh ever existed.

[112] "Monotheism and the Religion of Israel," *JBL*, LXI (1942), 34.

[113] *Archaeology and the Religion of Israel*, p. 96.

That Moses had an exalted conception of his God as a universal deity who ruled all nature Albright had made sufficiently plain. That was his essential contribution to the clarification of Old Testament religious ideology. But that Moses' exalted conception of God included the specific rejection of all other gods was not demonstrable in "the absence of direct documentation." For Albright, the rejection was implicit in the Mosaic conception; Moses had no need to state it explicitly.[114] For those, however, who read the Old Testament records from a critical point of view the silence of the records on this point was crucial.[115] "The belief that there is only one god is monotheism . . . no matter how the nature of God is conceived," but "that Moses and his followers were actually monotheists [in this sense] remains to be proved."[116] What Albright had accomplished was not proof of the existence of monotheism in the time of Moses but an enrichment of the understanding of Moses' conception of his deity, the one God whom Israel was to worship, whether other gods existed or not.

To insist, as Albright insisted, that Mosaic religion was monotheistic from the beginning was to lose the essential insight into its subsequent history which Ernst Sellin had contributed many years before. Sellin had also believed that, "since the days of Moses, the Old Testament belief in God was something new in the circle of ancient oriental religions," and that, while "ancient oriental conceptions were obviously made use of in order to clarify the conception of deity, . . . a completely new conception was introduced into the midst of the old ones: the teaching, the belief, the conviction that this highest God . . . was a spiritual, ethical, holy personality standing above all nature and history."[117] But Sellin had

---

[114] Cf. *Archaeology and the Religion of Israel*, p. 177.

[115] Cf. the discussion above, chap. III, pp. 101–2.

[116] Millar Burrows, in a review of Albright's *Archaeology and the Religion of Israel*, in the *Jewish Quarterly Review*, XXXIII (1942-43), pp. 475–76.

[117] *Die alttestamentliche Religion im Rahmen der andern altorientalischen* (Leipzig, 1908), pp. 59, 69.

made clear that this belief was not strict monotheism; it was "only incipient" monotheism. It was the germ from which the prophets developed the full content of the monotheistic conception of deity.[118] This view of the matter had the advantage of preserving a historical point of view in the interpretation of the data while recognizing such facts as Albright made much of.

Albright disregarded the developmental character of Old Testament history in favor of the unity of tradition which the records themselves imply existed from the beginning. But to do so is to forget that this unity was imposed upon the materials of history. Albright explains "divergences from basic historical fact" as "due to the nature of oral tradition, to the vicissitudes of written transmission, and to honest but erroneous combinations on the part of the Israelite and Jewish scholars." [119] As far as the explanation goes, it is correct; but it overlooks the much more significant factor of interpretation of the traditional data by those scholars in accordance with their own philosophy of history. The traditions of the Old Testament are not so much historical traditions as theological interpretations of the past.[120] "The accuracy of the history and the truth of the interpretation must not be confused." [121]

Archaeology has without doubt increased the historical value of the Old Testament records in many particulars. It has enhanced the general "historicity" of the patriarchal narratives; it has given support to the biblical account of the conquest under Joshua; and it has increased the probability that many minor portions of the records, formerly considered late and untrustworthy traditions, reflect authentic historical conditions. Not least of all, even Albright's interpretation of Moses' distinctive achievement in the

[118] Cf. H. H. Rowley, "The Antiquity of Israelite Monotheism," in *Expository Times*, LXI (1949-50), 333-38; and "The Growth of Monotheism," in his *Rediscovery of the Old Testament* (Philadelphia, 1946), chap. V.
[119] *Archaeology and the Religion of Israel*, p. 176.
[120] See above, chap. III, pp. 102-3.
[121] Millar Burrows, *What Mean These Stones?*, p. 5.

realm of religious ideology derived some enrichment of conception from being placed against the conceptual background of the ancient Near East as revealed by archaeological source materials. However, such results must not be allowed to obscure the fact that the apparent unity of tradition in the Old Testament does not reflect a historical reality but a philosophy of history.

Further enrichment of the details of Israel's historical experience can be expected from the renewal of archaeological exploration in the Near East since the end of World War II.[122] But with all the additions to the empirical evidence that may be made, it is to be hoped that scholarship will retain the new appreciation of the importance of interpreting the data which was born of intensive study of the previously accumulated materials. Interpretation, however, will be fruitful only in so far as it avoids subjective "frames of reference," on the one hand, and merely technical analysis of the archaeological materials, on the other. It must combine the technical results of archaeological research with the historical insights of the other significant approaches to biblical research.

ADDITIONAL NOTE

The most important find in Palestine in recent years was the discovery of a number of ancient Hebrew and Aramaic scrolls in a cave at Ain Fashkha near the Dead Sea. The scrolls include a complete text of the book of Isaiah in what is now the oldest existing Hebrew manuscript of a biblical book, a commentary on the book of Habakkuk, a "Sectarian Document," and some fragments of various other books of the Old Testament. On the basis of paleography and the evidence of the late Hellenistic jars in which the scrolls

---

[122] The Mesopotamian background of Hebrew law, for instance, has been further illuminated by the discovery of parts of two law codes older than that of Hammurabi, containing some of the social and economic laws and the early legal precedents upon which the Babylonian code was based. See Francis R. Steele, "The Lipit-Ishtar Law Code," *American Journal of Archaeology*, LI (1947), 158–64; "The Code of Lipit-Ishtar," *ibid.*, LII (1948), 425–50; Albrecht Goetze, "The Laws of Eshnunna Discovered at Tell Harmal," *Sumer*, IV (1948), 63–102. For the connections between these laws and the code of Hammurabi, see Goetze, "Mesopotamian Laws and the Historian," *JAOS*, LXIX (1949), 115–20.

were stored, they have been dated in the second and first centuries B.C. In the field of textual criticism these scrolls have great importance, for they provide material for extensive linguistic studies which promise to enrich the history of the Hebrew language considerably. The fact that the text of the Isaiah scroll is substantially in agreement with the Massoretic text is evidence that the standardization of the Hebrew text took place earlier than had formerly been supposed. See Millar Burrows, "The Newly Discovered Jerusalem Scrolls, II: The Contents and Significance of the Manuscripts," *Biblical Archaeologist*, XI (1948), 57–61; Lankester Harding, "The Dead Sea Scrolls," *PEQ*, 1949, pp. 112–16; R. de Vaux, "La grotte des manuscrits hébreux," *Revue biblique*, LVI (1949), 586–609; and "A propos des manuscrits de la Mer Morte," *ibid.*, LVII (1950), 417–29; B. J. Roberts, "The Jerusalem Scrolls," *ZAW*, LXII (1949–50), 224–45. Publication of the texts was begun with the volume edited by Millar Burrows, *The Dead Sea Scrolls of St. Mark's Monastery, I: The Isaiah Manuscript and the Habakkuk Commentary* (New Haven, 1950). See also A. Dupont-Sommer, *The Dead Sea Scrolls* (Oxford, 1952).

Another group of scrolls from the same cache is described by H. L. Ginsberg, "The Hebrew University Scrolls from the Sectarian Cache," *BASOR*, CXII (1948), 19–23, and Frank M. Cross, Jr., "The Newly Discovered Scrolls in the Hebrew University Museum in Jerusalem," *Biblical Archaeologist*, XII (1949), 36–46. A preliminary discussion of their contents, with publication of portions of the texts, was presented by E. L. Sukenik in *Megillot Genuzot* [in Hebrew] (Jerusalem, 1948).

VII

The Theological Approach to the Old Testament

Of all the important trends in Old Testament studies, the one which has given rise to the most vigorous discussion is the recent rebirth of Old Testament theology. For about a generation after Wellhausen had substituted the study of Israel's religious history for the study of Old Testament religious doctrine, systematic theology practically disappeared from the field. The last important work of a systematic nature was A. B. Davidson's discussion of Old Testament theology.[1] The works which came after it for a quarter of a century described the evolution of the historical religion rather than the content of its teachings.[2] Not until the twenties of the present century did a theological interpretation of the Old Testament data again interest scholars of standing in the field.[3] Then, slowly at first, but gathering momentum as the implications of the new approach awakened interest, the discussion of theological problems took on increasing importance, until in the last decade it predominated over the discussion of other problems.[4]

---

[1] *The Theology of the Old Testament* (Edinburgh, 1904).

[2] There were, however, a few brief manuals which successfully presented the religious ideas of the Old Testament, such as H. Wheeler Robinson's *The Religious Ideas of the Old Testament* (London, 1913), Albert C. Knudson's *The Religious Teaching of the Old Testament* (New York, 1918), and Charles F. Burney's *Outlines of Old Testament Theology* (Oxford, 1920).

[3] The first of the new systematic studies was Eduard König's *Theologie des Alten Testaments* (Stuttgart, 1922).

[4] See James D. Smart, "The Death and Rebirth of Old Testament Theology," *Journal of Religion*, XXIII (1943), 1–11, 125–36; William A. Irwin, "The Reviving Theology of the Old Testament," *ibid.*, XXV (1945), 235–46; Norman W. Porteous, "Old Testament Theology," in H. H. Rowley (ed.), *The Old Testament and Modern Study* (Oxford, 1951), pp. 311–44.

The Rebirth of Theology in Germany

The school of Wellhausen and his followers had reacted vigorously against the theologizing of a former generation. They objected to the practice of interpreting the Old Testament in terms of conceptions drawn from the doctrinal system of the New Testament. The idea that the Old Testament was but the preparation for the New they gave up as a guiding principle of interpretation. So also they rejected as inadmissible the supranaturalistic explanation of history. Not subjective traditions but empirical data were to be the basic materials for reconstructing the history of Old Testament religion. The critics, therefore, approached the Old Testament as a collection of historical sources and saw their task as a search for historical facts, from which were to be drawn only such conclusions as the facts indicated. They did not deny the prerogative of faith to make its own valuation of the evidence, but they regarded the terms in which such a valuation would be made as outside the scope of objective historical analysis. Religious devotion was here transmuted into intellectual enterprise.

Some theologians, like Oehler, Dillmann, and Schultz, had tried to compromise with the historical approach by giving "a historical presentation of revealed religion during the period of its growth." [5] But critical scholars ignored the possibility of rewriting theology from a historical standpoint, concerning themselves rather with the task of describing the evolution of Israel's religion. The resulting expositions of Old Testament religious history varied, of course, according to the extent of each author's commitment to the "scientific" point of view. A thorough historicist like Bernhard Stade presented Israel's religious history in terms of gradual growth

---

[5] Gustav F. Oehler, *Theologie des Alten Testaments* (3d ed., Stuttgart, 1891); August Dillmann, *Handbuch der alttestamentlichen Theologie* (Leipzig, 1895); Hermann Schultz, *Alttestamentliche Theologie: die Offenbarungsreligion auf ihrer vorchristlichen Entwicklungsstufe* (4th rev. ed., Göttingen, 1889); English translation: *Old Testament Theology* (Edinburgh, 1892). The quotation is from Schultz, *op. cit.*, p. 1.

from simple, primitive beginnings to a highly complex stage at the end.[6] On the other hand, a somewhat conservative scholar like Ernst Sellin, who gave due consideration to the critical analysis of the Pentateuch, nevertheless maintained the importance of the Mosaic era as the period of origins and put less emphasis on the later appearance of important religious conceptions.[7] Most typical, however, was the work of Rudolf Smend who, in a thorough study of the manifold religious conceptions in the Old Testament, eschewed a theological classification of the basic ideas and portrayed the development of Old Testament religion entirely in relation to the history of Israel.[8] This was the characteristic approach of most of the scholarly surveys of Old Testament religion until after the first World War.

Then, about the time when critical scholars themselves began to make modifications in the theories and conclusions of the Wellhausen system, dissatisfaction with the "objective" approach came to be expressed more and more frequently. Examination of the Old Testament writings by the same methods as were used in the study of other ancient books did not seem to result in an interpretation that gave significant meaning to these writings. The critical reconstruction of Old Testament religious history, setting forth as it did the ideas of the Old Testament only in relation to the circumstances from which they arose, made the viewpoints of the biblical writers simply an expression of an ancient way of life and the embodiment of a particular historic culture. It did not interpret them in terms that gave them universal validity as the expression of general principles. To those who were aware that the

---

[6] *Geschichte des Volkes Israel* (2 vols., Berlin, 1887–88); *Biblische Theologie des Alten Testaments, I: Die Religion Israels und die Entstehung des Judentums* (Tübingen, 1905).

[7] *Beiträge zur israelitischen und jüdischen Religionsgeschichte* (2 vols., Leipzig, 1896–97); *Die alttestamentliche Religion im Rahmen der andern altorientalischen* (Leipzig, 1908). See above, chap. III, pp. 106–7.

[8] *Lehrbuch der alttestamentlichen Religionsgeschichte* (Freiburg, 1893; 2d rev. ed., 1899).

importance of the Bible in human history was not due to the accuracy with which it reflected the viewpoints of an ancient culture, but to the permanent significance of its most basic ideas, the emphasis on descriptive fact rather than normative principle seemed like "mere antiquarianism." Even when the results of critical study were accepted as scientifically correct, the feeling remained that the real value of the Old Testament, as essentially religious in content and point of view, had somehow been missed.[9]

A change of emphasis, therefore, seemed to be called for in Old Testament studies. It was not enough to determine the course of the religious history, or even to analyze the viewpoints of the authors who interpreted the history. Both types of investigation, it seemed to some, were pointless unless they were undertaken with a view toward helping to explain the abiding truth of the Old Testament. Scholarship, that is, was meaningless if it remained entirely objective. It must not simply describe but interpret in terms of universal principles. And so there arose a demand for an approach to the Old Testament that would give it more substantial meaning than had been supplied by "objective" criticism. Without denying that the historical approach had its place in Old Testament studies, yet insisting that it had its limitations, scholars began asking for "elucidation of the specifically religious values" of the Old Testament in a systematic rather than historical form.[10] An approach that would do justice to what the Old Testament said about such basic concepts as God, man, and salvation offered a better way of arriving at the permanent significance of the Old Testament writings than historical investigation of their origin in a particular milieu. Not a history of ideas, merely, such as the

[9] Thus the point of view once expressed by Hermann Gunkel (see above, chap. IV, p. 122), but disregarded by the dominant scholarship of the day, was gradually being adopted—in this case, without his technique of literary appreciation.
[10] See Rudolf Kittel, "Die Zukunft der alttestamentlichen Wissenschaft," ZAW, XXXIX (1921), 84–99.

"religio-historical" school presented, but an exposition of their theological significance was desired.[11]

This demand for a new "theology of the Old Testament" claimed to be no mere revival of an older orthodoxy. It differed from conservative reaction in that it accepted the necessity of criticism. But it desired to supplement the critical history of Old Testament religion with a description of the ideological content. It was convinced that the Old Testament not only contained material of value as history but also conveyed a message concerning the ultimate meaning of history. Events reported in the Old Testament writings had not been included simply for the sake of their historical significance; they were made parts of a general scheme of history which had a significance beyond that of the particular events. As some scholars expressed it, the Old Testament was a "revelation" of the meaning of history, communicated progressively through the historical experience of a people. This way of looking at it was not quite the same as the orthodox view that the Old Testament writings were themselves an "inspired revelation," but it meant that those writings were to be taken seriously as the written record of a revelation in history. In form and completeness the "revelation" was conditioned by the human factors involved in making the record, so that there was some reason for studying its literary history. But the content of the revelation—the interpretation of the meaning of history which it embodied—was a subject for study even more important than the literary means by which it had been communicated.

For a Christian theologian there was an additional reason for taking the Old Testament record of revelation seriously. The content of the revelation had an "over-meaning" for him who saw it as part of a larger scheme of history which had its climax in the

[11] See Carl Steuernagel, "Alttestamentliche Theologie und alttestamentliche Religionsgeschichte," in Karl Budde (ed.), *Vom Alten Testament* (Marti Festschrift; Giessen, 1925), pp. 266–73.

New Testament. To the Christian theologian the Old Testament documents were meaningful not only in their original context but also in the context of later interpretation. Their deepest significance came from their relationship to the "final" revelation of the meaning of history given in the New Testament documents. By itself, the Old Testament revelation was not complete. But interpreted in the light of the New Testament revelation, its full meaning became clear. The new theology, therefore, did not content itself with the systematic description of theological conceptions in the Old Testament, nor with an analysis of the prophetic "revelation through history" which formed the general background of the Old Testament. It also sought an interpretation in terms of the Christocentric philosophy of history.

But such a program for a theology of the Old Testament, undertaken by scholars who recognized the necessity for historical criticism, and who often themselves had functioned as critics, raised the problem of the proper relationship between the original significance of an Old Testament passage and the "over-meaning" which Christian interpretation gave to it. If the latter was to be taken as the "true" meaning of the passage in relation to the sumtotal of revelation, how could the original meaning be related to it without resorting to an outmoded type of allegorical interpretation? The problem did not go unrecognized by those scholars who became interested in theological interpretation. Otto Eissfeldt discussed it in an important paper that seemed to offer a practicable solution.[12] Drawing the distinction between historical method and theological interpretation quite clearly, he suggested that both be recognized as legitimate, each in its own sphere, but that the two be kept strictly apart to operate on different planes. Knowledge of the historical movement was necessary to an understanding of the development of ideas in the Old Testament, but the eyes of faith

---

[12] "Israelitisch-jüdische Religionsgeschichte und alttestamentliche Theologie," ZAW, XLIV (1926), 1-12.

were also needed to read the revelation of eternal truth in those ideas. Knowledge and faith together were necessary for an adequate appreciation of the meaning of the Old Testament. The two planes of apprehension were parallel lines that never met except in the Infinite, but they could exist side by side in the same person. Thus Eissfeldt was arguing for the cultivation of two independent disciplines simultaneously, the one dealing objectively with the varied phenomena of Old Testament religion in such a way that scholars of all faiths might agree on the results, the other presenting in systematic form the fundamental meaning of the Old Testament for the confessional group to which the scholar belonged.[13]

But, if Old Testament theology were permitted to become a confessional matter, the historical approach might soon seem unimportant; the theologian might find himself more and more studying the Scriptures simply for "proof texts" to support the particular viewpoint of his religious community. Such a return to an outmoded method of theology was not what the new theologians had in mind. Eissfeldt had performed a service by at least making clear the nature of the problem. However, the proper scope of theological study and the proper method of interpreting the theology of the Old Testament needed more precise definition.

The next suggestion came from Walther Eichrodt, who was soon to be recognized as one of the most important theologians of the Old Testament. Instead of divorcing the historical method from theological interpretation, as Eissfeldt had done, Eichrodt maintained that a fruitful combination of the two was possible.[14] He assumed that the chief task of the theologian was to penetrate to the very essence of Old Testament religion and throw light upon the inner structure of its theological system. Hence he advocated the addition of a systematic method of describing theo-

[13] Cf. Gerhard von Rad, "Sensus Scripturae Sacrae duplex?", *Theologische Blätter*, XV (1936), 30-34.

[14] See his article, "Hat die alttestamentliche Theologie noch selbständige Bedeutung innerhalb der alttestamentlichen Wissenschaft?", *ZAW*, XLVII (1929), 83-91.

logical concepts to the usual historical approach to the data. The function of historical method was to provide the factual data regarding the development of Old Testament religion. The function of theology was to explain the permanently significant ideas that appeared in the religion. Accordingly, Eichrodt suggested that the Old Testament scholar, as historian, trace the stages in the growth of religious ideas and, as theologian, make a cross section through the historical process to bring out the interrelationships between the basic notions that constituted the essence of Old Testament religion. Such a method went beyond the descriptive possibilities inherent in historical criticism, without going so far as Eissfeldt would find it necessary to go in expressing a judgment on the ultimate validity of the theological concepts thus examined.

This program for acquiring a deeper understanding of the nature of Old Testament religion by means of a systematic synthesis of its essential doctrines was carried out, a few years later, by Eichrodt himself in the first volume of his comprehensive study of Old Testament theology.[15] Aware that, in the past, most efforts had been devoted to describing the historical development of Old Testament beliefs, with little or no attention to the content of the faith as a unified whole, Eichrodt set himself the task of presenting the religion as an entity which had kept its basic unity throughout the various stages of its history. In the main, he set aside the historical method of presentation, believing that the organic wholeness of the Israelite faith could not be successfully communicated in terms of the growth of its various parts.[16] Instead, as a means of showing its essential unity, he chose to relate all its elements to a central idea which had been characteristic of it from the beginning. This central idea was that of the Covenant. In opposition to the literary critics who ascribed the covenant idea to the prophets,

---

[15] *Theologie des Alten Testaments* (3 vols., Leipzig, 1933–39).

[16] See the excellent statement of his position in his review of Fosdick's *Guide to Understanding the Bible*, in *JBL*, LXV (1946), 205–17. (The first four pages are a summary in English.)

Eichrodt maintained that it was Moses who had originated the idea when he founded the religion on a Covenant between God and the people. Since all other aspects of Old Testament religion, according to Eichrodt, were determined by or influenced by the idea of the Covenant, he argued that the religion had always had the same basic character.[17] It was a religion in which the national God was thought of as a universal deity who had chosen this people as his own and had made a compact with them. Yahweh was not simply the God of the kingdom of Israel; they were the people of the Kingdom of God. In other words, the idea of the "kingdom of God," founded upon a covenant relationship between the ruler and the ruled, had existed, in essence if not in fully developed form, in Israel's theology from the beginning.[18]

While Eichrodt thus endeavored to portray the basic unity of Old Testament religion, he did not entirely neglect the fact of historical development in Israel's beliefs. His synthetic treatment left room for description of the changes that took place within the organic whole. For example, he made allowance for the growth of Israel's law through successive generations, while insisting that the basic character of the legal principles had been determined at the start by the ethical and cultic regulations of the Covenant established by Moses. His consciousness of forward movement in the religion of Israel led Eichrodt to describe the Old Testament as pointing ultimately toward the New. With all its uniqueness of character, he believed, Old Testament religion found its final

[17] In the light of Eichrodt's thesis Paul Volz's early study of the work of Moses (see above, chap. III, p. 97) was justified in its conclusions. As a matter of fact, the new edition of Volz's *Mose und sein Werk* (Tübingen, 1932) was quite in keeping with the viewpoint of the new theology.

[18] Cf. Martin Buber's *Das Kommende, I: Das Königtum Gottes* (Berlin, 1932; 2d ed., 1936), another attempt to show that the conception of "the kingdom of God" was a historical reality in the earliest period of Israel's history. While not specifically theological, this work reflected the contemporary effort to comprehend the theological content of Old Testament religion. It sought to improve the critical approach to the Old Testament by making use of critical method, not in the service of literary history, but to enrich the history of ideas.

significance in the fulfillment represented by the religion of the New Testament. Thus, Eichrodt combined his use of the historical method in the systematic description of Old Testament theology with the conviction that the guiding principle of interpretation was to be found in the Christian view of the significance of the two Testaments.

A similar conviction gave the exposition of Old Testament theology published by Ernst Sellin in the same year[19] an even more systematic character. Believing that the task of the theologian was to expound the content of the religious thought-world common to both the Old and New Testaments, he treated the entire range of biblical teaching as an essential unity and presented its major conceptions in systematic form. Sellin avoided Eichrodt's technique of building his system around some single great conception, as being too simple for such a complex subject-matter; instead, he discussed the doctrines of biblical religion under various topical headings: God and his relation to the world, man and his sinful nature, divine judgment and salvation. Even so, his scheme did not embrace all the religious ideas of the Old Testament. His method was selective. For Sellin sought to include only those basic doctrines regarding God, man, and salvation which were common to the various parts of the Old Testament and which gave its theology a consistent unity. He was aware, of course, of the variety of religious phenomena which the history of Israel's religion reveals, and conscious of the transformation which ideas and institutions suffered in the course of time.[20] In passing, he described the more important changes that some of the ideas had undergone, but his work was meant to be more than a history of ideas. To Sellin, Old Testament study was "not merely a historical

---

[19] *Alttestamentliche Theologie auf religionsgeschichtlicher Grundlage, II: Theologie des Alten Testaments* (Leipzig, 1933; 2d ed., 1936).

[20] Cf. his first volume, *Alttestamentliche Theologie auf religionsgeschichtlicher Grundlage, I: Geschichte der israelitischen und jüdischen Religion* (Leipzig, 1933), discussed above, chap. III, pp. 115–16.

discipline but also a discipline in Christian theology." He therefore made it his aim to "identify and present systematically the
current of religion which flowed from the time of Moses towards
its fulfillment in the divine revelation in Jesus Christ." [21] In other
words, Sellin treated the Old Testament as the foreground of the
New, distinguishing the permanently significant from the ephem-
eral in its religious content by looking at it from the vantage point
of the gospel.[22]

The climax of the Christocentric interpretation of Old Testament theology was reached in Wilhelm Vischer's avowed attempt
to find Christian doctrine in the Old Testament.[23] Vischer did not
merely deal with the Old Testament as a record of revelation imparting certain truths regarding God, man, and salvation; he found
in it the basis for the New Testament revelation regarding Jesus
Christ. On the surface his method was historical: it began by setting the texts examined in their original contexts. But mainly his
technique was typological, for the historical meaning of the texts
was allegorized so as to serve as figures for their "eternal" meaning
in relation to the "universal" revelation to which both Testaments
testified. What Vischer presented was a system of theology regarded as eternal truth, having significance for men of all ages,
including the twentieth century. His book thus represented the
culmination of the movement to go beyond criticism to an apprehension of the permanent theological significance of the Old
Testament.[24]

[21] *Op. cit.*, I, ix; II, 3.

[22] In this respect, Sellin was following the theological program which Otto
Procksch had called for, in "Die Geschichte als Glaubensinhalt," *Neue kirchliche
Zeitschrift*, XXXVI (1925), 485–99; "Ziele und Grenzen der Exegese," *ibid.*, pp.
715–30; and which Procksch himself carried out in his posthumous *Theologie des
Alten Testaments* (Gütersloh, 1950).

[23] *Das Christuszeugnis des Alten Testaments*, Vol. I (Leipzig, 1934; 2d ed.,
Munich, 1935); English translation: *The Witness of the Old Testament to Christ*
(London, 1949); Vol. II (Zurich, 1942). Cf. his *Die Bedeutung des Alten Testa-
ments für das christliche Leben* (Zurich, 1938).

[24] For a review of the "new theology" in Germany, see Ludwig Köhler,

Whatever ultimate judgment may be expressed on the new theology in Germany, one cannot but admire the force with which the German theologians presented their case for the permanent significance of the Old Testament. At a time when in their own country the Old Testament was being rejected as a Jewish book of no importance to Christians, and Christian doctrine itself was being displaced by the mythology of an artificially revived paganism, these scholars spoke out with a strong voice in defense of the Old Testament's relevance to Christian theology and the importance of the latter to their contemporaries. It was perhaps no accident that the movement towards a revival of theology began in Germany, or that the discussion of its scope and purpose was carried on there with the greatest vigor.[25] The collapse of Germany's spiritual heritage after World War I led to a serious questioning of the whole optimistic, progressive liberalism which had gone before; and the rise of a ruthless, nihilistic movement that challenged the accepted standards of the contemporary world led to a searching re-examination of fundamentals in the religious sphere. If, however, the new theology had been simply the product of special circumstances in the unhappy experience of one country, its significance in history would have been limited. But that was not the whole story.

The Neo-Orthodox Movement in England and America

The "new theology" was not confined to Germany. Its influence soon spread to other countries, but it was received there with

---

"Alttestamentliche Theologie, I: Vorfragen und Gesamtdarstellungen," *Theologische Rundschau*, VII (1935), 255–76; VIII (1936), 55–69, 247–84.

[25] Cf. the discussion of the purpose of Old Testament theology by Hermann Strathmann, "Zum Ringen um das christliche Verständnis des Alten Testaments," *Theologische Blätter*, XV (1936), 257–60; Hans Hellbardt, "Die Auslegung des Alten Testaments als theologische Disziplin," *ibid.*, XVI (1937), 129–43; Walther Eichrodt, "Zur Frage der theologischen Exegese des Alten Testaments," *ibid.*, XVII (1938), 73–87; Friedrich Baumgärtel, "Zur Frage der theologischen Deutung des Alten Testaments," *Zeitschrift für systematische Theologie*, XV (1938), 136–62.

so ready a response as to indicate that the way had been prepared
for it by conditions independent of the particular situation obtaining in Germany. The burgeoning of the "neo-orthodox" movement in England and America was patently more than the reflection of German theological developments. Had not the impulse
first come from the Continent, the movement must have started
spontaneously.

For the whole Western world, in the period between the wars,
was questioning the liberal humanistic faith of the prewar period
and was calling for an explanation of reality deeper than the previous generation had been satisfied with. The calamities attending
economic disaster and political chaos in the interwar period destroyed the shallow optimism of belief in steady progress, by
showing that history was not a continuous upward march to better
levels of human living; and the breakdown of civilization in World
War II, under circumstances of unimagined evil, shook the foundations of man's confidence in his ability to create a decent world
after the pattern of his best thinking. Frustration, bewilderment, and
a sense of despair prepared the way for a new interest in doctrines
of salvation. Hence, the revival of a theology which promised a
more profound insight into the ultimate realities than was represented by the optimistic liberalism of the nineteenth century
awakened a responsive chord in the minds of religious thinkers
far beyond the country in which the revival originated.

The result was that the last fifteen years have seen the publication of a spate of books attempting to interpret the significance
of theology to a bewildered generation. Many of these books have
dealt specifically with Old Testament theology, with the avowed
purpose of showing that the Old Testament still has meaning in
the present day, in relation to the question of fundamentals which
the times have raised. The basic assumption was that the Bible was
the basis for any significant development in religious thinking. The
task of the interpreter was to make an intelligible restatement of

its abiding truths. It was also assumed that these truths would not be found in the realm of facts that historical criticism dealt with, but in the more profound realm of ideas which had a permanent significance.[26] Hence, most recent books in the sphere of religion have sought to make clear the "abiding significance of the Bible" and the "relevance of its message" to the present day.

H. H. Rowley, for example, in one of the more influential books of this sort,[27] expounded the view that the Bible was rich in religious resources for readers who were willing to discover its timeless truths and abiding values.[28] He stressed the importance of going beyond scholarship and cultivating a spiritual receptivity to the basic message which the Bible conveyed. What that message was became the subject of a number of other books which attempted to assess the permanent significance of the religious ideas of the Old Testament. G. Ernest Wright dealt with the basic theological conceptions in Israel's faith in such a way as to emphasize their permanent validity.[29] W. A. L. Elmslie surveyed the content of Old Testament religion with a view to showing its significance for the modern world.[30] Of the same general nature were several works restricted to the prophets, designed to show the timelessness of their messages when applied to the problems and perplexities of the present day.[31] Characteristic of all these works

[26] See Stanley A. Cook, *The Old Testament: A Reinterpretation* (London, 1936), pp. 214–24; cf. his *The "Truth" of the Bible* (London, 1938).

[27] *The Relevance of the Bible* (London, 1942; New York, 1944). Cf. his *Rediscovery of the Old Testament* (London, 1946; Philadelphia, 1946), which endeavored to show that the Old Testament contained a message of importance not only for its own day but for all subsequent ages.

[28] Another book with the same general viewpoint was Frank Glenn Lankard's *The Bible Speaks to Our Generation* (New York, 1941). See also Wyatt A. Smart's *Still the Bible Speaks* (New York, 1948).

[29] *The Challenge of Israel's Faith* (Chicago, 1944).

[30] *How Came Our Faith: A Study of the Religion of Israel and Its Significance for the Modern World* (New York, 1949).

[31] R. B. Y. Scott, *The Relevance of the Prophets* (New York, 1944); Raymond Calkins, *The Modern Message of the Minor Prophets* (New York, 1947); George Pratt Baker, *The Witness of the Prophets* (New York, 1948).

was the combination of a certain respect for the historical method with emphasis on theological interpretation of the subject matter. The methodology for such interpretation was outlined by Hubert Cunliffe-Jones in a work that was typical of the "neo-orthodox" viewpoint.[32] He advocated first determining the original meaning of a passage of Scripture in relation to its own time, then examining its meaning in relation to the whole historical movement covered by the Old and New Testaments, and finally establishing its significance as part of the witness to the absolute revelation in Jesus Christ. For the final "authority of the biblical revelation" was its witness to the gospel.[33]

The conviction that the "relevance" of the Old Testament to modern needs could best be demonstrated in terms of the Christocentric view was the controlling principle of neo-orthodox interpretation. In some books the emphasis was specifically on Old Testament history as the opening portion of the great drama of history which centered around and received its significance from the redemptive act of Jesus, the climactic point of all history.[34] In others the emphasis was more generally on the self-revelation of God in history and the challenge which knowledge of God's redemptive purpose offered to man to make a fitting response in moral action.[35] Sometimes both emphases were skillfully combined in a single work.[36] But, whatever the emphasis, the Old Testament was treated as an integral part of the total record of revelation.

[32] *The Authority of the Biblical Revelation* (London, 1945).

[33] Bernhard W. Anderson's *Rediscovering the Bible* (New York, 1951) is a reinterpretation of the whole of Bible history from this point of view.

[34] A modern restatement of this Christian philosophy of history was made by C. Harold Dodd in *History and the Gospel* (New York, 1938). Otto Piper gave a more extended interpretation of the doctrine in his *God in History* (New York, 1939). Cf. the more recent discussion by Oscar Cullmann, *Christ and Time* (Philadelphia, 1950).

[35] Cf. Cuthbert A. Simpson, *Revelation and Response in the Old Testament* (New York, 1947).

[36] E.g., H. Wheeler Robinson's *Redemption and Revelation in the Actuality of History* (London, 1942).

This unity of the two Testaments was made clear by the new, historical definition of "revelation" which the neo-orthodox theologians applied to the interpretation of the Old Testament. As H. Wheeler Robinson explained it,[37] revelation was not the imparting of abstract truth regarding the moral imperatives of life, but rather the gradual revelation to mankind, through concrete experiences in life itself, of a pattern of divine purpose steadily unfolding in history.[38] It was possible, therefore, to interpret the whole process of historical revelation in the Old Testament as leading inevitably up to a climax in the New Testament, without which it would not have been complete.[39] The theologian could do justice to the notion of historical development by describing the various stages in man's gradual apprehension of the divine plan, and at the same time fulfill his theological task by showing how the Old Testament stages derived their ultimate significance from their relationship to the final stage of revelation in the New Testament.[40]

The strength of the neo-orthodox commitment to this type of interpretation reflected the conviction that, in biblical studies, a purely objective approach that failed to assume the truth of the biblical revelation defeated its own purpose. Scientific detachment was tantamount to divorcing oneself from the possibility of understanding. No merely intellectual understanding was adequate; there must be the kind of "spiritual" appreciation that comes from

[37] See his essay, "The Philosophy of Revelation," in the volume edited by himself, *Record and Revelation* (Oxford, 1938), pp. 303–20.

[38] The most recent restatement of this theory of revelation and the necessity for a historical approach to its interpretation is by C. Harold Dodd in *The Bible Today* (Cambridge, 1946; New York, 1947), chap. V: "History as Revelation."

[39] See, *ibid.*, p. 70. Cf. G. Ernest Wright, "Interpreting the Old Testament," *Theology Today*, III (1946), 176–91; and Robert C. Dentan, *Preface to Old Testament Theology* (New Haven, 1950).

[40] A good example of the results achieved by this method of interpretation is the conclusion reached by W. J. Phythian-Adams in his two volumes, *The Call of Israel* (London, 1934) and *The Fulness of Israel* (Oxford, 1938). The author, maintaining that the conceptions of a chosen people and a church of God in the Old and New Testaments were essentially the same, argued that "sacred history" thus revealed the existence from the beginning of a divine purpose working towards its consummation in the body of chosen ones represented by the church of God.

personal commitment as well.[41] As Hermann Schultz had once maintained, "Old Testament religion, like any other spiritual movement, reveals itself in all its truth only to one who has an inner experience of its essence." [42] Essentially, this viewpoint marked a return to the position of Luther, who had emphasized the importance of the subjective experience of sympathetic understanding as the prerequisite to exegesis. In modern times, it was the position of Wilhelm Dilthey, who stressed the necessity, for the highest type of interpretation, of an inner understanding of the writings to be interpreted.[43]

This return to a basic principle of the Reformation was justified by the fact that it led to results in Old Testament studies that were not attainable with objective criticism. It enabled the interpreter to point out significant values in the Old Testament which would enrich the religious life of present-day readers. Since revelation was the substance of what had been learned regarding God's purpose working out through the ages, and since the experience through which man had gained his knowledge of the divine plan had awakened in inspired individuals an insight into the meaning of existence so overpowering that it demanded a response in the form of action transforming their lives,[44] contact with the Old Testament figures whose understanding of life had been thus enriched provided a guide and an inspiration to a meaningful type of life.

Such a practically useful "revelation" gave the Old Testament what the neo-orthodox theologian meant by its "authority." It was not the "infallible external authority" of a revealed Scripture; for revelation, in the modern sense, did not mean the divine communication of abstract truths and principles. It was the inherent authority of truth learned from history and through experience.[45]

[41] See H. Wheeler Robinson, *Inspiration and Revelation in the Old Testament* (Oxford, 1946), pp. 281–82.
[42] *Alttestamentliche Theologie* (5th ed., 1896), p. 8.
[43] See Herbert A. Hodges, *Wilhelm Dilthey: An Introduction* (London, 1944).
[44] See C. H. Dodd, *The Bible Today*, pp. 57–58.
[45] See C. H. Dodd, *The Authority of the Bible* (London, 1929; rev. ed., 1948).

Current Problems of Old Testament Theology

(1)

In spite of similarities in purpose and aim between the work of the German theologians and of the neo-orthodox scholars in England and America, there was a significant difference in method which indicated the presence of an unresolved question regarding the nature of theological studies. Both groups had forcefully re-emphasized the view, forgotten by the historical critics, that the Old Testament had a meaning or message which gave it significance beyond the historical significance it had as a national literature. But each group set about examining that message and communicating it to the modern reader in its own way. The German theologians favored a systematic presentation,[46] which resulted in an interpretation setting forth the Old Testament "revelation" as a unified system of belief that had essentially the same significance throughout the historical period covered by the Old Testament. The neo-orthodox scholars, however, emphasized the historical character of the revelation and gave a dynamic interpretation which set forth "revelation" as a continuing process culminating in the New Testament. The unresolved question implicit here was the question of what constituted a proper method of Old Testament theology. The one group treated the revelation embodied in the Old Testament as an interrelated complex of theological conceptions which could be expounded systematically; the other group combined descriptive exposition of the content of revelation with an historical explanation of the nature of revelation. In current theological thinking this question of treatment is still under discussion, for both methods of exposition have produced results that showed they had value.

The virtue of the systematic method was that it eliminated the worst fault of the critical approach to Old Testament religion,

---

[46] "Systematic" is here used simply in the sense of "organized" according to some logical system of classification, not in the sense—which the word often had in the older German theological works—of organized according to some doctrinal system or some philosophical principle of valuation.

namely, the genetic interpretation which treated the early stages as necessarily primitive. The systematic theologian, starting from the premise that Old Testament religion had embraced a substantial body of belief from the beginning, could appreciate the possibility that conceptions which sounded primitive to the critical historian might very well be symbolic expressions of fully developed thought. For example, the anthropomorphic conception of God need not be explained away as a typical thought-pattern of an undeveloped theology; it could be taken as the expression of a rather profound understanding of God's essential nature.[47] In other words, the systematic theologian brought out a richness or depth of conception that was characteristic of Old Testament theology in all periods of its history.

On the other hand, the virtue of the neo-orthodox approach to theology was that it gave a clearer understanding of the nature of revelation. H. Wheeler Robinson's exposition of the process of revelation as the learning of God's will through a series of historical events, the meaning of which individuals of prophetic insight interpreted to the people,[48] for the first time provided a successful synthesis of the historical point of view with theological exposition. Robinson succeeded in finding the logical nexus between historical method and theological interpretation which Eissfeldt had been unable to perceive. Thus neo-orthodoxy made good its claim of taking the results of historical criticism seriously while, at the same time, going beyond them to the consideration of that which was more significant than the historical facts.

Another virtue of this combined technique, which made it superior to the systematic method of presentation, was that it avoided some of the difficulties inherent in the systematic method. Eichrodt admittedly had found it difficult to make Old Testament

[47] See the discussion of the divine "pathos" (feeling) in Abraham Heschel, *Die Prophetie* (Krakow, 1936), pp. 130–52.
[48] The latest (and most brilliant) statement of his views was *Inspiration and Revelation in the Old Testament* (Oxford, 1946).

theology amenable to systematic treatment, and Sellin had simply left out of consideration certain features of Old Testament religion, such as the national-cultic elements, which were not relevant to his scheme.[49] But recognizing the principle of historical development in Old Testament religion made it possible to treat all the data in perspective. As a matter of fact, Wheeler Robinson's definition of revelation as a process taking place through actual historical situations made it imperative to know the true course of events in Israel's history, as a foundation for the exposition of the revelation contained in the Old Testament.[50]

On the basis of such a historical interpretation of revelation, neo-orthodoxy was able to fulfill its practical purpose of making the Old Testament relevant to modern needs. C. H. Dodd, for example, in the volume already referred to,[51] presented an interpretation of the ultimate meaning of biblical history which was more acceptable to the modern mind than the theological systems of the older orthodoxy. Defining the nature of revelation as the insight of inspired individuals into the moral significance of life experiences, always followed by an ethical response on their part which changed the subsequent course of human events, Dodd described the course of "sacred history" as a succession of experiences through which prophetic personalities acquired an ever deeper understanding of the divine will. The climax came in the perfect response to the divine intention made in the life of Jesus, who demonstrated in the

---

[49] The only German theologian who rejected the systematic method in favor of a historical presentation was Ludwig Köhler, whose *Theologie des Alten Testaments* (Tübingen, 1936; 3d ed., 1953) was based on the viewpoint that revelation in the Old Testament was not a single body of doctrine but a progressive disclosure of many truths which gave great variety to the theological content of the Old Testament. His work, therefore, was more a historical survey of all the religious ideas and conceptions that had theological significance in Israel's religion than a selective treatment, as Sellin's had been, of those which had significance from the Christian standpoint.

[50] From this point of view, Vischer's tendency to allegorize everything in Old Testament history was open to criticism on the ground that he did not take seriously the biblical revelation mediated in and through history.

[51] *The Bible Today* (New York, 1947).

fullest manner what God willed life to be.[52] The value of this revelation for modern man was that the experiences through which it had been mediated and the meaning which those experiences had communicated could be shared through intimate acquaintance with the record of revelation left by those who had experienced it.

The present tendency of theological thinking, at least in England and America, is towards enriching this personal experience of the content of revelation contained in the Old Testament record.

(2)

Contemporary with the two major groups of theological works already discussed, there was another class of studies, the mere existence of which implied a second unresolved question—in this case, concerning the scope of Old Testament theology. In general, these works were devoted to the scholarly analysis of the content of Old Testament theology without reference to the doctrinal significance which the conceptions under inquiry might have in relation to the New Testament. Even so, such academic studies also contributed something of value to the understanding of the theological content of the Old Testament.

There were, for example, a number of competent studies in small compass of the characteristic doctrines or of particular conceptions.[53] One of the best was Norman H. Snaith's analysis of the distinctive ideas of the Old Testament.[54] Endeavoring to interpret the Old Testament by explaining its own categories of thought, Snaith showed how different the Hebrew modes of thought were from the Greek modes which influenced later Christian theology. Other studies of this nature, but with a more restricted scope, either described the historical development of particular doctrines[55] or

---

[52] See, *ibid.*, p. 111.

[53] See, e.g., H. Wheeler Robinson, "The Characteristic Doctrines," in the volume edited by him, *Record and Revelation* (Oxford, 1938), pp. 321–48.

[54] *The Distinctive Ideas of the Old Testament* (London, 1944).

[55] Wilhelm and Hans Moeller, in their *Biblische Theologie des Alten Testaments in heilsgeschichtlicher Entwicklung* (Zurich, 1938), with great erudition traced the

gave a semantic analysis of the connotations of certain conceptions.[56] Occasionally, both methods were combined to give an illuminating insight into the content of some specific idea.[57]

In addition to such monographs as these, a few comprehensive surveys of Old Testament theology were written from the "objective" standpoint. Millar Burrows published a manual of the theological conceptions of the Bible[58] which was essentially an exposition of the leading ideas of biblical religion in their original context and meaning. While avoiding the rigidity of the systematic method of presentation, it gave a synoptic view of the basic content of theology in the Old and New Testaments, collecting together all the pertinent data regarding the major conceptions and ideas, with a wealth of references to the texts themselves. A similar survey by Otto J. Baab[59] was the first work in English since Davidson's to call itself a "Theology of the Old Testament." Presenting the usual topics treated in a systematic theology, it recognized the fact of historical development in Old Testament religion and interpreted the major doctrines, for the most part, from within the Old Testament itself. The author emphasized, however, the importance of "religious experience" for the proper understanding of the doctrines.

The increasing concern of academic scholars with the theology of the Old Testament was also illustrated by the appearance of certain studies of the theological content of such documents as

doctrine of redemption through the Old Testament, coming to the conclusion that the Old Testament doctrine was not essentially different from that of the New.

[56] Good examples of the latter are J. J. Stamm, *Erlösen und Vergeben im Alten Testament: eine begriffsgeschichtliche Untersuchung* (Bern, 1940); Aubrey R. Johnson, *The One and the Many in the Israelitic Conception of God* (Cardiff, 1942); Gunnar Ostborn, *Tora in the Old Testament: A Semantic Study* (Lund, 1945).

[57] See, e.g., Johannes Lindblom, "Zur Frage der Eigenart der alttestamentlichen Religion," in Paul Volz (ed.), *Werden und Wesen des Alten Testaments* (Berlin, 1936), pp. 128–37 (for the most part an analysis of the Old Testament conception of God); H. H. Rowley, *The Biblical Doctrine of Election* (London, 1950).

[58] *An Outline of Biblical Theology* (Philadelphia, 1946).

[59] *The Theology of the Old Testament* (Nashville, 1949).

were formerly studied only from the literary or historical point of view. Gerhard von Rad added to his literary analysis of the Priestly Document[60] a short but penetrating discussion of its most important theological conceptions. Setting forth the view that the document was not primarily historical in character (as the critics had described it) but essentially theological in intention, von Rad endeavored to summarize the richness as well as the unity of its theological ideas. In similar fashion, Herbert Breit added to his form-critical analysis of the literary category of prophetic oratory, as exemplified in the book of Deuteronomy, a study of the theological content of the book;[61] while Martin Noth, seeking to prove that the origin of the Pentateuchal law was cultic rather than political, demonstrated the theological character of its thought-content.[62]

Scholarly inquiries of this sort showed how the influence of the theological approach was extending into other areas of Old Testament studies and was bringing home to non-theological scholars the fact that the Old Testament writings had never been intended by their authors as historical documents in the usual sense, but were literary works composed for theological and didactic purposes. However, the "objective" character of these inquiries, which generally restricted the scope of Old Testament theology to the data of the Old Testament itself, left open the question whether the relation of the Old Testament's "message" to New Testament theology could legitimately be left out of consideration.

Actually, there were a number of studies based on the assumption that the Old Testament "message" had a significance of its own, sufficiently important and meaningful to be examined in its own terms. The basic viewpoint from which the Old Testament writers had interpreted historical events and their own experience of life was presented by Christopher R. North[63] as a "philosophy of

[60] *Die Priesterschrift im Hexateuch* (Stuttgart, 1934).
[61] *Die Predigt der Deuteronomisten* (Munich, 1933).
[62] *Die Gesetze im Pentateuch: ihre Voraussetzungen und ihr Sinn* (Halle, 1940).
[63] *The Old Testament Interpretation of History* (London, 1946).

history" which itself had exerted a profound influence on the religious thinking of subsequent ages. It was not, to be sure, a unified point of view underlying all the Old Testament writings equally. It was rather the product of Israel's thinkers over the course of a long history of religious experience. But, in setting forth the various stages in their interpretation of Israel's history, North showed how they succeeded in developing a basic viewpoint that gave meaning to history.[64]

The dominant trend of theological studies in the present day is toward something more comprehensive than simply explaining the characteristic doctrines or the "philosophy of history" in the Old Testament. Nevertheless, such academic studies also served a useful purpose. They helped to give a depth to the interpretation of the Old Testament which the historical criticism of Wellhausen's generation had failed to achieve. The latter had missed the key to the real significance of the Old Testament when they disregarded the theological viewpoints of the writers in favor of a search for the "facts of history" behind their interpretations. To have persuaded a new generation of scholars of the paramount importance of the theology of the Old Testament, irrespective of the particular approach to its interpretation, is the real achievement of the theological movements described in this chapter. Although the current problems of method and scope have not been fully clarified, theology has become the most important field of Old Testament scholarship.

[64] Cf. Artur Weiser, *Glaube und Geschichte im Alten Testament* (Stuttgart, 1931); Jakob Obersteiner, *Biblische Sinndeutung der Geschichte* (Graz, 1946).

Summary

During the nineteenth century a changed conception of the nature of sacred Scripture resulted in a new attitude toward the study of the Old Testament. The liberal, humanistic spirit of the times had substituted for the traditional conception of a timeless revelation from God the view that the Old Testament was the product of man's attempt over many centuries to express his apprehension of moral and spiritual values in life. The task of the scholar, accordingly, was not to expound the theological doctrines of the Old Testament as the basis for faith, but to explain the origins and nature of the writings as significant products of religious experience. This conception of the scholar's task led to some highly interesting results that gave an entirely different view of the course of "sacred history" from the traditional one. It also opened the way for the use of secular techniques of investigation, so that the Old Testament came to be studied not only as a significant religious literature (to which the techniques of literary studies and the history of religions were applied), but also as a document of ancient history, a sourcebook for anthropological data, and a textbook of social history. The result was a broadening of the scope of Old Testament studies which, if it did not deepen the scholar's understanding of the religious significance of the Old Testament, considerably enlarged his knowledge of the nature of its contents and the character of the history portrayed therein.

The higher criticism had, first of all, shown the value of beginning with the analysis of biblical literature by the same methods as were applied to any other ancient literature (chap. I, sec. 1). Patient examination of the internal evidence in order to determine the literary structure of a book served to establish the basic facts regarding the composition of the Old Testament writings. Three major strands of literary material were found interwoven in the Hexateuch, with the core of Deuteronomy forming a separate block of material. This general classification—the result of purely literary criticism—has remained the common property of scholarship ever since, in spite of uncertainties and revisions in the textual scope of the "documents." The literary analysis was supplemented by historical criticism, which endeavored to discover the history of the biblical literature. Comparison of the contents of the major "documents," particularly of their ritual codes, with each other revealed an apparent development from the simple to the complex, which, when related to the major periods of Israel's history by comparison with the data of the historical books, established the historical sequence of the "documents" and their codes. In general outline, these results of historical criticism have also retained their validity in subsequent research.

The success of such criticism suggested the possibility of reconstructing the religious history of Israel on the basis of the history of its literature (chap. I, sec. 2). But here criticism left the field of objective analysis and entered that of subjective interpretation. Herder's humanistic appreciation of religious experience as a natural manifestation of human culture supplied the basic viewpoint. When it was combined, through Vatke, with the Hegelian notion of evolutionary development, the result was a description of Israel's religious history as having proceeded through three important stages: the stage of primitive worship exemplified by the popular religion of the early Israelites, the stage of ethical consciousness expressed by prophetic religion, and the final stage of formalized worship embodied in the ceremonial religion of the Law. Concurrently, there was a progressive evolution of religious institutions, beginning with practices of a spontaneous and natural character, developing through the reforms initiated by the prophets, and culminating in the formal practices of the ritual law. The general implication of this reconstruction was that the most characteristic features of Old Testament religion were late developments growing out of an evolutionary process from lower to higher forms.

This view of Israel's religious history was apparently strengthened by the results of the anthropological approach to biblical data (chap. II, secs. 1, 3). Since anthropologists approached the study of a historical religion through comparisons with the customs and rites of primitive peoples, they tended to interpret the early form of the religion entirely in terms of primitive belief and practice, and to find survivals of ancient customs and primitive thought beneath the surface of the later forms. Sir James G. Frazer's attempt to explore the Old Testament for traces of primitive superstition was designed primarily to recover the earliest beliefs of Israel's ancestors in prehistoric times, but the general effect of his interpretation was to make the religion of the historical period seem much more primitive than it probably had been. By concentrating attention on the antecedent primitive stages and shifting the focus of interest from the later development of the religion to the origin of particular conceptions and practices, the anthropological approach threw light upon many a feature of Hebrew religion that had previously been misunderstood and provided some insight into the nature of the nomadic religion with which the critical school had assumed the Hebrews entered Palestine. But it also led to undue emphasis on mere survivals and exaggeration of their significance, to the neglect of the more distinctive features of the religion. Moreover, it introduced into the Old Testament primitive modes of thought which may have once been effective in the thinking of the Israelites but which were no longer living conceptions in the religion at its height. However, the implication that there was little room for mature religious conceptions in the early periods bolstered the view of Israel's religious history established by the critical school.

After the initial success of the critical view in scholarly circles, a reaction very slowly but definitely set in against some of the conclusions which it had popularized (chap. I, secs. 3, 4). The younger members of the Wellhausen school made new analyses of the scope and structure of the major documents and came to the conclusion that the documents contained more or less material of varying age. No "document" was a unified literary work from the hand of a single author; it was the product of a literary school, which had added to the original work by inserting new matter in the style of the original, or old materials which had survived independently. The Priestly Law, in particular, was recognized as containing a good deal of old material from former ages of Israel's history, in spite of the late date of its final redaction. Fragments of older legislation and originally separate groups of laws were found embedded in the Priestly Code; it was not an entirely new creation of a late epoch but largely a compilation and codification of old laws and customs.

This tendency of the critics themselves to find an early origin for some portions of the documents which they dated comparatively late was paralleled by the attempt of the form critics to get behind the documents to the ultimate sources of the literature (chap. IV, secs. 1–3)—an attempt which led to the conclusion that the typical forms of Old Testament literature had originated at an early date (in the oral stage) and had attained the height of their development before the Exile. The narrative portions of the Pentateuch, for example, had acquired their characteristic features while they were current as popular tales, which had been taken up into the written "documents" without loss of their essential characteristics through the harmonizing tendencies of the redactors. Religious poetry, as exemplified by the psalms, showed conventions of literary form fixed by long usage; Gunkel and Mowinckel concluded that the psalms were the product of centuries of liturgical use in the religious life of the pre-exilic community. Various small groups of laws were now regarded as having been independent entities at one time. Each was a distinct unit dealing with a single subject and formulated in a single style. If, as some argued, the rituals covered by these laws were even older than the prescriptions, the latter may have grown out of early formulations of the cultic regulations transmitted orally. The most significant aspect of this supplementation of critical theory was its emphasis on the antiquity of the various types of legal formulation and its interpretation of the law as a living, growing thing.

The conclusion that many of the literary types were of great antiquity gave a new perspective to the history of Old Testament literature. Wellhausen and his school had made the postexilic period the most creative age in Old Testament history by attributing the bulk of the law, the majority of the psalms, and the whole of the wisdom literature to its priests, its poets, and its sages. But they had failed to appreciate how much of this literature had sprung from the life of the people in earlier times. Now much of the ritual law, various types of psalms, and some of the proverbial sayings were restored to what seemed like their natural place in the monarchical period, when Israel's culture was most vigorous.

This shift in critical theory was significant, not so much in itself, as because of its effect on the general interpretation of the history of Israel's religion. Much more was involved than the technical questions of the literary history of the Old Testament. The correctness of Wellhausen's evolutionary scheme of Old Testament religious history depended on whether he had been right in making the ritual law follow the prophetic movement. Now the theory that the Priestly Code was not all as late as its final compilation but contained prescriptions that were pre-exilic, both in substance and in form, made it possible to reconsider the history of the cultus and of ritual legislation among the Israelites. The anthropological investigations of Robertson Smith had shown that ritual had never been unimportant among the Semites, and that there had always been an anxious care to observe the rules of ritual correctly (chap. II, sec. 2). Similarly, Mowinckel's emphasis on the cultic factor in the religion of which the psalms were an expression counteracted the critical school's disparagement of the place of ritual in the religious life of the Israelites (chap. II, sec. 4). Not all that was vital and progressive in their religion was to be attributed to the prophets. In the early periods the cultus, too, expressed a genuinely religious spirit. Robertson Smith had also pointed out that the rituals embodied certain fundamental beliefs which were long significant in the religious life of the people and, in seeking the original meanings of the rituals, had found that certain ideas labeled "priestly" by the critical school (such as holiness and atonement) had early origins.

The reaction against making the roots of Israel's religion too primitive and against making the development of its distinctive features too late received its greatest strength from the researches of the religio-historical school (chap. III, secs. 1–2). Instead of the problems of the scope and structure of Old Testament documents, the new school devoted itself to the more fundamental problems of the provenance and historical development of the basic ideas in the documents. The older generation of critics, relying almost exclusively upon data within the Old Testament, had been unable to give a proper evaluation to the influence of external factors upon the development of biblical ideas. But the opening up of the ancient oriental world by archaeological discovery in the Near East, which revealed the larger milieu of Old Testament history, suggested that the development of Old Testament ideas could be truly understood only after a comparative study with ideas current in the external environment. The addition of the comparative method to historical criticism gave this school a better understanding of the history of ideas in the Old Testament and a clearer insight into their origins than the Wellhausen school had attained.

The sum-total of the extrabiblical evidence indicated that Israel's participation in the cultural heritage of the ancient Orient was richer than had been supposed before comparative studies in this field began. There were affinities and interrelationships between the cultural areas of the ancient Orient, and Israel was intimately involved in them. The fact that highly developed religious systems had preceded the beginning of Old Testament religion suggested that the early Hebrews were familiar with an initial stock of religious conceptions more complex than the critical school had thought possible. Mythological motifs relating to the creation of the world, ethical ideals affecting traditional codes of behavior, and universalistic conceptions of deity existed in the environment in which the fundamental beliefs of Israel had taken form. Hence, the religio-historical school drew the conclusion that certain ideas once thought to have been late went back to much older prototypes and had their beginnings in conceptions extant in the oriental world. Comparative studies pointed to several kinds of influence from the ancient oriental world that could have affected the thinking of the Israelites in the early stages of their history. There was seldom proof of actual derivation from an older culture at an early age, but the existence of analogies to certain Old Testament beliefs in the more mature cultures which had preceded Israel's was a strong argument against the assumption that such beliefs were necessarily late, just because they were embodied in late sources.

In the light of the external parallels, the Old Testament no longer appeared isolated from its environment. But, rather than diminishing the originality of Old Testament religion, comparative studies helped to emphasize the greatness of its achievement when properly interpreted. For they showed that, although partial imitations and even direct borrowings took place, the new context into which the derivative elements were transplanted quite often infused them with a different conceptual content. There were parallels, for example, to Babylonian hymns in the phraseology of the penitential psalms; but the religious experience which they expressed showed that the original magical notions had been displaced by a more highly developed conception of divine power. There was likewise more that was new than derived in Israel's ethical monotheism. Tendencies toward monotheism had existed in the ancient oriental environment, but the Mosaic conception of the uniqueness of God and the ethical substance attached to the conception by the prophetic interpretation of the covenant idea were Israel's own achievements.

The originality with which Israel had made use of the oriental heritage indicated that caution must be exercised in applying the new material to the interpretation of Israel's religion. S. H. Hooke's attempt to identify remnants of the ritual myth pattern of the ancient East in the pre-exilic New Year's rituals and to trace certain of its elements down into the thinking of very late times ignored the more distinctive features of Old Testament religion, in preoccupation with the similarities between Hebrew ritual and the practice of the oriental environment (chap. II, sec. 5). At its best, the religio-historical method did not content itself with the search for comparative analogies but supplemented it with a study of the history of ideas within the Old Testament.

The really significant aspect of Old Testament religious history was not its relationship to the oriental milieu, but the long struggle by which Israel's distinctive achievement had been accomplished —the struggle between the popular religion of the masses, affected as they were by the beliefs and practices of their environment, and the higher level of religious thinking of their spiritual leaders. The distinctive ideas of Israel's religion, as Rudolf Kittel and Ernst Sellin explained (chap. III, sec. 4), grew out of the tension between a spiritual minority, who endeavored to build upon the creative beginnings made by Moses, and the mass of the people, among whom the Yahweh cult had been assimilated to the Baal worship of the

Canaanites. The masses in Israel, unable to grasp the transcendence of the Mosaic conception of deity or the full implications of the Covenant idea, retained certain notions allied with the nature worship of their neighbors down to the period of the Exile. But a deeper understanding of the religion of Moses was kept alive in certain circles until it triumphed over the religion of the masses through the work of the great prophets.

The histories of Kittel and Sellin showed how the balance of interpretation was being restored after its swing to an extreme in the Wellhausen school. Whereas radical historical criticism had brought the basic ideas of the Old Testament down into relatively late periods, these scholars maintained that the ethical principles and the conception of deity taught by the prophets were not entirely new manifestations of religious insight but the heightening of original features of Israel's religion. The spirit of loyalty to the God of Israel alone and to the ethical ideal represented by the covenant reached full expression only in the ethical monotheism of the prophets, but the basic ideas could be traced back in germinal form to the very beginnings of the religion in Moses' time. Thus, as it became increasingly certain that much of importance in Old Testament religion was of greater antiquity than Wellhausen had concluded, scholarly opinion was gradually abandoning his strictly evolutionary view of its history.

Support for the new view of Old Testament religious history came from the sociological approach to the interpretation of the data (chap. V). Max Weber had emphasized the importance of the Covenant idea at the very beginning of Israel's history, and subsequent developments were interpreted by him and his successors in terms of the tension between Israel's attempt to maintain and develop its own spiritual and ethical ideals and the tendency to adapt them to new conditions in the land of Canaan. But, being an investigation of the social factors which influenced the formation and development of religion, sociology interpreted the conflict as a struggle for supremacy between the "nomadic ideal" of social organization, with its emphasis on the equality of all members of the group, and the "civilized" institutions of the Canaanites, which sanctioned class distinctions. Yet the sociological interpretation of the conflict supported the conclusion of the religious historians regarding the antiquity of the basic principles of Israel's religion. It showed how the prophets, in criticizing the social situation of their times, harked back to the ethical principles implicit in the Covenant idea. Essentially, according to this interpretation, what the prophets accomplished was to hammer out a higher meaning for the equalitarian ethics of the early nomadic society.

The most significant aspect of the new view of Israel's religious history was its emphasis on the continuity of certain basic features in Israel's religion. This emphasis was underscored by the most recent phase of anthropological research (chap. II, sec. 5). When the latter abandoned its initial attempt to construct a general scheme of cultural development for all mankind and turned instead to the study of specific culture-areas and the analysis of the "pattern" characteristic of each area, it set aside the unilinear evolutionary view of religious history and generated a new understanding of the unity within the complexity of the history of a particular culture. More important than the accidents of historical change were the basic characteristics which gave the culture a recognizable character throughout its history. From this point of view, the attempts of Robertson Smith and of Kittel and Sellin to describe Old Testament history as a progressive development which, at the same time, preserved elements fundamental to Israel's religion from the beginning were more illuminating than the evolutionary approach of the critical school; for they concentrated attention on those features which were continuously significant in Israel's religious development instead of the changing minutiae of successive periods. Such was also the value of Pedersen's attempt to describe the chief concepts of Hebrew psychology (chap. II, sec.

4). Although he slighted the factor of development too often, his description emphasized the continuity of basic thought-forms in Israel's thinking. The same may be said of recent attempts to find the continuously significant in the conceptual history of the ancient Near East (chap. VI, sec. 4). In spite of distortions resulting from too great a neglect of the historical principle, such surveys as those of Albright and Frankfort help greatly to increase a sense of what was most permanently important in the religious cultures with which they deal.

A similar point of view has affected recent interpretation of the history of Old Testament literature (chap. IV, sec. 4). The emphasis upon continuity within the diversity of religious history is paralleled by an appreciation of the unity within the complexity of religious literature. Literary historians have come to realize that more important than the details of minute analysis are the larger unities which bind the literature together. In the critical study of the Old Testament, accordingly, there has been a shift from preoccupation with "the smallest literary units" to a new interest in the factors which brought the various elements together into extensive, meaningful compositions. This trend is illustrated by an increasing appreciation of the work of the "creative writers" who imposed a unifying point of view upon the separate fragments of oral tradition and written record, in line with their religious philosophy of history. The literary achievements of the Yahwist and the "Deuteronomist" historian and the purposeful character of their histories are now being recognized, with the result that scholars are aware of a unity in these writings which had not been apparent to the critical school.

This recognition of the unifying religious motivation of Hebrew historiography was the most important development in Old Testament criticism of the last two decades. Form criticism's insight into the shaping influence of theological perspectives upon the more extensive "documents" in the Old Testament paralleled, if indeed it was not inspired by, the emphasis of contemporary theologians on the unity of purpose to be found in the Old Testament writings (chap. VII). The form critics showed that the guiding principles of the Old Testament writers were usually theological rather than historical; they illustrated in detail how the religious conceptions of the writers influenced their interpretation of historical events. The theologians were concerned with the more general task of explaining the over-all religious philosophy of history which gave unity of viewpoint to the varied writings of the Old Testament.

Some theologians, particularly the Germans, favored a systematic presentation (chap. VII, sec. 1), which treated the theology of the Old Testament as a unified complex of conceptions having essentially the same significance throughout the period covered by the Old Testament. Others, particularly the "neo-orthodox" group in England and America (chap. VII, sec. 2), emphasized more strongly the historical character of the "revelation" embodied in the Old Testament. The former brought out the richness of conception that characterized Old Testament theology in all periods of its history. The latter combined theological exposition with the historical point of view to give a clearer understanding of the nature of revelation as a continuing process taking place in and through history. Both groups, however, treated the Old Testament as an incomplete revelation which received its fulfillment only in the New. The ultimate significance of its theological concepts they derived from the "final revelation" embodied in the Gospel.

During this latest phase in the history of Old Testament studies, even academic scholars devoted increasing attention to the theological content of the Scriptures (chap. VII, sec. 3). They analyzed the characteristic doctrines or particular conceptions, either from the standpoint of historical development or with a view to explaining the semantic connotations. Such scholars maintained their academic "objectivity" by making their interpretations from within the Old

Testament itself, without reference to the doctrinal significance of the various concepts in relation to the New Testament. But, by taking seriously the fact that the Old Testament had a theological content, they helped to give a depth to recent Old Testament interpretation which the historical criticism of Wellhausen's generation had failed to achieve.

The theologians, however, consciously and purposely went beyond "objective" scholarship to consider what for them was more important than a mere historical interpretation. As responsible members of the Christian community, they had the duty of expounding the ultimate meaning of the Scriptures with which they dealt. Their works, accordingly, were devoted to the practical purpose of making clear the "abiding significance of the Bible" and the "relevance of its message" to the present day.

Survey of Recent Literature

Horace D. Hummel

Subject Headings

SCOPE

It would be impossible, within the brief compass of this survey, to take note of all the titles published in the field of the Old Testament since Hahn's work appeared in 1954. With the exception of some noted variations, therefore, only those titles have been included that would fit within the categories employed by Hahn. Similarly, the survey does not include literature published before about 1954, when this work first appeared, except when mention of earlier literature appeared necessary in order to give a complete and continuous picture. The survey cannot claim exhaustiveness even for the English-speaking audience toward which it is oriented, but it does attempt to do some justice also to major foreign-language works.

Limitations of space precluded listing of complete bibliographical data; only such details were included as seemed important in characterizing the publication or in helping the reader to locate it for study or purchase.*

1. BIBLIOGRAPHICAL SURVEYS

The *Internationale Zeitschriftenschau für Bibelwissenschaft und Grenzgebiete*, published since 1951 at Düsseldorf, has long since established itself as an indispensable aid to the researcher in all aspects of biblical studies. It has not, however, displaced the *elenchus bibliographicus* of *Biblica*, which maintains its usefulness. Similarly, the *Bücherschau* and *Zeitschriftenschau* of virtually every recent number of the *Zeitschrift für die alttestamentliche Wissenschaft* (*ZAW*) cannot be ignored. In the more specialized but vital field of cuneiform studies, the *Keilschriftbibliographie* and other bibliographies in *Orientalia* are especially valuable. Nearly every recent volume of the *Theologische Rundschau* contains one or more survey or bibliographical articles, many of which also treat Old Testament subjects. The annual *Book List* of the British Society for Old Testament Study, formerly edited by H. H. Rowley and now by G. W. Anderson, has proved invaluable; the lists for 1946-56 were published together under the title *Eleven Years of Bible Bibliography*, ed. H. H. Rowley (Indian Hills, 1957).

* I wish to thank Professor Albert E. Glock of Concordia Teachers College, River Forest, Illinois, as well as other Old Testament colleagues, who preferred to remain anonymous, for reading this survey in manuscript and making many useful suggestions. Final responsibility for the contents lies, of course, with me.

A few other general surveys are worthy of note here: G. H. Davies, "Contemporary Religious Trends: The Old Testament," *ET*, 67 (1955), 3-7; G. W. Anderson, "Old Testament Survey 1939-1964," *ET*, 76 (1964), 9-14; J. M. T. Barton, "Roman Catholic Biblical Scholarship 1939-60," *Theology*, 63 (1960), 101-09; C. Cantanzaro, "Some Trends and Issues in Old Testament Studies," *Anglican Theological Review*, 44 (1962), 251-63; H. W. Hertzberg, "Zur neueren Auslegung des Alten Testaments," *ThLZ*, 83 (1956), 527-40; R. Rendtorff, "Zur neueren Auslegung des Alten Testaments," *Verkündigung und Forschung*, 1-2 (1957), 142-50; James Muilenburg, "Old Testament Scholarship: Fifty Years in Retrospect," *JBR*, 28 (1960), 173-81; and the companion article in the same issue (pp. 182-93); G. E. Wright, "Old Testament Scholarship in Prospect."

2. THE HISTORY OF INTERPRETATION

Interest in the history of biblical interpretation, especially in the rise of the historical-critical method, has continued high in the past decade. A major effort in this area (which would merit translation into English) was Hans-Joachim Kraus, *Geschichte der historisch-kritischen Erforschung des Alten Testaments von der Reformation bis zur Gegenwart* (Neukirchen, 1956); among major reviews of Kraus's work may be noted that by W. Baumgartner, "Eine alttestamentliche Forschungsgeschichte," *Theologische Rundschau*, 25 (1959), 93-110.

Much research continues to be expended on the nineteenth-century founders of modern biblical criticism. Simon J. de Vries, in "The Hexateuchal Criticism of Abraham Kuenen," *JBL*, 82 (1963), 31-57, attempts to demonstrate that Kuenen was really more important than Graf in the formation of the classical documentary hypothesis. Wellhausen's self-acknowledged dependence on Vatke is explored in detail by L. Perlitt, *Vatke und Wellhausen* (*BZAW*, 94; Berlin, 1965). A similar interest in philosophical presuppositions is seen by R. Smend in "De Wette und das Verhältnis zwischen historischer Bibelkritik und philosophischem System im 19. Jahrhundert," *TZ*, 14 (1958), 107-19. Reflecting contemporary interest in the "historical Moses" are two works that have attempted to trace the rise of the problem: Eva Osswald, *Das Bild des Mose in der kritischen alttestamentlichen Wissenschaft seit Julius Wellhausen* (Berlin, 1962), and R. Smend,

Das Mosebild von Heinrich Ewald bis Martin Noth ("Beiträge zur Geschichte der biblischen Exegese," 3; Tübingen, 1959).

Not surprisingly, Genesis (and especially chapters 1-3) has received its share of attention from the historians of exegesis. A significant contribution is that of M. Metzger, *Die Paradieserzählung: Die Geschichte ihrer Auslugung von J. Clericus bis M. L. de Wette* ("Abhandlungen zur Philosophie, Psychologie und Pädagogik," 16; Bonn, 1959). Of related interest is G. T. Armstrong, *Die Genesis in der Alten Kirche: Die drei Kirchenväter* ("Beiträge zur Geschichte der biblischen Hermeneutik" 4; Tübingen, 1962); an English translation of this work will be published shortly.

As the last title indicates, the interest in the history of interpretation, overlapping with the concern for hermeneutics, has by no means limited itself to the modern era but has extended back to include the entire Christian era (not to speak of Jewish exegesis and other related areas). There is not space here even to sketch the many contributions in those areas, but a few broader works of general interest on the history of interpretation may be mentioned: E. G. Kraeling, *The Old Testament Since the Reformation* (Philadelphia, 1955); R. M. Grant, *The Bible in the Church* (New York, 1948; rev., paperback ed., 1963, entitled *A Short History of the Interpretation of the Bible*). A reprint of F. Farrar's classic *History of Interpretation* (Bampton Lectures, 1885) has appeared (Grand Rapids, 1962). A significant study of the Old Testament canon of the early church is A. C. Sundberg's *The Old Testament of the Early Church* ("Harvard Theological Studies," 20; Cambridge, Mass., 1964). Two studies of the Old Testament as interpreted by the two major reformers should also be mentioned: Heinrich Bornkamm, *Luther und das Alte Testament* (Tübingen, 1948; to appear soon in translation), and H. H. Wolf, *Die Einheit des Bundes: Das Verhältnis von Altem und Neuem Testament bei Calvin* ("Beiträge zur Geschichte und Lehre der Reformierten Kirche," 10; Neukirchen, 1948).

Roman Catholic scholars, too, as they have come to look upon the historical-critical enterprise with increasing favor and have begun to participate in it, have devoted attention to the history of Roman Catholic biblical studies since the Reformation. Here we may note J. Steinmann, *Richard Simon et les origines de l'exégèse biblique* (Bruges, 1960); F. M. Braun, *The Work of Père Lagrange* (Milwaukee, 1963; trans. from the French by Richard Murphy); and L. A. Schökel, *Understanding Biblical Research* (New York, 1963; trans. from the German by P. McCord).

3. THE PENTATEUCH

Pentateuchal criticism, now as before, probably easily retains pride of place in Old Testament study. While the classical isolation of four main sources (JEDP) remains as close to an "assured result" as anything in the nineteenth century's critical heritage, it has never lacked critics or at least would-be revisers, nor does it today. As Hahn pointed out, Engnell and other champions of "oral tradition" achieved a certain modification of the hypothesis, but not its demolishment. Virtually all contemporary work in the Pentateuch along form-critical and tradition-historical lines (see these sections below) understands itself as continuing and completing the earlier critical labors, not as replacing them (although the older conclusions tend to be repeated somewhat more cautiously and conditionally than was once the case). Similarly, archaeological and other comparative materials have led to an increasing consensus that much of the substance in all four sources (even P!) must be quite early, regardless of the date of final composition. At the very least, the classical source-theory of the Pentateuch remains the best "working hypothesis" in sight, and it will be regarded as established until a better hypothesis appears—if ever.

The common contemporary attitude on the subject (and on some related issues outside the Pentateuch) is excellently summarized in John Bright's "Modern Study of Old Testament Literature" in G. E. Wright (ed.), *The Bible and the Ancient Near East: Essays in Honor of William Foxwell Albright* (Garden City, 1961), 13-31. Bright's essay should be read in conjunction with the one following it, which is of kindred spirit: "Biblical History in Transition," by G. E. Mendenhall (pp. 32-53); Mendenhall points to the limits of literary criticism as well as to the increasingly acknowledged need for more objective, external criteria. An older article, by J. C. Rylaarsdam, is still useful: "The Present Status of Pentateuchal Criticism," *JBR*, 22 (1954), 242-47.

Otto Eissfeldt provides an illuminating introductory discussion of Pentateuchal study in his article on Genesis in *IDB*, 2, 366-80. (The article was published in German, with some alterations and additions, under the title *Die Genesis der Genesis: Vom Werdegang des ersten Buches der Bible* [Tübingen, 1958]). S. Mowinckel's tireless pen has also entered the lists on this question: *Erwägungen zur Pentateuch Quellenfrage* (Oslo, 1964). (Mowinckel's contribution to the knotty critical problems of the books of Ezra and Nehemiah should also be noted in passing: *Studien zu dem Buch Ezra-Nehemiah* [Oslo, 1964]). W. F. Albright expresses himself on some aspects of the wider issue in "Jethro, Hobab and Reuel in Early Hebrew Tradition (with some Comments on the Origin of 'JE')," *CBQ*, 25 (1963), 1-11. A popular but stimulating treatment by H. Guthrie, Jr., may also be noted: *God and History in the Old Testament* (Greenwich, 1960).

The coolness of much Jewish scholarship, particularly of the older generation, toward the classical documentary hypothesis, especially in its more radical form, is well-known. It received cogent expression in the work of U. Cassuto, whose study of the subject (Jerusalem, 1941) was belatedly translated into English in 1961 under the title *The Documentary Hypothesis and the Composition of the Pentateuch* (trans. from the Hebrew by I. Abrahams). Cassuto's critique is repeated and applied in his two-volume work, also translated by Abrahams, *A Commentary on the Book of Genesis* (Hebrew original, Jerusalem, 1944), Vol. 1, *From Adam to Noah* (Jerusalem, 1961), Vol. 2, *From Noah to Abraham* (Jerusalem, 1964).

Strong arguments for an early date of P have been assembled in S. R. Külling, *Zur Datierung der 'Genesis-P-Stücke' namentlich des Kapitels Genesis XVII* (Kampen, 1964), which also includes an excellent survey of the history of this particular issue. In his *Penitence and Sacrifice in Early Israel Outside the Levitical Law* (Leiden, 1963), R. J. Thompson attempts to demolish one of the classical Wellhausenian supports for the lateness of P, viz., the alleged absence of penitential or expiatory notions in connection with sacrifice until the post-exilic period.

Other major areas of Pentateuchal criticism may best be considered below in connection with form-critical and tradition-historical issues, which is the form taken by most contemporary investigation.

4. TEXTUAL CRITICISM

In textual criticism, an area not covered in the original edition of this work, we note a vast amount of work in recent years. Much of the activity in this area has been spurred by the Dead Sea Scrolls (see section 18 below). In their light it now appears that we can in the main distinguish three recensions of the prototypal text (or the oral tradition behind it), represented by the Massoretic tradition, the Septuagint, and (in the case of the Pentateuch) the Samaritan text. None of these is automatically to be favored over the other, and sometimes all may be correct, because the prototype was apparently often longer than any of the later surviving recensions. This aspect of the significance of the Qumran scrolls is described by W. F. Albright, "New Light on Early Recensions of the Hebrew Bible," *BASOR*, 140 (1955), 27-33, and M. Greenberg, "The Stabilization of the Text of the Hebrew Bible, Reviewed in the Light of the Biblical Materials from the Judean Desert," *JAOS*, 76 (1956), 157-67. A somewhat more popular explanation of the situation is offered by W. F. Albright, together with D. N. Freedman, in "The Continuing Revolution in Biblical Research," *JBR*, 21 (1963), 110-13 (this article introduces *The Anchor Bible* under Albright's and Freedman's general editorship, in which efforts have been made to apply the new insights).

D. Barthélemy's recent full publication and analysis of a previously unknown revision of the Old Greek text on the basis of a proto-Massoretic text, a revision that was also the basis of Aquila's later recension and identical with the "Quinta" of Origen's Hexapla, will certainly force full-scale revisions of current histories of the Old Testament text. Barthélemy's study is entitled *Les devanciers d'Aquila: Première publication intégrale du texte des fragments du Dodéca-prophéton* (SVT, 10; Leiden, 1963). In its wake we already note F. M. Cross, "The History of the Biblical Text in the Light of Discoveries in the Judean Desert," *HTR*, 57 (1964), 281-99; and P. Skehan, "The Biblical Scrolls from Qumran and the Text of the Old Testament," *BA*, 28 (1965), 87-100.

Other helpful material includes E. Würthwein, *The Text of the Old Testament: An Introduction to Kittel-Kahle's Biblia Hebraica* (New York, 1957; trans. from the German by P. Ackroyd); H. M. Orlinsky, "The Textual Criticism of the Old Testament," in Wright (ed.), *The Bible and the Ancient Near East*, the second half of which was published in *JBL*, 77 (1959), 26-33, as a separate article under the title "Qumran and the Present State of Old Testament Text Studies: The Septuagint Text"; F. M. Cross, "The Development of the Jewish Scripts," Wright (ed.), *The Bible and the Ancient Near East*, 133-202, a companion article to Orlinsky's, but pioneering in the important field of paleography, which is increasingly being established on a firm scientific basis; B. Albrektson, *Studies in the Text and Theology of the Book of Lamentations; with a Critical Edition of the Peshitta Text* ("Studia Theologica Lundensia," 21; Lund, 1963); P. Skehan, "Qumran and the Present State of Old Testament Studies: The Masoretic Text," *JBL*, 78 (1959), 21-25; J. Coppens, "La critique textuelle de l'Ancien Testament: Solutions anciennes et données nouvelles," *ETL*, 36 (1960), 466-75; M. H. Goshen-Gottstein, "The History of the Bible-Text and Comparative Semitics: A Methodological Problem," *VT*, 7 (1957), 199-201. The second edition of P. E. Kahle's *The Cairo Geniza* (Oxford, 1959), climaxing a life's dedication to textual problems, also takes the Qumran discoveries into account. Nor should one overlook Kahle's history of modern Old Testament textual criticism, *Der hebräische Bibeltext seit Franz Delitzsch* (Stuttgart, 1961). D. R. Ap-Thomas' *A Primer of Old Testament Textual Criticism* (2nd ed., Oxford, 1965; scheduled to appear in "Facet Books—Biblical Series") should fill a great need for beginning students. F. W. Danker's *Multipurpose Tools for Bible Study* (St. Louis, 1960) contains excellent introductory articles on many aspects of biblical bibliography, including those involved in textual criticism.

Much work is also currently in progress on the publication of new texts themselves. In 1957 the British and Foreign Bible Society published N. H. Snaith's new edition of the Hebrew Bible (cf. Snaith's introductory article, "New Edition of the Hebrew Bible," *VT*, 7 [1957], 207-08). In Germany an entirely new edition of Kittel's *Biblia Hebraica* based on the Leningrad Codex is being prepared. At Hebrew University in Jerusalem Israeli scholars are busy at their project of publishing a new edition of the Hebrew Bible based on the famous Aleppo Codex which was virtually inaccessible until recently. Studies in connection with the project are published in the annual, *Textus*, of which Volume 1 (Jerusalem, 1960) is noteworthy because of the articles it contains explaining the background and scope of the project. Three volumes of A. Sperber's *The Bible in Aramaic* (Leiden, 1959 ff.) have already been published. A critical edition of the Peshitta is also in progress at Leiden under the sponsorship of the International Organization for the Study of the Old Testament with P.A.H. de Boer as editor-in-chief. Work continues on the Cambridge and Göttingen editions of the Septuagint. It is obvious that exciting days lie ahead in this field.

5. OLD TESTAMENT INTRODUCTIONS

In spite of uncertainty about the role of classical literary criticism, traditional types of introductions (or new editions and translations of older ones) have continued to appear. However, nearly all of them show the impact of the newer emphases, which we shall consider shortly. A compact but highly serviceable original product is G. W. Anderson, *A Critical Introduction to the Old Testament* ("Studies in Theology," 52; London, 1959). All the others are German works now available in English translation, but all the more influential for that reason. Less detailed and more popular, but generally comparable to Anderson's, is C. Kuhl, *The Old Testament: Its Origin and Composition* (Richmond, 1961; trans. by C. Herriott from a 1953 original). Much more detailed and thorough, and including brief treatments of the apocryphal and pseudepigraphical books as well, is A. Weiser's *The Old Testament: Its Formation and Development* (New York, 1961; trans. by D. Barton from the 4th ed., 1957; 1st ed., 1948). Largest and most authoritative of all works of this type is O. Eissfeldt's *Einleitung in das Alte Testament;* the third edition recently appeared in Germany (Tübingen, 1964) and an English translation has now appeared under the title *The Old Testament: An Introduction* (New York, 1965).

A number of more popular "introductions," apparently intended primarily as college texts, but usually very reliable and helpful, have appeared. Among the best we note B. W. Anderson, *Understanding the Old Testament* (Englewood Cliffs, 1957, with a new edition in preparation), which is both highly readable and unusually successful in combining historical, theological, and isagogical aspects. Very similar, but with more literary and less theological accent, is N. K. Gottwald, *A Light to the Nations* (New York, 1959). B. D. Napier, *Song of the Vineyard* (New York, 1962), and W. Harrelson, *Interpreting the Old Testament* (New York, 1964), relate themselves somewhat more directly to the canonical arrangement of books in the Old Testament. S. Sandmel, *The Hebrew Scriptures: An Introduction to Their Litera-*

ture and Religious Ideas (New York, 1963), provides an interesting treatment from the standpoint of liberal Judaism, while Peter Ellis, *The Men and the Message of the Old Testament* (Collegeville, 1963), is a good sample of Roman Catholic efforts of the same type.

6. OLD TESTAMENT SACRIFICE

It is very doubtful if it is possible any longer to speak of an "anthropological approach to the Old Testament" as such (Hahn's chapter 2). Not only has the idea of a uniform "primitivism" throughout the world fallen into disrepute, but increasing knowledge of the ancient Near Eastern world surrounding Israel, and indeed long before Israel came into existence, have made it scarcely possible even to describe Israel any longer as "primitive" in any meaningful sense. Furthermore, Barthian influence, especially, often made it more congenial to think of "revelation" and "theology" than of "religion."

In this context, it is particularly striking that so little further exploration has been made into the nature and meaning of sacrifice. The relative neglect of this area is all the more surprising because of the intense interest in other areas of Israel's cult. A few studies may, however, be noted: R. Schmid, *Das Bundesopfer in Israel: Wesen, Ursprung und Bedeutung der alttestamentlichen Schelamin* ("Studien zum Alten und Neuen Testament," 9; Munich, 1964); R. de Vaux, *Studies in Old Testament Sacrifice* (Cardiff, 1964; trans. from the French by J. Bourke and R. Potter; the material in this work is essentially the same as in the chapters dealing with sacrifice in de Vaux's *Ancient Israel: Its Life and Institutions* [New York, 1961]); R. J. Thompson, *Penitence and Sacrifice in Early Israel Outside the Levitical Law* (Leiden, 1963; noted in section 3 above); a satisfying popular treatment by H. Ringgren, *Sacrifice in the Bible* (New York, 1962); L. Moraldi, *Espiazione sacrificale e riti espiatori nell' ambiente biblico e nell' antico testamento* ("Analecta Biblica," 5; Rome, 1956); R. Rendtorff, *Studien zur Geschichte des Opfers im alten Israel* (Göttingen, 1953); K. Koch, *Die israelitische Sühneanschauung und ihre historischen Wandlungen* (Erlangen, 1956); J. B. Segal, *The Hebrew Passover* (London, 1963).

7. THE NATURE OF "HEBREW THOUGHT"

Perhaps the most important offshoot of the earlier anthropological interest has been the semi-theological interest in "Hebrew thought-forms" or the like. In this form (and sometimes with a generous assist from the vitalistic philosophy of Henri Bergson) Pedersen's great work, *Israel: Its Life and Culture* (London and Copenhagen, 1920 ff.), has retained much of its usefulness. W. F. Albright has contributed signally to clarification in this field by his insistence that biblical "logic" should be described as "empirical logic" and not as "prelogical," to which "protological" is to be preferred even when speaking of mythological cultures; see especially the second and third essays ("The Human Mind in Action: Magic, Science, and Religion" and "The Place of the Old Testament in the History of Thought") in Albright's *History, Archaeology, and Christian Humanism* (New York, 1964), pp. 62-100. Other major works in this field include T. Boman, *Hebrew Thought Compared with Greek* (Philadelphia, 1960; trans. from the German by J. Moreau); and C. Tresmontant, *A Study of Hebrew Thought* (New York, 1960; trans. from the French by M. Gibson). Related works include L. Köhler, *Hebrew Man: How He Looked, Lived, and Thought* (New York and Nashville, 1956; English translation of the 1953 original by P. Ackroyd); A. R. Johnson, *The Vitality of the Individual in the Thought of Ancient Israel* (2nd ed., Cardiff, 1964; 1st ed., 1949); E. Sutcliffe, "Effect as Purpose: A Study of Hebrew Thought Patterns," *Biblica*, 25 (1954), 320-27 A. McAllister, "Hebrew Language and Israelite Faith," *Int.*, 14 (1960), 421-32; B. Childs, *Myth and Reality in the Old Testament* ("Studies in Biblical Theology," 27; Naperville, 1960).

So significant has H. Wheeler Robinson's theory of a "corporate personality" concept been in all such discussions that the publication of the pacemaking essay (see Hahn's text, p. 71) as a separate pamphlet in America must also be hailed: *Corporate Personality in Ancient Israel* ("Facet Books—Biblical Series," 11; Philadelphia, 1964); the second half of the pamphlet contains a related essay of Robinson's, "The Group and the Individual in Israel," first published in E. Hughes (ed.), *The Individual in East and West* (London, 1957). See also G. E. Mendenhall, "The Relation of the Individual to Political Society in Ancient Israel," in J. Myers *et al.* (eds.), *Biblical Studies in Memory of H. C. Alleman* (Locust Valley, 1960), 89-108. A recent related, but more detailed study is J. Scharbert's *Solidarität in Segen und Fluch im Alten Testament und in seiner Umwelt* ("Bonner Biblische Beiträge," 14; Bonn, 1958), and its sequel, *Heilsmittler im Alten Testa-*

ment und im Alten Orient (Freiburg, 1964). Cf. also J. de Fraine, *Adam et son lignage: Études sur la notion de "personnalité corporative" dans la Bible* (Louvain, 1959).

Other works concentrate more on the problem of language as such, especially that of the early, predominantly Jewish church in contact with Greek thought: G. Dix, *Jew and Greek: A Study in the Primitive Church* (London, 1953); J. Hessen, *Griechische oder Biblische Theologie? Das Problem der Hellenisierung des Christentums in neuer Beleuchtung* (2nd ed., Basel, 1956), as well as a second edition of the Hessen's earlier *Platonismus und Prophetismus: Die antike und die biblische Geisteswelt in strukturvergleichender Betrachtung* (Munich, 1955); J. L. Moreau, *Language and Religious Language: A Study in the Dynamics of Translation* (Philadelphia, 1961); S. Laeuchli, *The Language of Faith: An Introduction to the Semantic Dilemma of the Early Church* (New York & Nashville, 1962).

Not immediately related to any of the above works, but requiring mention in this connection, is the second edition of J. Hempel's well-established *Das Ethos des Alten Testaments* (*BZAW*, 67; Berlin, 1964).

More recently, many of the presuppositions and approaches of the researchers into "Hebrew thought" have been stoutly attacked, especially by J. Barr in two works, *The Semantics of Biblical Language* (London, 1961), and *Biblical Words for Time* ("Studies in Biblical Theology," 33; Naperville, 1962), the latter attacking especially the facile distinction often made between *chronos* and *kairos*. Barr's major barrages were directed against Boman's work cited above and certain articles in G. Kittel's *Theological Dictionary of the New Testament* (Grand Rapids, 1964 ff.; English translation by G. W. Bromiley). Inasmuch as the "biblical theology" movement had often come to be closely identified with "word studies" and conceptual studies, it appeared to some that Barr's attacks were directed against the biblical theology movement as such. However, it soon became apparent that this was not his intention, but that his purpose was, rather, to stress that the main force of a language lies in its phrases and sentences rather than in isolated vocables. In the balance, a consensus seems to have emerged to the effect that, although Barr often overstates his positions, he is correct in insisting that any difference between "Hebrew" and "Greek" thought cannot be linguistically (or ethnically) based.

Barr's polemic indicates the vast amount of attention which has been devoted to the semi-theological question of the ancient, and especially Old Testament, view of time and history. A sampling of that vast literature can be noted here: R. C. Dentan (ed.), *The Idea of History in the Ancient Near East* ("American Oriental Series," 38; New Haven, 1955); A. Richardson, *History Sacred and Profane* (Philadelphia, 1964); E. Rust, *Salvation History: A Biblical Interpretation* (Richmond, 1962) and *Towards a Theological Understanding of History* (New York, 1963); E. A. Speiser, "The Biblical Idea of History in Its Common Near Eastern Setting," *IEJ*, 7 (1957), 201-16; G. von Rad, "Les ideés sur le temps et l'historie en Israël et l'eschatologie des prophets," *Maqqel shaqedh: Hommage à W. Vischer* (Montpellier, 1960), 198-209; D. N. Freedman, "History and Eschatology: The Nature of Biblical Religion and Prophetic Faith," *Int.*, 14 (1960), 143-54; C. Ratschow, "Anmerkungen zur theologischen Auffassung des Zeitproblems," *ZTK*, 51 (1954), 360-87; J. Muilenburg, "The Biblical View of Time," *HTR*, 54 (1961), 225-52; H. Gese, "Geschichtliches Denken im alten Orient und in Alten Testament," *ZTK*, 55 (1958), 127-45; and E. Perry, "The Biblical Viewpoint [of Time]," *JBR*, 27 (1959), 127-32.

8. THE "SOCIOLOGICAL APPROACH"

Perhaps at this point a few remarks anent Hahn's chapter 5, "The Sociological Approach to the Old Testament." While it is doubtful if it is possible any longer to distinguish a special approach to the Old Testament which might be labelled "sociological," subsequent scholarship has by no means failed to tap the resources of this line of attack. It has often been observed that, although its major concerns are more archaeological and historiographical, the chief categories of W. F. Albright's *From the Stone Age to Christianity* (2nd ed., Garden City, 1957) are sociological. Likewise, archaeologists and other students of ancient Near Eastern cultures have nearly always had regard for sociological categories. A major example of such research among Israel's neighbors would be A. van Selms, *Marriage and Family Life in Ugaritic Literature* (London, 1954). A. F. Rainey's doctoral dissertation at Brandeis University on *The Social Stratification of Ugarit* is now available in microfilm (Grand Rapids, 1963), and related or derivative studies by the author have appeared in various places. I.

Gelb is writing a book on Old Babylonian society which should be very important. Many similar studies could be cited. In the case of Israel, the closest we come to a comprehensive sociological treatment is R. de Vaux, *Ancient Israel: Its Life and Institutions* (New York, 1961; trans. from the French by J. McHugh). Although de Vaux utilizes the latest archaeological and literary research, he attempts none of the more philosophical reconstructions of Israel's history often associated with the names of Max Weber and others of the sociological schools. Also worthy of note are R. North, *Sociology of the Biblical Jubilee* (Rome, 1954); I. Mendelsohn, "On Corvée Labor in Ancient Canaan and Israel," *BASOR*, 167 (1962), 31-35; C. Fensham, "Widow, Orphan, and the Poor in Ancient Near Eastern Legal and Wisdom Literature," *JNES*, 21 (1961), 129-39; E. Neufeld, "The Emergence of a Royal-Urban Society in Ancient Israel," *HUCA*, 31 (1960), 31-53.

In this connection it should be observed that the "nomadic ideal" supposedly cherished in Israel, as championed by Lods, Causse, Pedersen, and many others, has increasingly come under attack in the face of the evidence, and apparently must be abandoned or at least radically altered. The patriarchs or Israelite ancestors were not true nomads (camel nomads) like modern Bedouin, but semi-nomads (ass nomads), i.e., still largely dependent upon surrounding cultures and interacting with them. For defense of this view, see G. E. Mendenhall, "The Hebrew Conquest of Palestine," *BA*, 25 (1962), 66-87.

Closely related is the question of the history and religion of the patriarchs, where Alt's studies still remain basic. Note especially F. M. Cross's article, "Yahweh and the God of the Patriarchs," *HTR*, 55 (1962), 225-59, suggesting a symbiosis in classical (Mosaic) Yahwism of the Amorite (patriarchal) traditions of a family god and Canaanite accents on a high, monarchical, creator deity (El). Other research in this area (doubtless destined to become more prominent in the future) cannot be noted here, except to observe that in his commentary on Genesis in *The Anchor Bible* (Garden City, 1964), E. A. Speiser, working more independently and relying more on Mesopotamian sources, arrives at still more conservative conclusions with regard to patriarchal life and faith. Somewhat similarly, M. Segal, "The Religion of Israel before Sinai," *Jewish Quarterly Review*, 52 (1961), 41-68. A good popular survey of the entire question appears in J. M. Holt, *The Patriarchs of Israel* (Nashville, 1964).

9. "RELIGIONSGESCHICHTE" AND "SACRAL KINGSHIP"

It is my judgment that the types of approach labeled by Hahn as "religio-historical," "form-critical," and "archaeological" have become so interrelated that it will not serve our purposes here to try to maintain these distinctions. If there is any substantial difference in the last decade or two, it has been that these approaches, rather than having diminished in importance, have moved even more to the center of the stage. It is scarcely possible any longer for either the form-critic or the historian (or the historian of Israel's religion) to ignore the archaeological evidences, regardless of how they are ultimately judged and utilized. Indeed, as we shall note shortly, one of the deepest continuing divisions within the fraternity of Old Testament scholarship is the issue of how much comparative weight in the reconstruction of Israel's history and religion shall be placed on "external" (especially archaeological) evidence and how much on "internal" evidence, the latter based on various types of literary study of Israel's traditions preserved in the Old Testament. We turn first to the latter.

Even among those who emphasize external evidence, one notes an ever-increasing application of form-criticism to the various types of literature. Closely related are two other more controversial areas: varying degrees of emphasis on the history of tradition, including oral tradition, and varying degrees of emphasis on the role of the cult in the origination and transmission of the traditions. The last two questions, especially, raise immediate issues for Old Testament theology (see section 21 below).

The emphases on oral tradition and cult were especially prominent in the program of the "Uppsala School," whose influence, especially with the demise of its leader Ivan Engnell, now appears to be abating (although the 2nd ed. [1965] of Engnell's pioneering *Studies in Divine Kingship in the Ancient Near East* [1st ed., Uppsala, 1943] must not be overlooked). In this connection we may note G. Wingren's comments on the lessening disagreement on the Old Testament among the various Scandinavian theological faculties in his lecture *The Main Lines of Development in Systematic Theology and Biblical Interpretation in Scandinavia* (Richmond, 1964; trans. J. A. Mackenzie), especially pp. 2-4. Here we should note the belated (and posthumous) appearance in English translation of F. Hvidberg's *Weeping and Laughter in the Old Testament: A Study of Canaanite-*

Israelite Religion (Leiden, 1962; new ed. prepared by F. Løkkegaard, trans. by N. Haislund), which, when it first appeared in 1938, was a pioneering work in the history of the cult.

Certain works, quite representative of the classical "Uppsala" outlook, have nevertheless continued to appear in recent years. Most of these have centered on the vexed question of the nature of "kingship" in Israel and particularly the king's role in Israel's pre-exilic cultus, and here again especially in the New Year's or enthronement festival. The real issue, of course, is the extent to which the Israelite monarchy was influenced by an ideology found outside of Israel or to what extent Israel remained "unique" in its religious conceptions, even when often using identical or closely related forms. The literature provoked by this issue is far too immense to survey thoroughly here.

Quite representative of the standard "Uppsala" approach would be G. Widengren's, *Sakrales Königtum im Alten Testament und im Judentum* (Stuttgart, 1955); the same author's "King and Covenant," *JSS*, 2 (1957), 1-32; R. A. Carlson, *David, the Chosen King: A Traditio-Historical Approach to the Second Book of Samuel* (Uppsala, 1964); G. W. Ahlström, *Psalm 89, eine Liturgie aus dem Ritual des leidenden Königs* (Lund, 1959); and the same author's *Aspects of Syncretism in Israelite Religion* ("Horae Soederblomianae," 5; Lund, 1963). The extent, however, to which even "Uppsala" views have been modified is seen, e.g., in the works of H. Ringgren, Engnell's successor at Uppsala, perhaps especially in his *Israelite Religion* (Philadelphia, 1966; translated from the German by David E. Green) and *The Faith of the Psalmists* (Philadelphia, 1963; the author's own English version of a 1957 Swedish original); see also his commentaries on Proverbs, Canticles, and Esther in *Das Alte Testament Deutsch* (Göttingen, 1958 and 1962).

Similar modifications can be seen in the British "Myth and Ritual school," associated especially with the name of S. H. Hooke. These are best seen if one compares the recent *Myth, Ritual, and Kingship: Essays on the Theory and Practice of Kingship in the Ancient Near East and in Israel*, ed. S. H. Hooke (London, 1958), with its predecessor, *Myth and Ritual*, published in 1933. In this connection, note also the more independent contribution of T. Gaster, *Thespis: Ritual, Myth and Drama in the Ancient Near East* (New York, 1950; paperback, Garden City, 1961).

Increasing objections have been raised in many quarters against the "patternism" assumed by many cultic theorists and even against an alleged "parallelomania" (the latter term the title of a presidential address by S. Sandmel to the Society of Biblical Literature, published in *JBL*, 81 [1962], 1-13; although directed more to New Testament problems, the concern was easily applicable to Old Testament study as well. One of the most devastating attacks ever made upon this approach was H. Frankfort's *Kingship and the Gods: A Study of Ancient Near Eastern Religion as the Integration of Society and Nature* (Chicago, 1948; reprinted, 1955). In his stimulating work *The Religion of Israel* (Chicago, 1960; abridged from the seven-volume Hebrew original [1937-1948] and trans. by M. Greenberg) Y. Kaufmann goes so far as to assert that Israel was so little influenced by surrounding paganism that it was never even really understood! See also J. de Fraine, "Les implications du 'patternism,'" *Biblica*, 37 (1956), 59-73. An excellent recent discussion is C. Westermann's "Sinn and Grenze religionsgeschichtlicher Parallelen," *ThLZ*, 90 (1965), 489-96.

A few other general discussions of the subject of Israelite kingship may be noted: a helpful survey by C. M. Edsman, "Zum sakralen Königtum in der Forschung der letzten 100 Jahre," supplement to *Numen*, 4 (1959), 3-17; K. H. Bernhardt, *Das Problem der altorientalischen Königsideologie im Alten Testament unter besonderer Berücksichtigung der Psalmenexegese dargestellt und kritisch gewürdigt* (*VTS*, 8; Leiden, 1960); S. Amsler, *David, Roi et Messie: La tradition davidique dans l'Ancien Testament* ("Cahiers Theologiques," 49; Neuchâtel, 1963); G. Cooke, "The Israelite King as Son of God," *ZAW*, 73 (1961), 146-71; J. Porter, *Moses and Monarchy: A Study in the Biblical Tradition of Moses* (Oxford, 1963); A. R. Johnson, *Sacral Kingship in Ancient Israel* (Cardiff, 1955); W. S. McCullough, "Israel's Kings, Sacral and Otherwise," *ET*, 68 (1957), 144-48, a sharp criticism of Johnson's work; answered by Johnson in "Old Testament Exegesis, Imaginative and Unimaginative," *ibid.*, pp. 178-79; J. Gray, "The Kingship of God in the Prophets and Psalms," *VT*, 11 (1961), 1-29; *The Sacral Kingship: Contributions to the Central Theme of the VIIIth International Congress for the History of Religions—Rome, 1955* (Leiden, 1959); M. Noth, "Gott, König, Volk im Alten Testament: Eine methodologische Auseinandersetzung

mit einer gegenwärtigen Forschungsrichtung," a 1950 essay now reprinted in Noth's *Gesammelte Studien zum Alten Testament* (Munich,
1957), 188-229; W. Schmidt, *Königtum Gottes in Ugarit und Israel:
Zur Herkunft der Königsprädikation Jahwes* (*BZAW*, 80; Berlin,
1961); and H. Ringgren, *The Messiah in the Old Testament* ("Studies
in Biblical Theology," 18; Chicago, 1956).

Before we leave the subject of "comparative religion," we must note
the continuing independent researches of J. Morgenstern concerning
a possible solar cult in Jerusalem, especially in his *Fire Upon the Altar*
(Chicago, 1963). Of an entirely different sort, but a parade example
of concentration of this approach upon the exegesis of a single peri-
cope, is E. R. Dalglish, *Psalm Fifty-One in the Light of Ancient Near
Eastern Patternism* (Leiden, 1962). Finally, we must not neglect the
highly regarded work of Mircea Eliade, whose approach is quite
different from that of the patternism of older "comparative religion."
Eliade's concern is limited more to the "phenomenological," and the
term "history of religions" tends to be preferred. The implications of
Eliade's work have been little tapped formally as yet for biblical
studies, but the potentialities seem possibly revolutionary. Especially
to be noted are his *Patterns in Comparative Religion* (New York,
1958); *Cosmos and History: The Myth of the Eternal Return* (New
York, 1959; trans. from a 1949 original by W. Trask); *The Sacred
and the Profane: The Nature of Religion* (New York, 1959; trans.
W. Trask); and "History of Religions in Retrospect: 1912-1962,"
JBR, 31 (1963), 98-109.

10. Israelite Cult

The debate concerning Israelite kingship, putative enthronement
festival, etc., leads us into the broader issues of Israel's cult, to which
we next turn. Questions concerning form-criticism and history of
traditions are closely related, and to those we shall turn shortly.

Some of the difficulties inhere in varying definitions of "cult":
how "sacramental" it was (or the relation between "word" and "sac-
rament" or ritual), the relative merits of such terms as "repetition,"
"representation," "re-enactment," "renewal," "contemporization," "ac-
tualization," and others. Since, as usual, the Old Testament offers no
"theory" of cultus, agreement is not easy to achieve. In general, it
may be possible to say that Scandinavian scholars (especially

Mowinckel and those from Uppsala) have championed a "high" (objective, realistic, sacramental) view of Israel's cultus, while others have tended more to stress the verbal, subjective aspects. Among general discussions of the theory of "cult" may be noted S. Mowinckel, *Religion und Kultus* (Göttingen, 1953; trans. from the Norwegian by A. Schauer); H. Zirker, *Die Kultische Vergegenwärtigung der Vergangenheit in den Psalmen* ("Bonner Biblische Beiträge," 20; Bonn, 1964); M. Noth, "The 'Re-presentation' of the Old Testament in Proclamation," in C. Westermann (ed.), *Essays on Old Testament Hermeneutics* (Richmond, 1963; J. Mays, translation editor), 76-88.

As Hahn indicates, scarcely anyone has been more articulate and influential in urging a realistic approach to Israel's cult, especially in an "enthronement festival," than S. Mowinckel. The recent English translation of his 1951 *Offersang og Sangoffer* under the title *The Psalms in Israel's Worship* (2 vols.; New York and Nashville, 1962; trans. D. R. Ap-Thomas) will undoubtedly increase his influence in the English-speaking world. The most influential alternative hypothesis, at least in America, has probably been that of A. Weiser, who champions a quite objective, realistic "covenant renewal" accent as central to Israel's worship. His position is articulated in his "Zur Frage nach den Beziehungen der Psalmen zum Kult: Die Darstellung der Theophanie in den Psalmen und im Festkult," in *Festschrift für Alfred Bertholet* (Tübingen, 1950), 513-31; reprinted in Weiser's, *Glaube und Geschichte im Alten Testament und andere ausgewählte Schriften* (Göttingen, 1961), 303-21, and now conveniently summarized in the introduction to his commentary on the psalms, *The Psalms* ("The Old Testament Library"; Philadelphia, 1962; trans. by H. Hartwell from the 5th [1959] ed. of the original in *Das Alte Testament Deutsch*). It has been observed, however, that Mowinckel's and Weiser's positions overlap more than might initially appear, each one championing different ends of the possible total spectrum (nature and history; Jerusalem and Shechem); see H. Ringgren, "Enthronement Festival or Covenant Renewal," *BR*, 7 (1962), 45-48.

A third major position is taken by H.-J. Kraus, especially in his *Gottesdienst in Israel: Grundriss einer alttestamentlichen Kultgeschichte* (2nd ed., Munich, 1962; 1st ed., 1954); the imminent appearance of this work in English translation should vastly increase Kraus's influence in the English-speaking world, where he has been relatively

282   PROBLEMS IN THE STUDY OF ISRAELITE ORIGINS

little noted so far. A convenient introductory article is his "Gilgal: Ein Beitrag zur Kultusgeschichte Israels," *VT* 1 (1951), 181-99. Note also Kraus's major commentary on the psalms in the *Biblischer Kommentar* (2 vols.; Neukirchen, 1960). (Certain aspects of Kraus's work have been popularized by K. Crim, *The Royal Psalms* [Richmond, 1962]). Major aspects of Kraus's reconstruction include an early, combined Passover-unleavened bread festival, centering at Gilgal, and a later "royal Zion festival" at Jerusalem.

Two recent Dutch works also discuss the question of Israel's worship: H. Renckens, *De Godsdienst van Israël* (Roermond, 1962), and T. Vriezen's work with the same title (Zeist, 1963). We should also note the convenient popular summary of the subject of Israel's worship by A. S. Herbert, *Worship in Ancient Israel* ("Ecumenical Studies in Worship," 5; Richmond, 1959).

Other scholars are quite cool to the whole "cultic" approach, at least as applied to the psalms, and prefer to limit themselves to a more strictly form-critical stance (i.e., analysis of types without stressing cultic implications). Thus A. Szörenyi, *Psalmen und Kult im Alten Testament: Zur Formgeschichte der Psalmen* (Budapest, 1961), and especially C. Westermann, *The Praise of God in the Psalms* (Richmond, 1965; trans. from the 1961 original by K. Crim). Also note Westermann's "Struktur und Geschichte der Klage im Alten Testament," *ZAW*, 66 (1954), 44-88; now reprinted together with four other essays on the psalms and four new essays on various biblical topics in his *Forschung am Alten Testament* ("Theologische Bücherei," 24; Munich, 1964).

11. PROBLEMS IN THE STUDY OF ISRAELITE ORIGINS

Besides the psalms, the other major focus of contemporary interest in Israel's cult lies in the origins and early history of Israel. Here again cultic questions merge with those of archaeology, form-criticism, and history of traditions. Again a basic ambiguity in understanding of "cult" plagues us: When used to describe literature, does it refer to material originating primarily in the cult (and thus having little or no factual basis) or merely to traditions secondarily adapted to and transmitted by the cult? The confusion is serious enough to lead G. E. Wright to suggest dropping the very term "cult"; thus in his "The Nations in Hebrew Prophecy," *Encounter*, 26 (1965), 225-37, and in "Old Testament Scholarship in Prospect," *JBR*, 28 (1960), 182-93, and again similarly in "Cult and History," *Int.*, 16 (1962), 3-20. Desirable as it might be to cut the Gordian knot in that fashion, we shall probably have to resign ourselves to the same terminological confusion here as obtains with respect to "myth," "eschatology," and others.

The translation into English of the first volume of G. von Rad's *Theology of the Old Testament* (New York, 1962; trans. by D. Stalker from the 1957 original), of his commentary on *Genesis* ("The Old Testament Library"; Philadelphia, 1961; trans. from the 1956 original in *Das Alte Testament Deutsch* by J. Marks), and especially the forthcoming translation of *Das formgeschichtliche Problem des Hexateuch* ("Beiträge zur Wissenschaft vom Alten and Neuen Testament," 26; Stuttgart, 1938) under the title of *The Problem of the Hexateuch and Other Essays* should quicken the urgency of this debate in America. At the same time the imminent appearance in translation of W. Beyerlin's *Herkunft und Geschichte der ältesten Sinaitraditionen* (Tübingen, 1961), with powerful counter-arguments to von Rad's separation of faith and history in early Israel and especially his separation of the Exodus and Sinai traditions, should probably lead to some type of new synthesis.

Meanwhile, it is a pity that no one has apparently yet undertaken to translate Martin Noth's equally influential *Ueberlieferungsgeschichte des Pentateuch* (Stuttgart, 1948) and *Ueberlieferungsgeschichtliche Studien* (Tübingen, 1948). While his "amphictyonic" explanation of Israel's early institutional structure has won virtually unanimous acceptance, his emphasis upon aetiology and rigorous application of his tradition-historical methodology to the literary reports (generally implying little historical factuality behind the written materials) have become a major issue between the "Alt-Noth-von Rad" school of Germany and the "Albright-Bright-Wright" emphasis in America. At least the results of Noth's methodology are well-known to English-speaking readers through his *The History of Israel* (New York, 1958; rev. transl., 1960). (We should also note in passing the appearance in English translation of Noth's *The Old Testament World* [Philadelphia, 1966], treating Palestinian geography, archaeology, and textual criticism as well as ancient Near Eastern history.) The issues are sharply drawn in John Bright's *Early Israel in Recent History Writing:*

A Study in Method ("Studies in Biblical Theology," 19; Chicago, 1956) and worked out in the same author's *A History of Israel* (Philadelphia, 1959). Noth's rejoinder is probably most accessible in his review of Bright's work, "As One Historian to Another," *Int.*, 15 (1961), 61-66, and in "Der Beitrag der Archäologie zur Geschichte Israels," *SVT*, 7 (Leiden, 1960), 262-82.

Mention should be made in this context of S. Mowinckel's recent *Tetrateuch, Pentateuch, Hexateuch* (*BZAW*, 90; Berlin, 1964), which takes an independent position but supports Noth more than Bright; also Murray Newman's popular but provocative *The People of the Covenant: A Study of Israel from Moses to the Monarchy* (New York and Nashville, 1962); J. A. Soggin, "Ancient Biblical Traditions and Modern Archaeological Discoveries," *BA*, 23 (1960), 95-100; G. Fohrer, *Ueberlieferung und Geschichte des Exodus: Eine Analyse von Exodus 1-15* (*BZAW*, 91; Berlin, 1964); K.-D. Schunck, *Benjamin: Untersuchungen zur Entstehung und Geschichte eines israelitischen Stammes* (*BZAW*, 86; Berlin, 1963); H. Seebass, *Mose und Aaron, Sinai und Gottesberg* ("Abhandlungen zur evangelischen Theologie," 2; Bonn, 1962); R. Smend, *Jahwekrieg und Stämmebund: Erwägungen zur ältesten Geschichte Israels* ("Forschungen zur Religion und Literatur des Alten und Neuen Testaments," 84; Göttingen, 1963); S. Herrmann, "Neuere Arbeiten zur Geschichte Israels" (taking issue with Smend, Bright, and Weiser), *ThLZ*, 89 (1964), 813-24; H. B. Huffmon, "The Exodus, Sinai and the Credo" (supporting Beyerlin's position), *CBQ*, 27 (1965), 101-13; D. McCarthy, "Covenant in the Old Testament: The Present State of Inquiry," *CBQ*, 27 (1965), 217-40.

12. The History of Israel

A few other contributions to the study of Israel's history deserve to be mentioned. Above all, we must hail the collection of most of Albrecht Alt's germinal essays, many dealing directly with Israel's early history, into three volumes, *Kleine Schriften zur Geschichte des Volkes Israel* (Munich, 1953-1959). Similarly, many of O. Eissfeldt's essays, which though not so directly related to the problems of Israel's early history, are just as important in the broader perspective, have been published in two volumes, *Kleine Schriften* (Tübingen, 1962, 1963), with a third volume in preparation. A stimulating, independent treatment of Israel's history comes from the general historian E. Voegelin: *Israel and Revelation* (Baton Rouge, 1956, Vol. 1 of a projected six-volume study of world history entitled "Order and History"; cf. W. F. Albright's generally appreciative review in *History, Archaeology, and Christian Humanism*, 259-71). W. F. Albright has summarized many of his viewpoints in *The Biblical Period from Abraham to Ezra* (rev. ed., New York, 1963). Also noteworthy: K. Galling, *Studien zur Geschichte Israels im persischen Zeitalter* (Tübingen, 1964); A. Jirku, *Geschichte Palästina-Syriens im orientalischen Altertum* (Aalen, 1963); J. Hempel, *Geschichten und Geschichte im Alten Testament bis zur persischen Zeit* (Gütersloh, 1964); F. F. Bruce, *Israel and the Nations: From the Exodus to the Fall of the Second Temple* (Grand Rapids, 1963); M. Metzger, *Grundriss der Geschichte Israels* (Neukirchen, 1963); E. Ehrlich, *A Concise History of Israel from the Earliest Times to the Destruction of the Temple in A.D. 70* (London, 1962; trans. from the 1958 German original); M. Beek, *Concise History of Israel from Abraham to the Bar Cochba Rebellion* (New York, 1963; trans. from the 1957 Dutch original by A. Pomerans); M. Unger, *Israel and the Arameans* (Grand Rapids, 1957). The fixing of biblical and ancient Near Eastern chronologies is always an important part of the study of Israelite history. Here we can observe only that a new edition of E. Thiele, *The Mysterious Numbers of the Hebrew Kings* (Chicago, 1951), is scheduled to appear shortly.

13. FORM-CRITICAL STUDY OF ISRAEL'S HISTORY

Ever since the publication of G. E. Mendenhall's short but influential work *Law and Covenant in Israel and the Ancient Near East* (Pittsburgh, 1955; reprinted from *BA*, 17 [1954], 26-46 and 49-76), form-critical study of Israel's early period has focused especially on the covenant formulations and on their relation to the structure of Hittite treaties in the ancient Near East. Some of the same conclusions were reached independently by K. Baltzer in *Das Bundesformular* ("Wissenschaftliche Monographien zum Alten und Neuen Testament," 4; Neukirchen, 1960). Some other related studies include R. Smend, *Die Bundesformel* ("Theologische Studien," 68; Zurich, 1963); G. Schmitt, *Der Landtag von Sichem* ("Arbeiten zur Theologie," 1; Stuttgart, 1964); H. Reventlow, *Gebot und Predigt im Dekalog* (Gütersloh, 1962); J. Muilenburg, "The Form and Structure of the Covenantal Formulations," *VT*, 9 (1959), 347-65; and J. Stamm, *Der Dekalog im Lichte der neueren Forschung* (2nd ed., Bern, 1962; 1st ed., 1958).

A subdivision of the investigation of the background of the covenant forms is the study of the roots of the covenant curses and their forms; these curses were often apparently imitated by the prophets. See C. Fensham, "Common Trends in Curses of the Near-Eastern Treaties and *kudurru*-Inscriptions compared with Maledictions of Amos and Isaiah," *ZAW*, 75 (1963), 155-75; the same author's "Malediction and Benediction in Ancient Near Eastern Vassal-Treaties and the Old Testament," *ZAW*, 74 (1962), 1-9; E. von Waldow, *Der traditionsgeschichtliche Hintergrund der prophetischen Gerichtsreden (BZAW*, 85; Berlin, 1963); D. Hillers, *Treaty-Curses and the Old Testament Prophets* (Rome, 1964); S. Gevirtz, "West-Semitic Curses and the Problem of the Origins of Hebrew Law," *VT*, 11 (1961), 137-58.

H. Reventlow, often in sharp antithesis to older viewpoints, has been especially vigorous in promoting his form-critical and tradition-historical views of the later history of the cult and of the prophets' dependence upon it. Among his major writings: *Das Heiligkeitsgesetz formgeschichtlich Untersucht* (Neukirchen, 1961); *Das Amt des Propheten bei Amos* (Göttingen, 1962); *Wächter über Israel: Ezechiel und seine Tradition (BZAW*, 82; Berlin, 1962); *Liturgie und prophetisches Ich bei Jeremia* (Gütersloh, 1962). Many feel that Reventlow has overemphasized the role of the cult in shaping Israel's traditions, but his viewpoint remains a major catalyst to be reckoned with. Among the critiques of Reventlow may be mentioned Noth's comment, in his *Developing Ideas of Theological Thought in Germany* (Richmond, 1961), that Reventlow's work on the Holiness Code and Baltzer's on the covenant move from "form-history" to mere "formula history" to "formula non-history." As a major alternative to Reventlow we may note R. Killian's more traditional *Literarkritische und formgeschichtliche Untersuchung des Heiligkeitsgesetzes* ("Bonner Biblische Beiträge," 19; Bonn, 1963).

Inevitably, study of the covenant has merged with analysis of the book of Deuteronomy. (Cf. L. B. Cross's survey, "Commentaries on Deuteronomy," *Theology*, 64 (1961), 184-88). It is often noted that the major emphasis in von Rad's *Theology of the Old Testament* is "deuteronomic," as presented also in his *Studies in Deuteronomy*

("Studies in Biblical Theology," 9; Chicago, 1953; trans. from the 1948 original by D. Stalker), in his article on Deuteronomy in *IDB*, 1, 831-38, and now in his commentary on that book in *Das Alte Testament Deutsch* (Göttingen, 1964). Other writings on Deuteronomy include P. Buis and J. Leclerq, *Le Deutéronome* (Paris, 1963); F. Dumermuth, "Zur deuteronomischen Kulttheologie und ihren Voraussetzungen," *ZAW*, 70 (1958), 59-98; J. Wÿngaards, *The Formulas of the Deuteronomic Creed (Dt. 6/20-23; 26/5-9)*, (Tilburg, 1963); a very conservative study by M. G. Kline, *Treaty of the Great King: The Covenant Structure of Deuteronomy* (Grand Rapids, 1963). There have been a number of penetrating studies by Roman Catholic scholars: W. Moran, "The Ancient Near Eastern Background of the Love of God in Deuteronomy," *CBQ*, 25 (1963), 77-87; N. Lohfink, *Das Hauptgebot: Eine Untersuchung literarischer Einleitungsfragen zu Dtn. 5-11* (Rome, 1963); the same author's "Der Bundesschluss im Lande Moab: Redaktionsgeschichtliches zu Dt. 28, 69–32, 47," *Biblische Zeitschrift*, 6 (1962), 32-56; and D. J. McCarthy, *Treaty and Covenant: A Study in Form in the Ancient Oriental Documents and in the Old Testament* (Rome, 1963).

A basic methodological summary which has recently appeared is K. Koch, *Was ist Formgeschichte? Neue Wege der Bibelexegese* (Neukirchen, 1964). A recent reprint of Hermann Gunkel's pioneering *The Legends of Genesis: The Biblical Saga and History* (1901) with an introduction by W. F. Albright (New York, 1964) indicates how germinal the work of the "father of form-criticism" still is. See also J. Muilenburg, "Modern Issues in Biblical Studies: The Gains of Form Criticism in Old Testament Studies," *ET*, 71 (1960), 229-33.

14. ORAL TRADITION AND TRADITION HISTORY

As with other Scandinavian emphases, the Scandinavian accents on oral tradition are no longer urged so radically as was once the case. E. Nielsen's *Oral Tradition: A Modern Problem in Old Testament Introduction* ("Studies in Biblical Theology," 11; Chicago, 1954) remains unequalled as an introduction and exemplification of that approach. It is also amply illustrated in Nielsen's *Shechem: A Traditio-Historical Investigation* (Copenhagen, 1955). The application of the method is also concisely explained in chapter 4 of J. Lindblom, *Prophecy in Ancient Israel* (Philadelphia, 1962). We find a good theological analysis in C. Stuhlmueller, "The Influence of Oral Tradition upon Exegesis and the Senses of Scripture," *CBQ*, 20 (1958), 299-326. Turning to the broader issues of the history of traditions, we note first of all a helpful historical survey by H.-J. Kraus, "Zur Geschichte des Ueberlieferungsbegriffs in der alttestamentlichen Wissenschaft," *EvT*, 16 (1956), 371-87. Some general studies include P. Ackroyd, *Continuity: A Contribution to the Study of the Old Testament Religious Tradition* (Oxford, 1962); S. Segert, "Zur Methode der alttestamentlichen Literarkritik," *Archiv Orientalni*, 24 (1956), 610-21; J. Barr, "Tradition and Expectation in Ancient Israel," *Scottish Journal of Theology*, 10 (1957), 24-34. A number of studies have concerned themselves with the concept of "memory" or "remembrance" in ancient Israel, especially B. Childs, *Memory and Tradition in Israel* ("Studies in Biblical Theology," 37; Naperville, 1962), and W. Schottroff, "*Gedenken*" *im Alten Orient und in Alten Testament: Die Wurzel* zākar *im semitischen Sprachkreis* (Neukirchen, 1964).

A major challenge to the entire form-critical enterprise possibly comes now from Uppsala, especially in the works of H. Riesenfeld, e.g., his *The Gospel Tradition and Its Beginnings; A Study in the Limits of "Formgeschichte"* (London, 1957), and in more developed form in B. Gerhardsson's *Memory and Manuscript: Oral Tradition and Written Transmission in Rabbinic Judaism and Early Christianity* ("Acta seminarii neo-testamentici upsaliensis," 22; Uppsala, 1961). These works, emphasizing the role of the teacher and the power of memory in antiquity, are not applied to the Old Testament (note, however, B. Gerhardsson's "Mundliche und schriftliche Tradition der Prophetenbücher," *TZ*, 17 [1961], 216-20), but if they become established they are bound to be influential also there and may well merge with the critique of the "Albright school" to the effect that historical traditions in the ancient world were written down not at the end, but at the beginning of an era, in order to preserve and interpret for succeeding generations. Alongside these questionings perhaps we may juxtapose a stimulating study of parallel processes in Mesopotamia that invites exploration of the implications for biblical studies: W. W. Hallo, "New Viewpoints on Cuneiform Literature," *IEJ*, 12 (1962), 13-26. Pointing in the same general direction is the chapter on writing in A. Leo Oppenheim's *Ancient Mesopotamia: Portrait of a Dead Civilization* (Chicago, 1964), 228-87.

15. THE PROPHETS

In the meantime, much research along form-critical, tradition-critical, and cult-critical lines continues. Besides the psalms and Israel's early history, another area that is receiving increasing attention is the prophetical literature, beginning with studies of the transition from amphictyonic to monarchical structures, as in H.-J. Kittel's *Die Stammessprüche Israels: Genesis 49 und Deuteronomium 33 traditionsgeschichtlich untersucht* (Berlin, 1949) and W. Richter's *Traditionsgeschichtliche Untersuchungen zum Richterbuch* ("Bonner Biblische Beiträge," 18; Bonn, 1963). The latter work has now appeared in a revised and enlarged edition under the title *Die Bearbeitungen des "Retterbuches" in der deuteronomischen Epoche* ("Bonner Biblische Beiträge," 21; Bonn, 1964).

Attention has increasingly turned to Samuel as a pivotal figure in the transition. Three contrasting studies of the complex biblical traditions about him are especially noteworthy: W. F. Albright, *Samuel and the Beginnings of the Prophetic Movement* (Cincinnati, 1961); J. L. McKenzie, "The Four Samuels," *BR*, 7 (1962), 3-18; and A. Weiser, *Samuel: Seine geschichtliche Aufgabe und religiöse Bedeutung* ("Forschungen zur Religion und Literatur des Alten und Neuen Testaments," 81; Göttingen, 1962).

Interest in Samuel has lead to greater concentration on Deuteronomy 32 ("The Song of Moses"), which increasingly is given a date in the eleventh century, i.e., about the time of Samuel. Its setting in the "council of Yahweh" and its employment of the "covenant lawsuit" form has led to considerable research in that area, especially since the prophets, conscious of their role as God's heralds or messengers, continued to use the same form freely. Among other studies we may note H. B. Huffmon, "The Covenant Lawsuit in the Prophets," *JBL*, 78 (1959), 285-95; G. E. Wright, "The Lawsuit of God: A Form-Critical Study of Deuteronomy 32," in B. W. Anderson and W. Harrelson (eds.), *Israel's Prophetic Heritage: Essays in Honor of James Muilenburg* (New York, 1962), 26-67; M. Newman, "The Prophetic Call of Samuel," *ibid.*, 86-97; J. Ross, "The Prophet as Yahweh's Messenger," *ibid.*, 98-107; J. Harvey, "Le 'Rîb-Pattern' réquisitoire prophétique sur la rupture de l'alliance," *Biblica*, 43 (1962), 172-96; R. Rendtorff, "Botenformel und Botenspruch," *ZAW*, 74 (1962), 165-77; B. Gemser, "The *rîb-* or Controversy-Pattern in

Hebrew Mentality," in M. Noth and D. W. Thomas (eds.), *Wisdom in Israel and in the Ancient Near East* (*SVT*, 3, Leiden, 1955). Some of the other significant general literature on the prophets may now be mentioned. A basic form-critical study which has not yet attracted the attention it deserves is C. Westermann's *Gundformen prophetischer Rede* ("Beiträge zur evangelischen Theologie," 31; Munich, 1960). Much of the earlier furor over "cultic prophecy" has abated (although terminological imprecision plagues us here too), but some work along this line continues. We have noted Reventlow's several studies above. Aubrey Johnson's *The Cultic Prophet in Ancient Israel* (Cardiff, 1962; 1st ed., 1944) is still more representative of earlier viewpoints. Using "cultic" more in the sense of liturgically transmitted historical traditions is W. Beyerlin's *Die Kulttraditionen Israels in der Verkündigung des Propheten Micha* (Göttingen, 1959). R. E. Clements, *Prophecy and Covenant* ("Studies in Biblical Theology," 43; Naperville, 1965) is an excellent survey of the relatively conservative plateau that has been reached by most recent scholarship on such issues as prophecy and cult, prophecy and "law," etc.

Probably the two most influential of all recent studies on prophecy are both of Scandinavian origin: S. Mowinckel, *He That Cometh: The Messiah Concept in the Old Testament and Later Judaism* (Oxford, 1956; trans. from the 1951 original by G. W. Anderson), which deals especially with the issues of kingship (cf. section 9 above) and eschatology; and J. Lindblom, *Prophecy in Ancient Israel* (Philadelphia, 1962), which summarizes a lifetime's research, particularly into the question of prophetic ecstasy.

A. Heschel's *The Prophets* (New York, 1955; an expansion of his 1936 volume *Die Prophetie*) is an entirely independent study that defies classification but is perhaps all the more noteworthy as a result. N. K. Gottwald's *All the Kingdoms of the Earth: Israelite Prophecy and International Relations in the Ancient Near East* (New York, 1964) fills a gap in its concentration on the "Gentile oracles." A comparable study is H. Donner, *Israel unter den Völkern: Die Stellung der klassischen Propheten des 8. Jahrhunderts v. Chr. zur Aussenpolitik der Könige von Israel und Juda* (*SVT*, 11; Leiden, 1964). Bruce Vawter's more popular *The Conscience of Israel: Pre-Exilic Prophets and Prophecy* (New York, 1961) has deservedly been well-received. W. McKane's *Prophets and Wise Men* ("Studies in Biblical Theology,"

44; Naperville, 1965) explores the reasons for the frequent tension between these two groups. Finally, we note B. Napier's fine survey, *Prophets in Perspective* (New York and Nashville, 1963) which is a recasting of his article "Prophet, Prophetism" in *IDB* 3, 896-918.

16. BIBLICAL ARCHAEOLOGY

How does one begin to summarize the vast amount of archaeological work in Palestine and the rest of the Near East in the past fifteen years, let alone its influence on biblical studies? Some aspects of its influence we have already noted in previous sections. An excellent discussion of how archaeology interacts with other aspects of biblical studies, both inciting new hypotheses and also helping to check their excesses, is G. E. Wright's "Archaeology and Old Testament Studies," *JBL*, 77 (1958), 39-51. A much more conservative viewpoint is expressed in J. P. Free, "Archaeology and Biblical Criticism," *Bibliotheca Sacra*, 113 (1956), 123-29, and 114 (1957), 23-39 and 123-32. G. E. Wright has a very comprehensive survey, "The Archaeology of Palestine," in Wright (ed.), *The Bible and the Ancient Near East*, 73-112. See also H. N. Richardson, "A Decade of Archaeology in Palestine," *JBR*, 27 (1959), 91-109. More restricted in scope, but very useful is S. Yeivin, *A Decade of Archaeology in Israel, 1948-1958* (Istanbul, 1960).

Among the best surveys and summaries of new excavations and finds bearing on biblical studies are those appearing regularly in certain more general biblical journals, especially *Revue Biblique* and *The Catholic Biblical Quarterly*. The popular *Biblical Archaeologist*, of course, concerns itself exclusively with this topic. In addition there are the more technical journals, e.g., the *Bulletin of the American Schools of Oriental Research*, the *Israel Exploration Journal*, the *Quarterly of the Palestine Department of Antiquities*, the *Palestine Exploration Quarterly*, the *Zeitschrift des Deutschen Palästina-Vereins*, and *'Atiqot*.

We shall make no attempt here to survey recent excavation reports, but at least three popular reports by the excavators themselves should be noted: K. Kenyon, *Digging Up Jericho* (New York, 1957); J. B. Pritchard, *Gibeon, Where the Sun Stood Still* (Princeton, 1962), and G. E. Wright, *Shechem: The Biography of a Biblical City* (New York, 1965). In this category also belongs Nelson Glueck's fascinating report of his surface survey in Israel's southern region, *Rivers in the Desert: A History of the Negev* (New York, 1959), and his study of the fabulous Nabateans entitled *Deities and Dolphins* (New York, 1965).

Only some of the more important of the more general and relatively popular works on biblical archaeology can be noted here. Easily heading the list are new editions of two of W. F. Albright's major works: *From the Stone Age to Christianity* (2nd ed., Garden City, 1957; 1st ed., Baltimore, 1940); *The Archaeology of Palestine* (4th ed., Baltimore, 1960; 1st ed., 1949). G. E. *Wright's Biblical Archaeology* (2nd ed., Philadelphia, 1961; 1st ed., 1957), which has also appeared in an abridgement by R. Tomes (Philadelphia, 1960), treats the material chronologically. Kathleen Kenyon's contributions appear in her popular study of methodology *Beginning in Archaeology* (3rd ed., New York, 1961; 1st ed., 1952) and in her historical survey *Archaeology in the Holy Land* (New York, 1960). Certain minor methodological differences (concerning the relative importance of pottery and stratigraphical analysis) between the Kenyon and Albright traditions have been loudly aired by one of Kenyon's devoted disciples, especially in a work co-authored with his wife: H. J. Franken and C. A. Franken-Battershill, *A Primer of Old Testament Archaeology* (Leiden, 1963); cf. Wright's rejoinder in a review of the work in *Archaeology*, 18 (1966), 74-75. J. B. Pritchard's *Archaeology and the Old Testament* (Princeton, 1958) is an unusually readable introduction to all aspects of the subject. John Gray's *Archaeology and the Old Testament World* (New York, 1962) is distinguished by the emphasis placed on ancient Near Eastern institutions and social conventions. The two volumes of *The Biblical Archaeologist Reader* cull choice articles from past issues of the journal (Vol. 1, ed. G. E. Wright and D. N. Freedman [Garden City, 1961]; Vol. 2, ed. D. N. Freedman and E. F. Campbell, Jr. [Garden City, 1964]). From very conservative quarters come G. F. Owen, *Archaeology and the Bible* (Westwood, 1961); M. F. Unger, *Archaeology and the Old Testament* (Grand Rapids, 1954); and J. Thomson, *The Bible and Archaeology* (Grand Rapids, 1962). In 1959 a new edition of Jack Finegan's *Light from the Ancient Past: The Archaeological Background of the Hebrew Christian Religion* appeared (Princeton; 1st ed., 1946). Further we may mention I. Price, O. Sellers, and E. Carlson, *The Monuments and the Old Testament* (a thorough revision of a popular classic; Philadelphia, 1958); and W. G. Williams, *Archaeology in Biblical Research* (New York and Nashvlle, 1965). Finally, we must not fail to note two popular series containing volumes treating many different archaeological sites and topics: "Studies in Biblical Archaeology," general editor, A. Parrot (New York, 1955 ff.), and the "Baker Studies in Biblical Archaeology," general editor, Charles Pfeiffer (Grand Rapids, 1962 ff.).

Two significant works dealing with pre-biblical history may be noted. E. Anati, *Palestine Before the Hebrews: A History, from the Earliest Arrival of Man to the Conquest of Canaan* (New York, 1963), provides an excellent survey of the Paleolithic through the Bronze Age in Palestine. Far more controversial is Cyrus Gordon's *Before the Bible: The Common Background of Greek and Hebrew Civilizations* (New York, 1962), championing, as the subtitle indicates, the thesis of an eastern Mediterranean civilization that was parent to both the later Greek and Hebrew cultures; cf. Albright's scathing review in *Int.*, 18 (1964), 191-98.

On archaeological methodology we may note (besides the works of Kenyon and Franken mentioned above) one excellent popular treatment: L. A. Sinclair, "Two Basic Principles of Biblical Archaeology," *JBR*, 28 (1960), 437-43. On the more technical side, a few basic studies of pottery typology should be noted: a semi-popular study of the *Ancient Pottery of Erez-Yisra'el* by Ruth Amiran, which contains a useful bibliography by M. Cassuto-Salzmann (Jerusalem, 1959); R. Amiran's longer *Ancient Pottery of Erez-Yisra'el* (Jerusalem, 1961; written in modern Hebrew); a reprint of G. E. Wright's basic study, *The Pottery of Palestine from the Earliest Times to the End of the Early Bronze Age* (Ann Arbor, 1962; 1st published, New Haven, 1937); and Paul Lapp's *Palestinian Ceramic Chronology 200 B.C.-A.D. 70* (New Haven, 1961).

We have also been favored with two major collections (in English translation) of documents which have been uncovered in excavations and bear on biblical research. Virtually indispensable to the serious researcher is J. B. Pritchard (ed.), *Ancient Near Eastern Texts Relating to the Old Testament* (2nd ed., Princeton, 1955; 1st ed., 1950). The derivative *The Ancient Near East: An Anthology of Texts and Pictures* (Princeton, 1958) is now available also in paperback. Shorter but handy is D. W. Thomas (ed.), *Documents from Old Testament Times* (New York, 1958).

17. ARCHAEOLOGY AND THE PATRIARCHAL AGE

There are those who feel that biblical archaeology has now "matured" to the point where the discipline is moving beyond the "prove-the-Bible-true" stage to a more objective, scientific level. It is very doubtful, however, if any general conclusion of poor scientific quality in the Palestinian archaeology of the past would pass muster, as has sometimes been charged (although, of course, there have been notable exceptions, as in other geographical areas); and there certainly is no indication in the literature of any growing disinclination to relate new finds to biblical studies—whether or not these efforts be construed in any sense as "proofs" or "disproofs."

A major effort to summarize for the non-specialist the revolutionary developments in biblical studies in the past century, which are attributable to no little exent directly or indirectly to archaeological finds, is represented in the appearance of *The Anchor Bible* under the general editorship of W. F. Albright and D. N. Freedman (Garden City, 1964 ff.).

We have already noted above some of the recent research into the history and religion of the patriarchs. Since the biblical documents are exceptionally brief and otherwise problematic here, archaeology naturally plays an important role in attempts to interpret the patriarchal age in terms of modern historiography, and increasingly so in recent discussions. Here, as with the later period of Exodus-Judges, the more archaeologically oriented American scholars, particularly those in the Albright tradition, are generally pitted against the Alt-Noth-von Rad tradition in Germany. As concerns the patriarchs the issues were highlighted by G. E. Wright in "Modern Issues in Biblical Studies: History and the Patriarchs," *ET*, 71 (1960), 272-76; a rejoinder by G. von Rad, entitled "History and the Patriarchs," appeared in the next volume (72) of the same journal (pp. 213-16). Easily one of the most potentially revolutionary articles on the subject is W. F. Albright, "Abraham the Hebrew: A New Archaeological Interpretation," *BASOR*, 162 (1961), 36-54, which describes Abraham as originally a *ḫabiru* (Hebrew), i.e., a "donkey caravaneer" (which Albright regards as the original meaning of the word). On the subject see also R. de Vaux, *Die hebräischen Patriarchen und die modernen Entdeckungen* (Düsseldorf, 1959; a translation of articles originally appearing in *RB*, 1946-1949).

The subject is closely related to the whole vexed question of the relation of the *ḫabiru* to the patriarchs and the later Israelite invaders of Canaan. Among the major publications on the subject: M. Greenberg, *The Hab/piru* ("American Oriental Series," 39; New Haven, 1955); J. Botterto, *Le problème des Habiru à le 4e Recontre Assyriologique Internationale* ("Cashiers de la Société Asiatique," 12 [1954]); M. Gray, "The *Habiru*-Hebrew Problem in the Light of the Source Material Available at Present," *HUCA*, 29 (1958), 135-202; and H. Cazelles, "Hébreu, ubru et ḫapiru," *Syria*, 35 (1958), 198-217.

Study of the patriarchs (as of many other aspects of Old Testament study) is also closely linked with study of the texts from the great Amorite city-state, Mari, on the upper Euphrates. Some of the literature on the subject: J. Gibson, "Light from Mari on the Patriarchs," *JSS*, 7 (1962), 44-62; C. Gadd, "The Mari Letters, Past and Present," *ET*, 66 (1955), 174-77; J. N. Schofield, "Mari and the Old Testament, Past and Present," *ibid.*, 250-52; M. Noth, "Das alttestamentliche Bundschliessen im Lichte eines Mari-Textes," a 1953 essay now reprinted in Noth's *Gesammelte Studien zum Alten Testament*, 142-54; M. Noth, *Die Ursprünge des Alten Israel im Lichte neuer Quellen* (Köln, 1961); A. Malamat, " 'Prophecy' in the Mari Documents" (in modern Hebrew), *Eretz Israel*, 4 (1956), 74-84; G. E. Mendenhall, "Mari," *BA*, 11 (1948), 1-19, reprinted in the *Biblical Archaeologist Reader*, Vol. 2, 3-20. The recent appearance of H. B. Huffmon's *Amorite Personal Names in the Mari Texts: A Structural and Lexical Study* (Baltimore, 1965) should hasten the study of the Mari materials and their application to biblical studies.

In addition, we may note D. Gard, "Power for Life: The Rise of Organized Law in Mesopotamia and Its Bearing upon the Mosaic Book of the Covenant," *Int.*, 11 (1957), 41-47; D. N. Freedman, "The Babylonian Chronicle," *BA*, 19 (1956), 50-60, reprinted in the *Biblical Archaeologist Reader*, Vol. 1, 113-27; and D. N. Freedman, "The Prayer of Nabonidus," *BASOR*, 145 (1957), 31-32.

18. THE DEAD SEA SCROLLS

As Hahn's note on pp. 224-25 indicates, the veritable deluge of literature on Qumran or the Dead Sea Scrolls had only begun when his book went to press, and only now does it appear to be abating somewhat. While their chief application to Old Testament studies is in the field of textual criticism, especially in restoring respect for the Massoretic text (see section 4 above), because of their significance for New Testament and other studies the scrolls still rank as among the most important of all archaeological finds. We must confine ourselves to noting a few useful surveys, collections, and the like. An entire periodical devoted solely to the subject, *Revue de Qumran*, has sprung up, but hundreds of articles have appeared in other periodicals as well. Probably the most comprehensive bibliography on the subject are the two volumes of C. Burchard, *Bibliographie zu den Handschriften vom Toten Meer* (*BZAW*, 76 and 89; Berlin, 1957 and 1965). The story of the excavations at Qumran is told by R. de Vaux, *L'archéologie et les manuscrits de la Mer Morte* (London, 1961), and in J. Van der Ploeg, *The Excavation at Qumran* (New York, 1958; Dutch original, 1957). K. G. Kuhn's *Konkordanz zu den Qumrantexten* (Göttingen, 1960) is a vital tool for the study of the scrolls. Publication of the texts (plates and transcriptions) and commentary on them proceeds slowly but surely in the series "Discoveries in the Judaean Desert" (London, 1955 ff.), three volumes of which have appeared thus far. Other text editions include M. Burrows (ed.), *The Dead Sea Scrolls of St. Mark's Monastery* (2 vols.; New Haven, 1950 and 1951), and E. L. Sukenik and N. Avigad (eds.), *The Dead Sea Scrolls of the Hebrew University* (Jerusalem, 1955). The two most important English translations of most of the Qumran material are probably T. H. Gaster, *The Dead Sea Scriptures in English Translation* (2nd ed., New York, 1965; 1st ed., 1956), and G. Vermes, *The Dead Sea Scrolls in English* (Baltimore, 1962).

Of the many studies of the scrolls' significance, we may mention the following as possibly most helpful. H. Bardtke (ed.) *Qumran-Probleme: Vorträge des Leipziger Symposiums über Qumran-Probleme vom 9.-14. Oktober, 1961* (Berlin, 1963). M. Burrows' two works, *The Dead Sea Scrolls* (New York, 1955) and *More Light on the Dead Sea Scrolls* (New York, 1958), were among the earliest comprehensive discussions of the subject and remain among the best. Also at the top of the list: F. M. Cross, *The Ancient Library of Qumran and Modern Biblical Studies* (Garden City, 1958), and J. T. Milik, *Ten Years of Discovery in the Wilderness of Judaea* ("Studies in Biblical Theology," 26; Naperville, 1959; trans. from a 1957 French original). We mention four other noteworthy publications: J. M. Allegro, *The*

Dead Sea Scrolls (Baltimore, 1956); W. H. Brownlee, *The Meaning of the Qumran Scrolls for the Bible with Special Attention to the Book of Isaiah* (New York, 1964); M. Mansoor, *The Dead Sea Scrolls: A College Textbook and a Study Guide* (Grand Rapids, 1964); and H. Ringgren, *The Faith of Qumran: Theology of the Dead Sea Scrolls* (Philadelphia, 1963).

19. RAS SHAMRA

Easily the most important of all archaeological sites for Old Testament study is that of Ras Shamra, the ancient Ugarit on the northern Phoenician coast. It has become the major source of our knowledge of both Canaanite culture and religion, which were previously known mostly from the Old Testament polemics. It has also given us revolutionary insights into the history and development of the main Canaanite language, of which biblical Hebrew is only one dialect. Except during the war, excavation under the direction of the French archaeologist, Claude F. A. Schaeffer, has continued at the site almost annually since shortly after its discovery in 1928; work still is far from complete. Preliminary reports on the excavations by Schaeffer (as well as many other articles on the subject) have appeared in *Syria* (1929 ff.).

Two good popular introductions to the entire subject are A. Kapelrud, *The Ras Shamra Discoveries and the Old Testament* (London, 1962), and C. F. Pfeiffer, *Ras Shamra and the Bible* ("Baker Studies in Biblical Archaeology," 1; Grand Rapids, 1962). Cf. also Kapelrud's earlier *Baal in the Ras Shamra Texts* (Copenhagen, 1952); J. Gray, "The Excavation of Ras Shamra, Past and Present," *ET*, 64 (1953), 205-08 and 227-29; the same author's "The Ras Shamra Texts: a Critical Assessment," *Hibbert Journal*, 53 (1955), 115-26; and N. C. Habel, *Yahweh versus Baal: A Conflict of Religious Cultures, A Study of the Relevance of Ugaritic Materials for the Early Faith of Israel* (New York, 1964). A definitive edition of the earliest Ugaritic texts discovered has been published by Andrée Herdner, *Corpus des Tablettes en Cunéiformes Alphabétiques Découvertes à Ras Shamra-Ugarit de 1929 à 1939* (2 vols.; "Mission de Ras Shamra," 10; Paris, 1963).

Most collections of translations of the Ugaritic texts have appeared since 1950. Probably most easily accessible are those of H. L. Ginsberg in Pritchard (ed.), *Ancient Near Eastern Texts*, 129-55. We also have G. R. Driver, *Canaanite Myths and Legends* ("Old Testament Studies," 3; Edinburgh, 1956); J. Aistleitner, *Die mythologischen und kultischen Texte aus Ras Shamra* (Budapest, 1959); A. Jirku, *Kanaanäische Mythen und Legenden aus Ras Schamra-Ugarit* (Gütersloh, 1962); and a more popular treatment by T. Gaster, *The Oldest Stories in the World* (New York, 1952).

Ugaritic lexicography has been handled for the English-speaking world by C. H. Gordon in four successive editions, each with different titles: *Ugaritic Grammar* ("Analecta Orientalia," 20; Rome, 1940); *Ugaritic Handbook* ("Analecta Orientalia," 25; Rome, 1947); *Ugaritic Manual* ("Analecta Orientalia," 35; Rome, 1955); and *Ugaritic Textbook* ("Analecta Orientalia," 38; now in press). In German we now have J. Aistleitner, *Wörterbuch der ugaritischen Sprache*, ed. O. Eissfeldt (2nd ed., Berlin, 1964; 1st ed., 1963). There is also G. D. Young's *Concordance of Ugaritic* ("Analecta Orientalia," 36; Rome, 1956).

There are those who fear that we currently suffer from a patternism of a "pan-Ugaritic" or "pan-Canaanite" type, comparable to the earlier "pan-Babylonianism." The charge is not entirely without foundation, but, in general, the danger is surely far greater that the Ugaritic materials will not be mined sufficiently by biblical scholars, rather than the opposite. The literature on biblical applications is ample, but hardly what one might expect in terms of the potential.

Among the more important recent studies we note: E. Jacob, *Ras Shamra-Ugarit et L'Ancien Testament* (Neuchatel, 1960); M. Pope, *El in the Ugaritic Texts* (*SVT*, 2; Leiden, 1955); J. Gray, *The Legacy of Canaan: The Ras Shamra Texts and Their Relevance to the Old Testament* (*SVT*, 5; Leiden, 1957); U. Cassuto, *The Goddess Anath* (Jerusalem, 1958); O. Kaiser, *Die mythische Bedeutung des Meeres in Ägypten, Ugarit, und Israel* (Berlin, 1959). In the periodical literature a sampling of the articles discussing Ugaritic contributions to biblical studies would include W. F. Albright, "Some Canaanite-Phoenician Sources of Hebrew Wisdom," in Noth and Thomas (eds.), *Wisdom in Israel and in the Ancient Near East*, 1-16; M. Dahood, "The Value of Ugaritic for Textual Criticism," *Biblica*, 40 (1959), 160-70; M. Dahood, "Ugaritic Studies and the Bible," *Gregorianum*, 43 (1962), 55-79; R. De Langhe, "Myth, Ritual, and Kingship in the Ras Shamra Tablets," in Hooke (ed.), *Myth, Ritual, and Kingship,*

122-48; L. Fisher, "Abraham and His Priest-King," *JBL*, 81 (1962), 264-70 (gives possible Ugaritic illumination of Gen. 14); J. Gray, "Cultic Affinities between Israel and Ras Shamra," *ZAW*, 62 (1949), 207-20; W. Hallo, "Is. 28:9-13 and the Ugartic Abecedaries," *JBL*, 77 (1958), 325-38; F. Hvidberg, "The Canaanite Background of Gen. I-III," *VT*, 10 (1960), 285-94; I. Mendelssohn, "Samuel's Denunciation of Kingship in the Light of the Akkadian Documents from Ugarit," *BASOR*, 143 (1956), 17-22; R. O'Callaghan, "Echoes of Canaanite Literature in the Psalms," *VT*, 4 (1954), 164-76; and T. Worden, "The Literary Influence of the Ugarit Fertility Myth on the Old Testament," *VT*, 3 (1953), 273-98.

Limitations of space do not allow us to survey other areas, equally relevant to Old Testament studies, that have risen to prominence as a result of archaeological finds, such as the Amarna tablets, the Egyptian, Akkadian, Sumerian or Hittite literature, the inscriptional materials, and others. For these the reader is referred to the bibliographical helps cited in section 1 above, perhaps especially Wright (ed.), *The Bible and the Ancient Near East*.

20. LINGUISTIC STUDIES

One basic area of biblical study which has benefited immeasurably from archaeological finds, especially at Ugarit, is linguistic studies (Hebrew grammar, lexicography, etc.). This important field, like textual criticism, was left unsurveyed in the original edition of Hahn. In America the "Albright school" especially has been active in exploring and applying the new materials to the study of the Hebrew literature and especially to the poetic materials which often swarm with archaisms. Creative hypotheses are needed, of course, to come to terms with the mass of new evidence, but when the ballast of actual knowledge of the Hebrew language is missing (as it commonly is in American theological education), the hypotheses easily become purely speculative or fall prey to assumptions not readily compatible with the canonical literature itself.

Among the major pioneering efforts in this area in the past decade and a half we note the following: three studies by W. F. Albright, "The Psalm of Habakkuk," in H. H. Rowley (ed.), *Studies in Old Testament Prophecy Presented to Professor Theodore H. Robinson* (Edinburgh, 1950), 1-18; "A Catalogue of Early Hebrew Lyric Poems

(Psalm 68)," *HUCA*, 23 (1950-51), 1-39; "Some Remarks on the Song of Moses in Deuteronomy XXXII," *VT*, 9 (1959), 339-46; a series of works by F. M. Cross and D. N. Freedman, including *Early Hebrew Orthography: A Study of the Epigraphic Evidence* ("American Oriental Series," 36; New Haven, 1952; the first of two joint doctoral dissertations at Johns Hopkins University under W. F. Albright); "The Blessing of Moses," *JBL*, 67 (1948), 191-210; "A Royal Song of Thanksgiving—II Samuel 22 = Psalm 18," *JBL*, 72 (1953), 15-34; "The Song of Miriam," *JNES*, 14 (1955), 237-50 (the original form of these last three studies together with a study of "The Blessing of Jacob" and a very helpful introduction, i.e., the second half of the joint dissertation, is now available in photostatic copy, Pittsburgh, 1964); D. N. Freedman, "Archaic Forms in Early Hebrew Poetry," *ZAW*, 72 (1960), 101-07; four studies by M. Dahood, *Canaanite and Phoenician Influence in Qoheleth* (Rome, 1952); an article with the same title in *Biblica*, 43 (1962), 349-65 (the latest in a series of articles by Dahood defending and expanding his original thesis); "Northwest Semitic Philology and Job," in J. L. McKenzie (ed.), *The Bible in Current Catholic Thought* ("St. Mary's Theology Studies," 1; New York, 1962), 55-74; "Some Northwest Semitic Words in Job," *Biblica*, 38 (1957), 306-20; *Proverbs and Northwest Semitic Philology* ("Scripta Pontificii Instituti Biblici," 113; Rome, 1963); A. Jirku, "Eine Renaissance des Hebräischen," *Forschungen und Fortschritte*, 32 (1958), 211-12; M. Held, "The YQTL-QTL (QTL-YQTL) Sequence of Identical Verbs in Biblical Hebrew and in Ugaritic," in M. Ben-Horin, B. Weinryb, and S. Zeitlin (eds.), *Studies and Essays in Honor of A. A. Neuman* (Leiden, 1962), 281-90; two studies by J. Huesman, "Finite Uses of the Infinitive Absolute," *Biblica*, 37 (1956), 271-95; and "The Infinitive Absolute and Waw + Perfect Problems," *Biblica*, 37 (1956), 410-34; H. D. Hummel, "Enclitic *Mem* in Early Northwest Semitic, Especially Hebrew," *JBL*, 76 (1957), 85-107; S. Gevirtz, *Patterns in the Early Poetry of Israel* (Chicago, 1963); R. G. Boling, "Synonymous Parallelism in the Psalms," *JSS*, 5 (1960), 221-55; M. H. Goshen-Gottstein, "Semitic Morphological Structures: The Basic Morphological Structure of Biblical Hebrew," in *Studies in Egyptology and Linguistics in Honor of H. J. Polotsky* (Jerusalem, 1964), 178-96; W. Moran, "The Hebrew Language in its Northwest Semitic Background," in Wright (ed.), *The Bible and the Ancient*

Near East, 54-72; F. Nötscher, "Zum emphatischen Lamed," *VT*, 3 (1953), 372-80; C. S. Rodd, "Modern Issues in Biblical Study: Rediscovered Hebrew Meanings," *ET*, 71 (1960), 131-34; M. Sarna, "The Interchange of the Preposition *Beth* and *Min* in Biblical Hebrew," *JBL*, 78 (1959), 310-16; B. Vawter, "The Canaanite Background of Genesis 49," *CBQ*, 17 (1955), 1-18.

In the broader field of major reference works much effort has also been expended. By 1953 L. Köhler's and W. Baumgartner's *Lexicon in Veteris Testamenti Libros* (Leiden) was complete, with a supplement appearing in 1958. However, since it was generally agreed that the Hebrew part was less reliable than the Aramaic (done by Baumgartner), Professor Baumgartner is now at work on a revised edition of the entire lexicon. Similarly, work on a new *Oxford Hebrew Lexicon* (to replace the old "Brown, Driver, Briggs") is in progress under the editorship of G. R. Driver and D. W. Thomas, assisted by J. Snaith.

In the field of grammars and concordances, we hail the reprinting of three indispensable reference tools: H. Bauer and P. Leander, *Historische Grammatik der hebräischen Sprache des Alten Testaments* (Hildesheim, 1962; first published, 1922); C. Brockelmann, *Grundriss der vergleichenden Grammatik der semitischen Sprachen* (2 vols.; Hildesheim, 1961; first published, 1912); S. Mandelkern, *Veteris Testamenti Concordantiae Hebraicae Atque Chaldaicae* (Graz, 1955; first published, 1937). A smaller and handier substitute for the latter has now appeared: G. Lisowsky, *Konkordanz zum hebräischen Alten Testament* (Stuttgart, 1957). F. Blake's *A Resurvey of Hebrew Tenses* (Rome, 1951) challenged the commonly accepted interpretations of S. R. Driver, but the established "aspect theory" was defended by C. Brockelmann, *Hebräische Syntax* (Neukirchen, 1956). Cf. also J. Watts, *A Survey of Syntax in the Hebrew Old Testament* (Grand Rapids, 1964; 1st ed., 1951). In comparative Semitic grammar, the only recent work in English is S. Moscati, *An Introduction to the Comparative Grammar of the Semitic Languages* ("Porta Linguarum Orientalium"; Wiesbaden, 1964).

In the area of elementary grammars we have a new edition (the 25th!) of A. Davidson's *An Introductory Hebrew Grammar*, ed. J. Mauchline (Edinburgh, 1962), and a second edition (London, 1959) of J. W. Weingreen's *A Practical Grammar for Classical He-*

brew. New efforts include A. Bertsch, *Kurzgefasste hebräische Sprachlehre* (Stuttgart, 1956); J. Marks and V. Rogers, *A Beginner's Handbook to Biblical Hebrew* (New York and Nashville, 1958); G. Beer and D. Meyer, *Hebräische Grammatik* (2 small vols.; Berlin, 1952 and 1955); and M. Greenberg, *Introduction to Hebrew* (Englewood Cliffs, 1965). Also noteworthy is George Landes' *A Student's Vocabulary of Biblical Hebrew Listed According to Frequency and Cognate* (New York, 1961). In its area, F. Rosenthal's *A Grammar of Biblical Aramaic* ("Porta Linguarum Orientalium"; Wiesbaden, 1961) is very useful.

21. OLD TESTAMENT THEOLOGY

The past decade has seen intense activity in the field of Old Testament theology, but also increasing uncertainty concerning its actual role. One of the best surveys of the field, together with the elucidation of its problems, is R. Dentan's *Preface to Old Testament Theology* (2nd ed., New York, 1963; 1st ed., 1950). An extremely useful survey is found throughout Vol. 73 (1962) of *ET*, where major Old Testament scholars review and discuss major Old Testament theologies.

In the actual production of Old Testament theologies, most of the significant activity in the English-speaking world has consisted of translation of continental works, very few of which were available in English in 1952. However, much of the original work was produced within the period since as well. It is our judgment that probably the two most serviceable works of this type for the ordinary reader (prescinding here from methodological debates) are E. Jacob, *Theology of the Old Testament* (New York, 1958; original French, 1955) and T. Vriezen, *An Outline of Old Testament Theology* (Oxford, 1958; original Dutch, 1949, 2nd ed., 1954). L. Köhler's *Old Testament Theology* (London, 1957; original German, 1935; 3rd ed., 1953) was translated after its major usefulness had been outlived (there is general agreement that it followed too rigid and too dogmatic a scheme). The first volume of one of the earliest full-scale theologies has finally appeared in English translation: W. Eichrodt, *Theology of the Old Testament* ("The Old Testament Library"; Philadelphia, 1961; translated from the 6th German edition [1959]; original German, 1933, Vols. 2 and 3, 1935 and 1939); in spite of its age it remains one of the best, perhaps all the more so because of its running dialogue with *Religionsgeschichte*. Likewise, only the first volume of von Rad's *Old Testament Theology* has been translated (New York, 1962; German original, 1957). It is fervently hoped that von Rad's second volume (Munich, 1960) as well as Eichrodt's remaining two volumes will also appear in translation soon. However, the subtitles of von Rad's volumes, "The Theology of Israel's Historical [Vol. 2: Prophetic] Traditions" indicates the methodological impasse which became critical in this discipline with the publication of von Rad's work (see below); as von Rad remarks in his preface, his work differs so radically from Jacob's and Vriezen's that it is hard to see how they can all be entitled "Old Testament Theology." In this connection, note the appendix to the English translation of Eichrodt's theology, written after von Rad's work had appeared: "The Problem of Old Testament Theology" (pp. 512-20).

Before we pursue this issue further, a few works of lesser scope, especially English-language ones may be noted. As its title indicates, G. A. Knight's *A Christian Theology of the Old Testament* (Richmond, 1959) touches another controversial point in the entire issue of "biblical theology." For this reason it received a very mixed reception, and, indeed, in a way, it belongs less in this classification than in succeeding ones on hermeneutics, especially typology. John McKenzie's popular but penetrating *The Two-Edged Sword* (Milwaukee, 1956) is a significant contribution from the Roman Catholic side, and the same may be said of R. A. F. MacKenzie's *Faith and History in the Old Testament* (Minneapolis, 1963). H. H. Rowley, *The Faith of Israel: Aspects of Old Testament Thought* (Philadelphia, 1956) is selective but helpful (and is itself, of course, only a sample of the indefatigable British scholar's many other contributions). G. E. Wright is one of the few scholars who has made significant contributions to Old Testament theology as well as to biblical archaeology; his *The Old Testament Against Its Environment* ("Studies in Biblical Theology," 2; Chicago, 1950) and especially his *God Who Acts: Biblical Theology as Recital* ("Studies in Biblical Theology," 8; Chicago, 1952)—which treats also the question of the relation between "biblical" and "systematic" theology—have long since established themselves as classics. (Indeed, virtually the entire "Studies in Biblical Theology" series falls within the period we are discussing, and its varied titles are themselves an excellent indicator of the variety and

vigor—as well as uncertainty—which characterizes the movement.)
J. N. Schofield's *Introducing Old Testament Theology* (Philadelphia,
1964) competently fulfills the promise of the title.

Among other works we may mention W. Zimmerli, *Das Alte Testament als Anrede* (Munich, 1956); the same author's *Das Gesetz und
die Propheten: Zum Verständnis des Alten Testaments* (Göttingen,
1963; English translation promised shortly); and a provocative essay
(with also major ecumenical implications) by F. Leenhardt, *Two
Biblical Faiths: Protestant and Catholic* (Philadelphia, 1964; trans.
from the 1962 French original by H. Knight). A somewhat similar
work, but more restricted in scope, is M.-L. Henry, *Jahwist und
Priesterschrift: Zwei Glaubenszeugnisse des Alten Testaments* ("Arbeiten zur Theologie," 3; Stuttgart, 1960). Beyond this brief sampling,
of course, there is a host of books, monographs, and periodical literature on various topics and themes of Old Testament theology, often
merging wth other aspects of Old Testament study, the sum of which
almost "no man can number."

The influence of the theological emphasis on the commentary
literature (most of which also cannot be surveyed here) should be
observed, however. In contrast to the nearly exclusively historical,
critical, grammatical, textual content of many of the older commentaries, increasing efforts are being made at least to supplement
that foundation with theological commentary (although at times it
may be feared that the foundation will now be neglected and a "theological" commentary be attempted which relates itself only very
superficially to the text). Certainly not superficial, however, is the
theologically oriented *Das Alte Testament Deutsch*, which is now
nearly complete. Some of its volumes are finally now appearing in
English translation in the "Old Testament Library" series (together
with some original commentaries and some non-commentary volumes).
(It is our judgment that the "Old Testament Library," stressing
theology, and *The Anchor Bible*, stressing historical-critical and philological concerns, offer a nearly ideal combination for the average
non-specialist Old Testament student who, if he uses both side by
side, will probably be in a better position than he has been for at least
half a century.) The new *Biblischer Kommentar* is a more "scientific"
commentary than *Das Alte Testament Deutsch*, but even it concerns
itself with the question of the Old Testament's relation to the New,

often along typological lines, in a way we have rarely seen heretofore. Further examples are provided by two recent "theological" commentaries on Second Isaiah: James Smart's *History and Theology in Second Isaiah* (Philadelphia, 1965) and G. A. Knight's *Deutero-Isaiah: A Theological Commentary on Isaiah 40-55* (New York and Nashville, 1965). Whatever one's final judgment of these works, they do represent quite a contrast to C. R. North's almost contemporaneous *The Second Isaiah* (London, 1964), a much more "scientific" commentary and the distillation of a lifetime's labors in this area (particularly on the Servant problem).

However, beneath the surface of this intense activity it is plain that the discipline of "biblical theology" suffers increasingly from nagging uncertainties. The conflict with *Religionsgeschichte*, out of which the modern "biblical theology" movement arose, has largely disappeared, partly out of reaction to the former's "patternism" (see section 9 above), partly through acceptance of its valid insights, and few protests of this nature are heard any longer. In a way, what has happened is that the more recent debate with *Religionsgeschichte* and its historicistic or positivistic presuppositions has given away to a return to the even earlier debate with dogmatic or systematic theology, i.e., to the point where "biblical theology" first arose at the end of the eighteenth century. Understandably, systematics saw "biblical theology" as a threat to its own integrity. In the church as a whole concern mounted over the lack of communication between the biblical scholars and the systematicians. As the latter were asked whether they were implicitly ignoring their biblical foundations or exchanging them for others, so it was asked in return whether the claim of the biblical scholars to be able to proceed entirely independently did not, in fact, conceal naturalistic or positivistic prepossessions incompatible with the historic Christian faith. In other words, was not biblical theology continuing *Religionsgeschichte's* claim to "objectivity"? Was there any such thing as "presuppositionless exegesis"? Or, to use Hahn's original captions, was there really *any* approach to the Bible which was not ultimately "theological"?

Within the discipline of Old Testament theology itself, one of the chief manifestations of the problem has been the methodological debate concerning the proper subject or arrangement of such a work: Was it to attempt to unify all the material under the traditional dog-

matic categories (God, man, salvation) as in Köhler, Jacob, and
Vriezen, or around some inner-biblical category such as the "covenant," as in Eichrodt's work? But could any such arrangement do
justice to the biblical richness and variety? Or should it abjure any
such attempt and simply explore the "theology" of individual traditions, as is done especially in von Rad's work? But, if so, in what
sense could this be called a "biblical" (or even "Old Testament")
theology? Was there no more discernible unity to the canonical collection than this? Or was the discipline merely to be an extension
of historical exegesis (which, indeed, is the great merit of von Rad's
effort), abandoning more "ultimate" issues to the systematician?

Among the studies discussing these issues, we may include (besides
those already mentioned) E. J. Young, *The Study of Old Testament
Theology Today* (London, 1958), which registers objections from
the viewpoint of fundamentalism and "inerrancy"; H. Vorgrimler
(ed.), *Dogmatic vs. Biblical Theology* (Baltimore, 1965), an attempt
to come to terms with "biblical theology" from a Roman Catholic
viewpoint; J. Barr, "Revelation through History in the Old Testament and in Modern Theology," *Int.*, 17 (1963), 193-205; B. Childs,
"Interpretation in Faith," *Int.*, 18 (1964), 432-49; E. L. Allen, "The
Limits of Biblical Theology," *JBR*, 25 (1957), 13-18; O. Piper,
"Biblical Theology and Systematic Theology," *JBR*, 25 (1957), 106-11;
H. Reventlow, "Grundfragen der alttestamentlichen Theologie im
Lichte der neueren deutschen Forschung," *TZ*, 17 (1961), 91-98; J.
van der Ploeg, "Une 'Théologie de l'Ancien Testament' est-elle pos-
sible?", *ETL*, 38 (1962), 417-34; P. Wernberg-Möller, "Is There an
Old Testament Theology?", *Hibbert Journal*, 59 (1960), 21-29; J.
Hempel, "Alttestamentliche Theologie in protestantischer Sicht heute,"
Bibliotheca Orientalis, 15 (1958), 206-14; H. Wildberger, "Auf dem
Wege zu einer biblischen Theologie," *EvT*, 19 (1959), 70-90; R.
Martin-Achard, "Les voies de la théologie de l'Ancien Testament,"
Revue de Theologie et de Philosophie, 3 (1959), 217-26; L. B. Gilkey,
"Cosmology, Ontology, and the Travail of Biblical Language," *Journal
of Religion*, 41 (1961), 194-205.

Closely related to these questions is that of the relation between
faith and fact, between "history" in the more ordinary sense and the
"kerygma" of the "history of Israel's traditions," i.e., of Israel's own
theological interpretations of events (or presumed events). Again,

discussion of this issue focuses on von Rad's theology, and especially on his treatment of the early traditions concerning the patriarchs, Exodus, Sinai, and conquest, where, following Alt and Noth (cf. section 11 above on the Noth-Bright debate over history), he posits "interpretation" or theology with little or any discernible historical basis in fact. Recently, some of von Rad's own students, notably Rolf Rendtorff, have attempted to improve upon von Rad's position and thus defend him against his critics. They try to transcend what they regard as a false dichotomy of history and interpretation by arguing that, since there is no history without interpretation, the interpretation must itself be viewed as part of history. Cf. the following essays by Rendtorff: "Hermeneutik des Alten Testaments als Frage nach der Geschichte," *ZTK*, 57 (1960), 27-40; "Geschichte und Überlieferung," in R. Rendtorff and K. Koch (eds.), *Studien zur Theologie der alttestamentlichen Überlieferungen* (Neukirchen, 1961), 80-94; "Die Offenbarungsvorstellungen im Alten Israel," in W. Pannenberg (ed.), *Offenbarung als Geschichte*, 21-41; ("Kerygma und Dogma, Beiheft 1"; 2nd ed., Göttingen, 1963; 1st ed., 1961); "Geschichte und Wort in Alten Testament," *EvT*, 22 (1962), 621-49 (part of a debate with Zimmerli).

Of course, these efforts are inseparable from the activity of the entire Pannenberg circle, of which Rendtorff is a member (for a concise and incisive survey of which I refer the reader to Carl E. Braaten, "The Current Controversy on Revelation: Pannenberg and His Critics," *Journal of Religion*, 45 [1965], 225-37). Although it is not clear if Pannenberg does not merely represent a resurgence of some sort of historicism and semi-Hegelianism, it is nevertheless evident that we have here a welcome return to the importance of history. At the same time, it is to be doubted if this more or less philosophical improvement can ultimately accomplish much if it does not pay more attention also to the external evidences of historicity supplied in increasing measure by the archaeological historians. Quite apart from the more speculative debates, a corrective of the earlier excessively "kerygmatic" approaches can be documented elsewhere; thus Krister Stendahl's now nearly classic article, "Biblical Theology, Contemporary," *IDB*, 1, 418-32, with its stress on the discipline's "descriptive" task of "what it *meant*." Cf. also W. L. Reed, "The Bible and North Arabia," *Encounter*, 26 (1965), 143-53.

22. HERMENEUTICS

All this leads us, finally, into the discussion of "hermeneutics," which has bulked so large in recent years. Virtually none of the Old Testament discussion of the question has followed the lead of contemporary existentialist philosophy, which has been central in New Testament discussions; one of the relatively few essays even to discuss it as such was H. W. Wolff, "Das Alte Testament und das Problem der existentialen Interpretation," *EvT*, 23 (1963), 1-17; reprinted in Wolff's, *Gesammelte Studien zum Alten Testament* ("Theologische Bücherei," 22; Munich, 1964), 325-44. This, of course, does not mean that Old Testament scholars could remain neutral toward the essentially negative conclusions regarding their discipline championed by Bultmann and his disciples. This is best documented in B. W. Anderson (ed.), *The Old Testament and Christian Faith* where each essayist answers (mostly negatively) the initial essay by Bultmann. The appearance of this volume and of another similar to it, C. Westermann (ed.), *Essays on Old Testament Hermeneutics* (Richmond, 1963; translation of a 1960 German original, itself a collection of older essays on the question, including another by Bultmann) are, at least in America, the major indications of the changed climate in Old Testament studies.

For the Old Testament, the major issue of hermeneutics is how to defend and formulate the unity of the testaments, without which one might speak of "Old Testament theology" or "New Testament theology," but scarcely of a "biblical theology" (it is significant that the latter has virtually never been attempted). If historicism is to be overcome, the Old Testament must somehow become more than merely "relevant" and must have an authority which is not entirely subjectively determined. In general, we may say that there are currently two main stresses concerning the unity of the testaments: typology and *sensus plenior* (plenary or fuller sense). In one way or another, prophecy-fulfillment, *Heilsgeschichte* (which in spite of mounting attacks and varying definitions still retains a commanding position), and christological approaches tend to merge with both of these major stresses (although the christological is very rarely defended on a programmatic basis as in Vischer and traditionalist exegesis).

In general, von Rad has become the major exponent of a typological view, especially in the second volume of his *Theologie des Alten Testaments*, part 3 (329-424). Probably von Rad's major opponent, and not only on the question of typology, has been F. Baumgärtel, especially in his *Verheissung: Zur Frage des evangelischen Verständnisses des Alten Testaments* (Gütersloh, 1952). In the Westermann volume cited above the English-speaking reader obtains a sample of Baumgärtel's thought as well as that of F. Hesse, who champions very similar viewpoints. In almost the sharpest possible contrast to the rather spiritualistic views of these two men stands the work of the Dutch theologian, A. A. van Ruler, *Die christliche Kirche und das Alte Testament* (Munich, 1955), with its strong accent on the material, this-worldly content of the Old Testament, an accent van Ruler believes should also inform the Christian church (two essays in the Westermann volume respond to van Ruler's thesis).

While typological hermeneutics used to be especially popular among Roman Catholics, a certain clear shift toward the "plenary sense" seems to have developed in recent years. On the latter point, see the unique essay of James M. Robinson, "Scripture and Theological Method: A Protestant Study in *Sensus Plenior*," *CBQ*, 27 (1965), 6-27. A partly comparable, obverse study might be R. Philben's, "Some Modern Protestant Attitudes Toward Hermeneutics," *CBQ*, 21 (1959), 115-35.

Out of the vast area of recent literature on all aspects of hermeneutics we cite the following: J. L. McKenzie, "Problems of Hermeneutics in Roman Catholic Exegesis," *JBL*, 77 (1958), 197-204; a series of articles on "Messianism" in Vol. 19 (1957) of *CBQ;* an entire number of *Concordia Theological Monthly*, 25 (October, 1964), devoted to conservative Lutheranism's wrestling with these problems; J. A. Soggin, "Geschichte, Historie und Heilsgeschichte im Alten Testament: Ein Beitrag zur heutigen theologisch-hermeneutischen Diskussion," *ThLZ*, 89 (1964), 721-36; and J. C. K. von Hofmann, *Interpreting the Bible* (Minneapolis, 1959; trans. C. Preus from the 1860 original, published in 1880). Surprisingly, this is virtually all of von Hofmann's influential work ever to appear in English; cf. Preus's article, "The Contemporary Relevance of von Hofmann's Hermeneutical Principles," *Int.*, 4 (1950), 311-21. Further: J. Coppens, *Vom christlichen Verständnis des Alten Testaments* (Louvain, 1952); J. Jocz, *The Spiritual History of Israel* (London, 1961); K. Frör,

Biblische Hermeneutik (Munich, 1961; scheduled to appear in English shortly); H. Duesberg, *Les valeurs chrétiennes de l'Ancien Testament* (Tournai, 1960); C. Larcher, *L'actualité chrétienne de l'Ancien Testament d'après le Nouveau Testament* (Paris, 1962); P. Grelot, *Sens chrétien de l'Ancien Testament; esquisse d'un traité dogmatique* (Tournai, 1962); N. Lohfink, *Das Siegeslied am Schilfmeer: Christliche Auseinandersetzungen mit dem Alten Testament* (Frankfurt, 1965).

More specifically on the "plenary sense" we may mention R. E. Brown, *The Sensus Plenior of Sacred Scripture* (Baltimore, 1955), in many ways the pioneering work on the subject, and his subsequent "The *Sensus Plenior* in the Last Ten Years," *CBQ*, 25 (1963), 262-85 (this article lists and responds to most of the subsequent literature on the subject); B. Vawter, "The Fuller Sense: Some Considerations," *CBQ*, 26 (1964), 85-96 (urging a "fuller understanding" rather than a "fuller sense"); J. Coppens, "Le problème du sens plenier," *ETL*, 34 (1958), 1-20.

On the subject of typology we may note, further, two examples of J. Danielou's influential studies on patristic hermeneutics: *From Shadows to Reality: Studies in the Biblical Typology of the Fathers* (London, 1960); and *The Bible and the Liturgy* (Notre Dame, 1956). Others: G. W. Lampe and K. J. Woolcombe, *Essays on Typology* ("Studies in Biblical Theology," 22 London, 1957); R. Poelman, *Times of Grace: The Sign of Forty in the Bible* (New York, 1964; note, too, J. L. McKenzie's introduction); H. Hummel, "The Old Testament Basis of Typological Interpretation," *BR*, 9 (1964), 38-50; D. Daube, *The Exodus Pattern in the Bible* (London, 1963); and B. W. Anderson, "Exodus Typology in Second Isaiah," in Anderson and Harrelson (eds.), *Israel's Prophetic Heritage*, 177-95.

It is hoped that this essay will have given the reader a fair notion of "what is the breadth and length and height and depth" of contemporary Old Testament scholarship—and perhaps also ultimately of "the love of Christ" (Eph. 3:18-19).

Indexes

INDEX OF BIBLE PASSAGES

GENERAL INDEX

Type, 11 on 14 and 9 on 11 Janson
Display, Garamond
Paper, Spring Grove E. F. (Sized for offset)